BARRON'S

Guide to Making

Investment Decisions

REVISED & EXPANDED

BARRON'S
Guide to Making
Investment
Decisions

NEW YORK INSTITUTE OF FINANCE
NEW YORK • TORONTO • SYDNEY • TOKYO • SINGAPORE

Douglas Sease and John Prestbo

Library of Congress Cataloging-in-Publication Data

Sease, Douglas.
    Barron's guide to making investment decisions / Douglas R. Sease
and John A. Prestbo.—Rev. and expanded.
       p. cm.
    Includes bibliographical references and index.
    ISBN 0-7352-0044-0 (pbk.).—ISBN 0-13-798530-4 (pbk.:Dow Jones)
    ISBN 0-13-011608-4 (pbk.)
    1. Investments—Handbooks, manuals, etc. I. Prestbo, John A. II. Title.
    HG4527.S393 1998
    332.6—dc21   98-27594
                                                      CIP

Printed in the United States of America

10 9 8 7 6 5 4 3 2 1   10 9 8 7 6 5 4 3 2
ISBN 0-13-798530-4 (Barron's)   ISBN 0-7352-0044-0 (Prentice Hall Press)

10 9 8 7 6 5 4 3 2
ISBN 0-13-011608-4 (Prentice Hall Direct)

This publication is designed to provide accurate and authoritative information in regard to the subject matter covered. It is sold with the understanding that the publisher is not engaged in rendering legal, accounting, or other professional services. If legal advice or other expert assistance is required, the services of a competent professional person should be sought.

    ...From the Declaration of Principles jointly adopted by a Committee of the American Bar Association and a Committee of Publishers and Associations

 NEW YORK INSTITUTE OF FINANCE
An Imprint of Prentice Hall Press
Paramus, NJ 07652
A Simon & Schuster Company

On the World Wide Web at http://www.phdirect.com

Prentice Hall International (UK) Limited, *London*
Prentice Hall of Australia Pty. Limited, *Sydney*
Prentice Hall Canada, Inc., *Toronto*
Prentice Hall Hispanoamericana, S.A., *Mexico*
Prentice Hall of India Private Limited, *New Delhi*
Prentice Hall of Japan, Inc., *Tokyo*
Simon & Schuster Asia Pte. Ltd., *Singapore*
Editora Prentice Hall do Brasil, Ltda., *Rio de Janeiro*

Contents

9 Real Estate and Other "Hard" Assets 292

10 Collectibles Aren't Investable 314

Tax Strategies for Investors   326

BARRON'S

Guide to Making

Investment
Decisions

Introduction

The first edition of this book, published in 1994, began with our two-word summation of investment advice:

Caveat emptor!
Buyer, beware!

Fortunately for us, people brushed that warning aside and purchased copies in sufficient number that our publisher encouraged this new edition. We are flattered, to be sure, but the truth is that conditions in the economy and the markets have changed considerably in the past several years. As we write, the longest bull market in history is long in the tooth, but still going strong. Stock prices have climbed rapidly to levels that few dreamed were possible. Mutual funds have become far and away the preferred vehicle for most individual investors. Indeed, there are now more mutual funds than there are stocks listed on the New York Stock Exchange. The American economy is the strongest and most productive of any on earth. Our technology and finance sectors are the envy of the world. While growth is unusually strong, so far there has been no evidence of inflation. And Washington—in a tardy but nonetheless welcome recognition of the fact that most voters are also investors, directly or indirectly—sharply cut capital gains taxes. In short, it's a different world from the one that existed when the first edition of the *Barron's Guide* was published, and it is time we freshened these pages with more recent examples and expanded discussion of certain topics.

Most of our advice remains sound, however, and we retained the overall approach and tone. We're grateful for the feedback we received from readers of the first edition. We'd like to share some excerpts to help explain what we are about with this book.

"Your book shies not from the many complexities in investment areas, and doles out advice and counsel succinctly and without hyperbole, a formidable task in itself," writes a retired gentleman from Florida. "Above all, as an editorial product, it has balance."

We indeed aim to make investing understandable, but without oversimplifying. Furthermore, while we certainly have opinions that we don't hesitate to convey as forcefully as we can, in most instances we devote some space to alternate views. Our ultimate goal isn't to convert you into disciples of the way we handle our money but to get you thinking about making your own investment decisions—and to raise your confidence in your ability to make them yourself.

In his syllabus for beginning MBA students at a university out on the Great Plains, a professor observed: "Unfortunately, when it comes to the published investments literature, that which is 'short and snappy' often tends to be wrong. At the same time, much of the correct and useful literature tends to be long and boring." Then he proceeds to assign readings from our first edition. "This is an excellent investment guide for both beginning and advanced investors. Students with no experience or a limited background in investments will find this guide to be especially well organized and readable."

We're flushed from the praise, but the good professor (how could he be otherwise with such excellent taste?) makes an important point: Our book is not just for beginners. Experienced investors can get sidetracked, hustled by salespeople and so focused on trees that they stray from the forest. This book can help them regain their bearings.

One such reader of our first edition, a millionaire several times over, penciled his thanks on a sheet from a yellow pad: "As a result of your book, I've changed my whole (and my company's) investment program." In his case, he dropped his broker, who was making so much money off this guy that he treated our reader to lunch at a fancy New York restaurant every once in a while. Our reader signed up with a consultant who finds—and monitors—professional money managers for his personal and company accounts. "I don't perform my own dentistry," he told us during a visit, "so why would I think I could invest this much money very well?"

Some people simply aren't interested in investing. But in this day and age they can't afford not to be investors, or they will find themselves more than a dollar short when retirement rolls around. What to do? We address such conflicts in this book in the course of showing how laying out an investment program depends very much on the kind of person you are. For those of you without millions to dangle in front of a money manager, we repeat the good news of the first edition: You can reach your financial goals with an uncomplicated program that you are capable of managing yourself.

As with the first edition, you should know what this book will *not* do. It will not tell you which stocks or other investments to buy. That is your responsibility. You know yourself, your financial circumstances, and your investment objectives far better than anyone else.

This book won't steer you to this broker or that financial adviser. To the extent that you choose to delegate to

someone else part or all of the responsibility of picking specific investments, it is up to you to find qualified financial
advisers who understand your goals, are aware of what
resources you have, and who will act in *your*—not *their*—best
interest.

This book certainly won't reveal a system for beating
the market, for earning 20% annually with no risk, or even
for avoiding losses. Someone may have such systems and be
using them, but we don't know about them. And if we did,
would we tell you for less than $20?

But don't despair. Though we won't give you specific
how-to-invest advice, you will get your money's worth out of
this book by learning how to *think* about investing. We will
help you devise your own approach to investing, taking into
account your goals and your willingness to take risks to
achieve them. We'll show you how to assess the risks and the
rewards of various investment vehicles and strategies; and we
will share with you some of the insights we have picked up in
years of interviewing money managers, corporate executives,
and investment strategists.

We will help you acquire an attitude about investing,
which should bolster your resistance to the get-rich-quick
siren songs they are forever playing on Wall Street. We certainly have an attitude, and it will become apparent to you as
you read along. It's there not for you to adopt as your very
own—although if you want to, be our guest—but to show you
how helpful it can be in sorting through the confusing investment possibilities. If we were to propose a subtitle for this
book, it would be "Investing with an Attitude."

We'll also direct you to sources of more detailed
information about specific securities and other investments.
One of these—no surprise here—is *Barron's*. The statistical
data in *Barron's* are invaluable for tracking the performance
of investments. The interviews with financial pros and articles about companies provide another type of capital that no

investor can afford to ignore: ideas. And if there is any publication that has an attitude about investing, it's *Barron's*.

In preparing this guide to making investment decisions, we made a few assumptions about our readers. The main one is that you already have your financial house in order. We assume you know whether you can afford a house and how to shop for a mortgage if you need one. We assume you aren't so foolish as to be planning an investment program while paying 19.8% interest on credit card balances. Frankly, we assume you have enough money to *invest*—which means life's necessities and, yes, a modest number of luxuries are provided for.

We also assume you have a working knowledge of the economy. You don't need to be able to recite how much durable goods orders grew last month or where the consumer price index stood in January. But we do assume you know whether the economy is growing or shrinking, and whether interest rates are rising or falling. For economics and beyond, we expect you to be reading a daily newspaper or two to keep abreast of the world.

We do *not* assume that you have a Master's of Business Administration degree. It certainly isn't necessary, and as a good investor you probably know that an MBA isn't worth nearly as much as everyone used to think it was. We also don't assume that you know how to read a balance sheet and an income statement. If you're interested enough in investing in stocks, that skill is picked up easily along the way.

As you embark on an investment program—or salvage the remains of a previous, unsuccessful one—there are certain things we think you must keep in mind. Collectively, they add up to:

Colloca sapienter.
Invest wisely.

■ You alone are responsible for your investment decisions. Don't blame this book, your broker, Congress, or your spouse and children for the mistakes you will invariably make. On the other hand, take credit for the decisions that work well, and don't let anyone else (like your broker) take bows *ex post facto*.

■ Your broker is not your friend. He or she may be cordial, competent, and clever, but never forget: Brokers make money whether you win or lose. There's a simple test you can conduct to eliminate the worst brokers right away. Find two mutual funds with similar objectives and performance, one of which rewards the broker with a sales commission while the other, known as a "no-load" fund, doesn't. Ask a broker which is best for you. Be prepared for a long search.

■ The markets are not your friends, either. A common misconception among investors is that they are owed something by the financial markets. You give the market some money, and it gives you more back. But markets have no emotions and no commitments. The stock market isn't some friendly pet that roams Wall Street. It's an arena in which lots of very smart people want to take your money and put it in their pockets.

■ Never buy an investment you don't understand. Some brokers and financial advisers work hard at leaving their clients slightly mystified about whatever it is they peddle. This creates a dependency that the broker then continues to exploit for years at his clients' expense. Even worse are the brokers who themselves don't really understand what it is they are selling.

■ Don't buy anything over the phone if you didn't originate the call. We can't begin to count the number of otherwise perfectly sane people who, beguiled by an unsolicited sales pitch, have sent huge checks off to total strangers. These folks spend the rest of their lives trying to get even a portion of their money back and hating themselves for being duped. Life is far too short for that.

■ Simplicity is better than complexity. By this we don't mean be unsophisticated. We don't recommend putting all your money into a single stock, for example, though that's a lot simpler than buying 50 of them. But be a good engineer, constructing a portfolio no more complicated than it has to be to accomplish your goals.

■ Leverage is dangerous. Investing with borrowed money can produce immense returns and also immense losses. Unless you thoroughly understand a leveraged investment and are financially and psychologically prepared to accept the worst that might happen, confine your use of leverage to buying a house in which to live. Even that can be highly risky, but at least you can come in out of the rain to contemplate life's cruelties.

■ As your coach might have told you in school, play heads-up ball. You have to know when to hold 'em and when to fold 'em, when to make your move and when to sit back. No amount of advice can supplant paying attention to what you're doing and knowing exactly why you're doing it. If you don't know, don't do it. Remember, a lost opportunity is better than lost money.

■ Base your investment decisions on investment criteria, not something related perhaps but in reality quite different. For example, don't go into an investment *solely* for its supposed tax benefits or because your son got a job with the company. Above all, superstition has no place in an investment program. If you think the alignment of planets has something to do with total return, please put this book back on the shelf without bending the corners.

■   Enjoy the investment process. There are bound to be frustrations in any investment program, and you must live with them. But if you're constantly fretting about whether you have made the right decision regarding a particular investment, it is almost a sure bet that you haven't. Not that it's a bad investment from a financial point of view but because it's one you can't be comfortable with. Unwind it at the first opportunity and put the money somewhere that allows you to relax and enjoy life.

We know you want to get right down to the business of picking some stocks that will make you wealthy. Chapter Three of this book is aimed at helping you decide how to pick stocks. But don't be in such a hurry. Investing in haste has been the undoing of many a portfolio. Instead, spend a little time in Chapters One and Two. We wrote them to help you devise a *systematic* approach to investing that will stay with you for the rest of your life, subject only to your changing financial circumstances.

CHAPTER ONE.   You will be asked to assess your own tolerance for risk, taking into account such variables as age and investment objectives. It is to your advantage to be brutally honest with yourself. There's no room for reluctant heroes in the financial markets. If you don't like risk, no one is going to think less of you for choosing a conservative approach to investing. On the other hand, we hope you'll see that, given sufficient time, seemingly risky investments might not be so risky after all and some "safe" ones could end up costing you plenty.

We'll also discuss some of the costs of investing, not the least of which can be the time you spend monitoring and managing your investment portfolio. Again, we want you to be honest with yourself. If you really enjoy following the ups and downs of a portfolio of stocks, deciding what to buy and, perhaps more difficult, when to sell, that's wonderful. You're exactly the kind of person for whom *Barron's* is published. But if you'd really rather be out playing golf Saturday mornings instead of poring over the stock tables, that's fine, too. You can still have a sophisticated investment program that will produce substantial gains over time; you'll just need some help in running it. And we can assist you there as well. The financial services business has more than its share of shysters, fakes, and plain old crooks. But it's also full of many very smart, creative, and interesting people from whom you can learn and profit. The key is knowing what you are getting for your money. That's where Chapter One comes in.

CHAPTER TWO. The next step in establishing your lifetime investment program is deciding how to distribute your investment capital among the various markets and instruments available to the individual investor. Professional money managers often try to make the asset allocation process some kind of mysterious ritual, the secrets of which are known only to those in the investment advisory business. Bah, humbug! There's nothing the least bit mysterious about the process once you recognize your own tolerance for risk and identify your investment objectives. We have devised a few simple asset allocation programs to illustrate how the process works. But they're only illustrations. Part of the challenge and the fun of investing is to devise your own program, one that is uniquely suited to your personality, your financial resources and your investment goals.

CHAPTER THREE. *Now* you can start looking for those hot stocks. But be careful. Hot stocks can burn you as assuredly as hot pots. In Chapter Three you will get an overview of the risks and rewards of the stock market. You'll probably notice that this is the longest chapter in the book, and that's no accident. The U.S. stock market is probably the single most fascinating playground in the world for true investors. The rich menu from which to choose—from staid old blue chips to tiny companies that exist only to bring to fruition an idea lurking in some scientist's mind—has something for everybody. The dynamics of the U.S. economy, the world's largest and most influential, keeps the market churning with activity. And the securities laws and enforcement agencies make this the world's most open market as well. Nobody guarantees profits in the U.S. stock market, but there is no place better to give it your best shot.

CHAPTER FOUR. Bonds are often thought of as the *safe* investment, which they certainly can be. Indeed, probably nothing is safer than a U.S. Treasury bond held to maturity. But the bond market is seething with products that can take a big bite out of your portfolio and never give it back. Perhaps you weren't aware that municipal bonds, those havens for the heavily taxed, can be highly risky. And junk bonds didn't get their name by accident. Chapter Four takes you on a walk through this deceptively quiet forest, pointing out the dangers lurking behind bonds of every stripe.

CHAPTER FIVE. Mutual funds aren't just for investment wimps. You will see in Chapter Five that mutual funds can get you into places you can't go by yourself, such as to many foreign markets. They offer instant diversification and, as long as you stick to no-load funds, relatively inexpensive access to some top-notch money managers. You can even set up an entire portfolio based on mutual funds. But they can be deceiving, too. If you're one of the millions of Americans who hate to pay taxes, beware of municipal bond funds: Part of their gains come from trading bonds, and you'll owe taxes on those gains. Another caution: Sector funds, which concentrate on investments in only one industry, force you to make asset allocation decisions that you might not be prepared to make. We'll look at fee structures as well as the perils and pitfalls of old standbys, especially index funds. And we'll tell you about a new kind of fund that is traded on a stock exchange.

CHAPTER SIX. If you need or want more personal attention than mutual funds can provide, a competent money management firm may be the answer. Just be aware that you will pay for the service. What's more, you'll already have to be something of a successful investor yourself because many firms require minimum investments. Those minimums are coming down a bit, however, because of competition. Banks compete with insurance companies, which compete with stock brokers, who compete with fee-based advisers—all to get their hands on fees and commissions for helping investors run their finances. We survey this fast-growing money-management scene.

CHAPTER SEVEN. Americans are only beginning to feel comfortable sending some of their investment money abroad. Yet as you will see in Chapter Seven, foreign markets, which make up half of the investment universe, have produced superior long-term results. The wise investor will put at least a portion of his portfolio in international stocks and bonds. But you probably can't do it alone. International investing is expensive, cumbersome, and risky for the individual, but mutual funds and closed-end funds can help smooth the process.

CHAPTER EIGHT. As we said, leverage is dangerous. But futures and options have their uses, not least of which are the potential of enhancing returns on your portfolio and reducing your exposure to market risk. Trouble is, you will have to study long and hard to master this part of the investment world. If you leave it all up to brokers and advisers and don't make the effort to understand what they are doing and why, you deserve the losses you are certain to sustain.

CHAPTER NINE. If you own your home, you already are a certified real estate investor. Indeed, this real estate could well constitute the largest single asset in your portfolio. If you don't own a home, think twice before buying one. We'll show you in Chapter Nine that there are powerful demographic trends working against real estate prices, and you might be better off investing some of that money elsewhere. You can still get exposure to real estate in much smaller quantities through real estate investment trusts, or REITs, which trade on the stock exchanges. But steer clear of limited partnerships; they are usually much too limited.

CHAPTER TEN. Each season you read in the newspapers about the fabulous prices paid for works of art. What you don't read about are all the paintings hanging on walls or sitting in attics and basements that were bought not for their beauty or interest but for investment. In Chapter Ten we explore the fascinating but treacherous world of collectibles. You might one day make money by selling your baseball card collection, your toy soldier collection, or the decorated egg collection, but don't bet on it. Collect for enjoyment, yes, but don't collect as an investment.

CHAPTER ELEVEN. Uncle Sam is such a pain in the neck. He does damn little to help you make good investment decisions, but he sure wants his cut when the score is settled. He has been nice to investors lately by reducing the tax rate on capital gains. Still, there are ways to lighten your tax burden even further, which we elaborate on in Chapter Eleven. But never, ever invest just to avoid taxes.

1 Setting Investment Objectives

"Someone keeps moving the finish line."

Investing is only half about money. The other half is time. Any successful investment program is based on the identification of objectives that can be placed somewhere on a time line. You can decide if each objective is a reasonable goal, given how much time you have to achieve it. To undertake an investment program at age 40 with the aim of retiring to a Caribbean island in five years is probably ludicrous (unless you're starting with an awfully big grubstake or are willing to accept a humbling decline in your standard of living). It isn't nearly so unreasonable if you have 20 years to get there.

It's always later than you think when it comes to starting an investment program. But while it's always better to start early rather than late in life, it's also better to start late rather than never. You just have to remember to set objectives that are reachable within the time frame you have. And don't make those objectives too specific. If buying that house or boat requires you to earn 20% per year for five years, you're going to be disappointed and frustrated. Trying to force the market to march to your drumbeat is a losing proposition.

In fact, this is the time and place for an important reality check. Although it is always possible that the future holds tremendous surprises for us, you probably shouldn't count on earning much more than about 12% annually from a long-term investment program—and that's assuming you're willing to take more risk than the average investor. Although the past doesn't necessarily predict the future, that's roughly the average return from a diversified stock portfolio since World War II; it's a little on the rich side if you go back to World War I. You might be really smart (lucky is more likely) and do better than that. Or you might make more than your share of dumb mistakes and do worse. In any case, that's *before* taxes and *before* inflation. If you're in the top tax brackets, kiss more than a third of that return good-bye and make sure your investment objectives reflect an anticipated 8% annual return *after* taxes. Taxes are what make 401k plans and IRAs so attractive to smart investors. Taxes also make tax-free municipal bonds attractive to many investors, but they aren't always a bright buy.

Now subtract inflation from the equation. If it's running at a relatively modest 4% annually, subtract that 4% from your return for a *net return* of 4%. That's right, 4%. Horrible, isn't it? But what if you're a very conservative investor and have all your money tied up in a money market account yielding 7% before taxes and inflation? You'll end the year with a *net loss.* More horrible, isn't it? Avoiding that trap is the entire reason behind having a long-term investment plan.

There is no need to limit your entire portfolio to a single time frame. Just because your child is going to Outrageous U. in five years doesn't mean you should neglect the care and feeding of your retirement nest egg. (Remember what we said about getting started early.) Instead, have a separate time frame for each objective: the kid to college; new car or furniture (please don't finance these purchases unless you use them in your business and

SETTING INVESTMENT OBJECTIVES **19**

Figure 1.1 Stock Market Performance, 1950-1997
Annual Percentage Change

Year	Dow Jones Industrial Average	Standard & Poor's 500 Index	Year	Dow Jones Industrial Average	Standard & Poor's 500 Index
1950	17.63%	21.78%	1974	-27.57%	-29.57%
1951	14.37%	16.46%	1975	38.32%	31.55%
1952	8.42%	11.78%	1976	17.86%	19.14%
1953	-3.77%	-6.62%	1977	-17.27%	-11.50%
1954	43.96%	45.02%	1978	-3.15%	1.07%
1955	20.77%	26.40%	1979	4.19%	12.31%
1956	2.27%	2.62%	1980	14.93%	25.77%
1957	-12.77%	-14.31%	1981	-9.23%	-9.73%
1958	33.96%	38.06%	1982	19.60%	14.76%
1959	16.40%	8.48%	1983	20.27%	17.27%
1960	-9.34%	-2.97%	1984	-3.74%	1.40%
1961	18.71%	23.13%	1985	27.66%	26.33%
1962	-10.81%	-11.81%	1986	22.58%	14.62%
1963	17.00%	18.89%	1987	2.26%	2.03%
1964	14.57%	12.97%	1988	11.85%	12.40%
1965	10.88%	9.06%	1989	26.96%	27.25%
1966	-18.94%	-13.09%	1990	-4.34%	-6.56%
1967	15.20%	20.09%	1991	20.32%	26.31%
1968	4.27%	7.66%	1992	4.17%	4.46%
1969	-15.19%	-11.36%	1993	13.72%	7.06%
1970	4.82%	-0.07%	1994	2.14%	-1.54%
1971	6.11%	10.82%	1995	33.45%	34.11%
1972	14.58%	15.79%	1996	26.01%	20.26%
1973	-16.58%	-17.53%	1997	22.64%	31.01%

can gain some tax advantages); the boat of your dreams; and a comfortable retirement. Bear in mind, though, that these objectives vary not only in when they are to be reached but also in the amount of money they require. An Ivy League college education costs more than a degree from a state university. And a comfortable retirement, although perhaps further away, will require far more money than a degree from any college. As you set these objectives down on your time line, you will understand why it is never too early to start that investment program. The less time you have, the more likely it is you will find yourself having to make some hard choices: a kid with a degree *or* that boat.

TIME AND RISK

Time also plays an important role in the relative risk of investment vehicles or strategies. A bank certificate of deposit or money market account are usually considered "safe" in that there is little risk of losing some of your invested capital. But it also isn't likely to grow very much. Over a long period—and the definition of what constitutes a "long period" seems to be growing shorter all the time—the money parked so safely faces much larger risks than most people realize. Inflation can eat into it much more quickly than you suspect. If it doesn't, then you may face "reinvestment risk"—having to roll over that maturing CD into some similar instrument with even lower returns or higher risks. Millions of retirees came face-to-face with that unpleasant picture in the 1990s as interest rates plunged. And don't forget the fact that money tied up in a five-year CD can't be put to work more profitably elsewhere.

Conversely, investments that seem risky on their face—small growth stocks, for instance—are indeed risky in the short run. It's quite easy to conceive of putting $20,000 into a portfolio of small stocks and watching it plunge in price for a year or two. That $20,000 can become $10,000 awfully fast. But over a period of 10 years—better yet, 20 years—a portfolio of small stocks is likely to provide among the best returns of any investment you probably are going to be comfortable making.

To get an idea about the relative long-term risks of investments, consider that since 1926 there have been 20 calendar years in which Standard & Poor's 500-stock index declined. Some of those drops were breathtaking, especially the 43% plunge in 1931, the worst of them all. Since 1926, however, stocks have produced an annual return of 10.4%, including reinvested dividends. In that same period, long-term government bonds, considered relatively "safe" investments, produced a total return (price changes plus interest payments) of 4.8% annually. And Treasury bills, regarded as about the safest investment one can make, returned 3.7% annually, barely above the average 3.1% annual rate of inflation. So, which is really the "safest" investment for the long-term investor?

On the basis of all this, we feel free now to make these grossly generalized statements about time, money, and risk:

- Risky investments can turn a lot of money into a little money very quickly. But over the long haul, risky investments can turn a little money into a lot of money.

- Safe investments can turn a lot of money into a little more money over the short term. And they can turn a lot of money into a little less money over the long term.

Please remember that we mean *reasonable* risk. If you want to take on some really big risks, such as playing the commodities markets, this should be your principle: Commodities can make any amount of money disappear damned fast.

At this point we'll assume you have firmly in mind some investment objectives and have set them down on some kind of time line that gives you a clear picture of when those objectives need to be met. What you must do now is determine how much money will be required to meet them. Suddenly, our old friend time becomes an enemy. The further away your objectives, the more difficult it will be to estimate accurately how much money will be required to meet your goal. What's more, inflation, even if it runs at only a modest rate, will be steadily working against you, quietly robbing you of some of the value of your future investment gains.

Consider a simple goal like financing your kids' college education. If your son or daughter is 17 years old, it isn't hard to know approximately what you will need for four years of college. You probably know which college your child will be attending, have the schedule of tuition, fees, room and board for next year, and can project 5%-to-10% increases in each of the following years. But if your kids are, say, four years old, you face a lot more uncertainty. College costs have been rising substantially faster than the annual rate of inflation, and there isn't any reason to expect that trend to stop anytime soon. What will be the cost of a four-year college

Figure 1.2 Life's Events Requiring Financial Planning

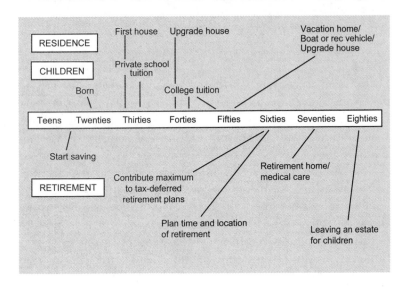

education that begins 14 years from now? You can't be certain, but assuming a 10% annual increase in each of those 14 years will probably—but not necessarily—lead you to set an investment goal that will be adequate to do the job. If you fall short, it most likely won't be by much. And if you find 14 years from now that you have overestimated the cost, congratulate yourself on the savings and invest it in your retirement portfolio. But remember, achieving a 10% annual return isn't going to be easy, especially if you have other investment objectives or if you tend to be on the conservative side.

A good way to get a feel for how much money you need to be investing now—or how much risk you need to be taking—is to use the table in Figure 1.3. It shows the *present value* of money extended into the future. Take one of your goals—let's say the purchase of a new car in five years when the old one is surely going to be ready for the junk heap. You figure you'll need $25,000 for the new buggy, and you can invest money in five-year bonds yielding 6%. Work across the top of the chart to 6%, then go down that column to five years. That number, .747, tells you that to have a dollar five years from now you should immediately invest nearly 75 cents at 6%. To fund your car purchase, in other words, you'll need to invest $18,675 right away. Now let's look at some big numbers. Say you figure you'll need $800,000 in 20 years when you retire, and you think your aggressive investment tactics can net you an 8% annual gain after taxes. Find 8% across the top, drop down that column to 20 years, and you see the number, .215. That means to get a dollar 20 years hence you need to invest about 22 cents now at 8% interest. If you don't make any further contributions to your retirement, you need to have $172,000 working away, earning an average 8% per year after taxes. Awesome, isn't it? Frightening, really.

Figure 1.3 Present Value Table

Years Hence	1%	2%	4%	6%	8%	10%	12%	14%	15%	16%
1	0.990	0.980	0.962	0.943	0.926	0.909	0.893	0.877	0.870	0.862
2	0.980	0.961	0.925	0.890	0.857	0.826	0.797	0.769	0.756	0.743
3	0.971	0.942	0.889	0.840	0.794	0.751	0.712	0.675	0.658	0.641
4	0.961	0.924	0.855	0.792	0.735	0.683	0.636	0.592	0.572	0.552
5	0.951	0.906	0.822	0.747	0.681	0.621	0.567	0.519	0.497	0.476
6	0.941	0.888	0.790	0.705	0.630	0.564	0.507	0.456	0.432	0.410
7	0.933	0.871	0.760	0.665	0.583	0.513	0.452	0.400	0.376	0.354
8	0.923	0.853	0.731	0.627	0.540	0.467	0.404	0.351	0.327	0.305
9	0.914	0.837	0.703	0.592	0.500	0.424	0.361	0.308	0.284	0.263
10	0.905	0.820	0.676	0.558	0.463	0.386	0.322	0.270	0.247	0.227
11	0.896	0.804	0.650	0.527	0.429	0.350	0.287	0.237	0.215	0.195
12	0.887	0.788	0.625	0.497	0.397	0.319	0.257	0.208	0.187	0.168
13	0.879	0.773	0.601	0.469	0.368	0.290	0.229	0.182	0.163	0.145
14	0.870	0.758	0.577	0.442	0.340	0.263	0.205	0.160	0.141	0.125
15	0.861	0.743	0.555	0.417	0.315	0.239	0.183	0.140	0.123	0.108
16	0.853	0.728	0.534	0.394	0.292	0.218	0.163	0.123	0.107	0.093
17	0.844	0.714	0.513	0.371	0.270	0.198	0.146	0.108	0.093	0.080
18	0.836	0.700	0.494	0.350	0.250	0.180	0.130	0.095	0.081	0.069
19	0.828	0.686	0.475	0.331	0.232	0.164	0.116	0.083	0.070	0.060
20	0.820	0.673	0.456	0.312	0.215	0.149	0.104	0.073	0.061	0.051
21	0.811	0.660	0.439	0.294	0.199	0.135	0.093	0.064	0.053	0.044
22	0.803	0.647	0.422	0.278	0.184	0.123	0.083	0.056	0.046	0.038
23	0.795	0.634	0.406	0.262	0.170	0.112	0.074	0.049	0.040	0.033
24	0.788	0.622	0.390	0.247	0.158	0.102	0.066	0.043	0.035	0.028
25	0.780	0.610	0.375	0.233	0.146	0.092	0.059	0.038	0.030	0.024
26	0.772	0.598	0.361	0.220	0.135	0.084	0.053	0.033	0.026	0.021
27	0.764	0.586	0.347	0.207	0.125	0.076	0.047	0.029	0.023	0.018
28	0.757	0.574	0.333	0.196	0.116	0.069	0.042	0.026	0.020	0.016
29	0.749	0.563	0.321	0.185	0.107	0.063	0.037	0.022	0.017	0.014
30	0.742	0.552	0.308	0.174	0.099	0.057	0.033	0.020	0.015	0.012
40	0.672	0.453	0.208	0.097	0.046	0.022	0.011	0.005	0.004	0.003
50	0.608	0.372	0.141	0.054	0.021	0.009	0.003	0.001	0.001	0.001

EXAMPLE: Suppose you need $20,000 10 years into the future. How much must you invest today to achieve it assuming a 12% rate of return? First, enter the chart at "10 Years Hence" and move right until you intersect

Figure 1.3 *continued*

18%	20%	22%	24%	25%	26%	28%	30%	35%	40%	45%	50%
0.847	0.833	0.820	0.806	0.800	0.794	0.781	0.769	0.741	0.714	0.690	0.667
0.718	0.694	0.672	0.650	0.640	0.630	0.610	0.592	0.549	0.510	0.476	0.444
0.609	0.579	0.551	0.524	0.512	0.500	0.477	0.455	0.406	0.364	0.328	0.296
0.516	0.482	0.451	0.423	0.410	0.397	0.373	0.350	0.301	0.260	0.226	0.198
0.437	0.402	0.370	0.341	0.328	0.315	0.291	0.269	0.223	0.186	0.156	0.132
0.370	0.335	0.303	0.275	0.262	0.250	0.227	0.207	0.165	0.133	0.108	0.088
0.314	0.279	0.249	0.222	0.210	0.198	0.178	0.159	0.122	0.095	0.074	0.059
0.266	0.233	0.204	0.179	0.168	0.157	0.139	0.123	0.091	0.068	0.051	0.039
0.225	0.194	0.167	0.144	0.134	0.125	0.108	0.094	0.067	0.048	0.035	0.026
0.191	0.162	0.137	0.116	0.107	0.099	0.085	0.073	0.050	0.035	0.024	0.017
0.162	0.135	0.112	0.094	0.086	0.079	0.066	0.056	0.037	0.025	0.017	0.012
0.137	0.112	0.092	0.076	0.069	0.062	0.052	0.043	0.027	0.018	0.012	0.008
0.116	0.093	0.075	0.061	0.055	0.050	0.040	0.033	0.020	0.013	0.008	0.005
0.099	0.078	0.062	0.049	0.044	0.039	0.032	0.025	0.015	0.009	0.006	0.003
0.084	0.065	0.051	0.040	0.035	0.031	0.025	0.020	0.011	0.006	0.004	0.002
0.071	0.054	0.042	0.032	0.028	0.025	0.019	0.015	0.008	0.005	0.003	0.002
0.060	0.045	0.034	0.026	0.023	0.020	0.015	0.012	0.006	0.003	0.002	0.001
0.051	0.038	0.028	0.021	0.018	0.016	0.012	0.009	0.005	0.002	0.001	0.001
0.043	0.031	0.023	0.017	0.014	0.012	0.009	0.007	0.003	0.002	0.001	
0.037	0.026	0.019	0.014	0.012	0.010	0.007	0.005	0.002	0.001	0.001	
0.031	0.022	0.015	0.011	0.009	0.008	0.006	0.004	0.002	0.001		
0.026	0.018	0.013	0.009	0.007	0.006	0.004	0.003	0.001	0.001		
0.022	0.015	0.010	0.007	0.006	0.005	0.003	0.002	0.001			
0.019	0.013	0.008	0.006	0.005	0.004	0.003	0.002	0.001			
0.016	0.010	0.007	0.005	0.004	0.003	0.002	0.001	0.001			
0.014	0.009	0.006	0.004	0.003	0.002	0.002	0.001				
0.011	0.007	0.005	0.003	0.002	0.002	0.001	0.001				
0.010	0.006	0.004	0.002	0.002	0.002	0.001	0.001				
0.008	0.005	0.003	0.002	0.002	0.001	0.001	0.001				
0.007	0.004	0.003	0.002	0.001	0.001	0.001					
0.001	0.001										
the column headed by the label "12%." The factor is 0.322. Multiply $20,000 by											
0.322; you will find that the present value of this amount (discounted at 12%) is											
$6440.00.											

TO SPEND OR INVEST, THAT IS THE QUESTION

Now that you have a better idea of the time and money it takes to reach your financial goals, it's time to face up to the self-discipline that also is required.

We all have finite financial resources, and there are two basic choices we face for every dollar we have or will get in the future: spend it or invest it. If we spend it, we get something in return, whether it's a fine restaurant meal, a new dress, or a spiffy car. Those things are all fine, but they're somewhat ephemeral: The memory of the meal fades, we outgrow the dress, and the car eventually falls apart. If we invest a dollar, we hope to get back both the dollar plus some return. It doesn't always work out that way because we sometimes make bad investments, but for the most part a dedicated long-term investor will wind up with more money than he or she started with.

The fact that we have a choice of investing or spending brings us to a simple but very important concept in running a successful investment program: *opportunity costs*. In essence, this concept requires us to think each time we either spend or invest a dollar about what else we could do with that dollar. In its simplest form it becomes a question of whether to eat out for $50 (that includes the tip but not a bottle of wine) or eat at home for a total cost of $8 and save the other $42. Put that way, it doesn't sound like much is at stake; an occasional $50 meal won't break most of us, and it's fun to go out. But apply the same logic to something considerably more expensive, such as a new car. And apply it also over an extended period of time, say 10 or 12 years. During that time many of us wind up buying a new car every four years or so.

Now you may think you know what those cars cost you. After all, you dickered with the salesman, who knocked

$1,000 or so off the sticker price, and he gave you a generous trade-in offer on your old car, as well. But what if instead of buying three new cars during a 12-year period you bought just one and kept it for all 12 years, investing what you would have paid for new cars in the fourth and eighth year?

Let's look at two individuals who follow these very different strategies. Ralph likes tooling around town in a relatively new car; Jane figures a car is a device to get her from Point A to Point B and doesn't much care what it looks like. We'll start them out buying identical $25,000 sedans. Ralph buys a new car every four years. His old car depreciates about 50% over four years (that means he gets half the purchase price back when he trades it in on a new model), but car prices also rise at the rate of 4% per year. Jane used up all her available cash to buy her new car, so she can't start investing for four years. When she does, she'll invest the same amount that Ralph had to pay out of pocket for a new car, after his trade-in. Jane's stock portfolio rises at an annual rate of 10%, about the long-term average for stocks. At the end of the eighth year, she'll add to her portfolio the same amount Ralph paid out of pocket for his third new car.

At the end of 12 years, Ralph is driving around in a four-year-old car worth about $16,450. Jane, on the other hand, is riding around in a car worth about $1,000, but she is comforted by the fact that her investment portfolio is now worth $61,066. How much did those new cars really cost Ralph? A lot more than he thought!

We aren't telling you to never eat out, never buy a new dress, or never drive a new car. All we're doing is pointing out that spending and investing decisions we make now have much larger long-term implications than many of us realize. A fine, expensive meal is a true delight. So is the freedom from financial worry that comes with a healthy savings and investment program. Maybe the best advice we can offer is that old saw: all things in moderation.

MAKING THE FIRST CUT

Now is the time for you to make the first cut in the investment process. If, because of your age or because of the particular investment goals you have identified, your investment "horizon" is five years or less, you are by default a conservative investor who accepts a lower return in exchange for less risk. Without thinking much about it, you probably have the bulk of your investment program in short-term (one year or less) and intermediate-term (one to seven years) Treasury notes. As we'll see later, that isn't necessarily the best portfolio for your situation, but it recognizes reality. If you're entirely in stocks, then you're a gambler, not an investor. Taking risks without the benefit of time to correct or smooth the peaks and valleys of returns is foolish. If you can't meet your investment objective without taking undue risks, then you need to change the objective. Either place it farther in the future or scale down your expectations.

If, however, your main objective falls somewhere between five and ten years on your investment horizon, you can afford to step up the risk component of your portfolio a bit, devoting more of it to stocks instead of keeping it all in Treasury notes. As your objective approaches, though, you probably should skew your portfolio increasingly toward conservative investments. If you see that you aren't going to hit your target, don't, as many people are prone to do, step up the risky portion of the portfolio hoping to regain the lost ground. You could easily wind up even farther from the target. Instead, recognize that the error lay in setting too ambitious a target for the time available. Lower your sights to a level that you can hit.

Once your horizon extends to ten years or more you can start to enjoy the flexibility of a full-blown investment program that encompasses the entire range of stocks as well as other interesting, albeit more risky, investments. The farther out you go, the more risks you can take. If you just have to try your hand at a little commodity trading, go ahead. Better to learn how risky commodity trading can be now, when you have plenty of time to recover, than later when unexpected losses could have disastrous consequences for reaching your financial goals. Besides, you'll get it out of your system and have one less regret in your old age.

THE NATURE OF RISK

In grappling with the concept of risk, most people try to reduce it to a matter of chance. What are the chances that I will make a big profit or suffer a big loss? Certainly you need to have a sense of whether the odds are for or against you. But there's a second aspect of risk that is much more important for investors: What are the *consequences* of taking risks? In other words, if the odds go against you, what will be the results? If, for instance, you are 30 years old and just beginning to invest for your retirement, what are the consequences if the market goes against you next year? Minor, at worst. You'll be 31 instead of 30, and you'll have 34 years instead of 35 to invest for your retirement. But what if you're 45, have a kid who has been accepted into Harvard, and you have to ante up for tuition, room, and board in six months? The consequences of a big drop in stock prices could be disastrous for you if you were counting on paying junior's college bills out of your stock portfolio. And that's why setting realistic investment objectives and knowing the period of time in which they are to be reached is so critical to the construction of a lifetime investment portfolio.

The Psychology of Risk

To understand risk you have to think about it. Not everyone likes to do that. Some time back, in a well-intentioned effort to prevent panic in stalled elevator cars, the Los Angeles city government required each elevator to carry a placard that said: "There is little danger of the car dropping uncontrollably or running out of air." It wasn't long before the stairwells in every building were clogged with people who were willing to trudge up and down rather than endure the thought of the "little" risks that the placards mentioned.

We have seen that time is an important factor in making investment decisions. But knowing rationally that time can help reduce risk doesn't eliminate the psychological burden of risk. So, as an investor, you need to think carefully—and as unemotionally as possible—about your own attitude toward risk.

Our nation was built by people who took risks, and it thrives because of them. From the first adventurers who sailed here across the stormy North Atlantic to the young entrepreneur creating new software for personal computers, risk takers have been the engines driving our economy. We tend to admire people who take risks, such as mountain climbers, fighter pilots, and aggressive business executives. We also tend to think of ourselves as risk takers. To do otherwise is to think of ourselves as, heaven forbid, chickens.

There have been innumerable tests devised by psychologists and money managers that purport to measure your willingness to take risk. Some of them ask questions like this:

> You are playing blackjack in Las Vegas. You have lost $1,000 so far. How much are you prepared to lose to win the $1,000 back?

A) Nothing. You're heading for the bar.

B) $200

C) $500

D) $1,000

E) More than $1,000.

Obviously, the less you are willing to lose to win back your $1,000, the more conservative you are. Did you need a Ph.D. to figure that out? What we want to know is what a really smart investor was doing in Las Vegas in the first place? Isn't investing in the financial markets risky enough without having to go somewhere expensive to play a game in which you know the odds are against you?

Properly constructed tests can help you get a grasp on your own ability to tolerate risk as long as you realize a few things about the tests. First, the results of any tests provide only a general description of risk tolerance and shouldn't be used in any formula for setting up an investment portfolio. Use the tests only as one part of your effort to understand your own attitude toward risk. Second, be brutally honest with yourself. There isn't any room in the financial markets for posturing and bluff. We suspect one reason that tests haven't proven very useful in many instances—even when the results won't be known by anyone other than the test taker—is that people just aren't willing to admit, even to themselves, that they don't like to take risks.

Many money managers who use tests have found that the tests in and of themselves aren't very helpful. If a client knows his own risk tolerance and admits it up front, there is no need for a test. And a client who doesn't know his level of risk tolerance—or isn't willing to admit it—invalidates the test. Instead, the tests and its results provide a basis for *discussing* the role of risk in an investment program. It's from the discussions that the money managers find they learn most about their clients' attitudes toward risk. The tests simply serve as a starting point for the discussion.

A lot of myths are floating around about what kinds of people seek or avoid risk. It is commonly assumed, for instance, that the wealthy are much more willing to take financial risks than the rest of us. Certainly they have more money to throw around, but it isn't that simple. People who made their money by starting and growing their own business frequently are more willing to take higher risks. And money managers who handle their portfolios love entrepreneurs as clients. Entrepreneurs don't chew out money managers for an occasional bad call. They know the money manager will make a mistake because they made mistakes in running their own businesses. Not so the wealthy heirs who did little or nothing but outlive their parents to become rich. They tend to feel entitled to big gains and no losses. Money managers secretly hate them because of their intolerance of occasional mistakes and their insistence on impossibly fat returns.

It is often thought that sex makes a difference in the willingness to take on risk. Older women, for example, are regarded as the most risk averse of investors. But surveys and studies of investment patterns show that women of a given age group tend to be no more or less risk averse than men in the same age group. And younger women tend to be more risk averse than older women.

How, then, does one determine one's risk tolerance? We suggest that you review your willingness to take risks so far in your life and use that as your guideline. Have you ever quit a good, well-paying job without having another already in place? Without knowing the specific circumstances, we'd consider that somewhat risky. Or do you worry about losing your job even though you're doing good work and have been commended by your boss? You may not be a big risk taker. Do you keep a sizable amount of cash on hand to meet unexpected emergencies? That's probably evidence of a conserv-ative bias toward investing. Finally, ask yourself why you made any previous investments. Were you looking to make a killing? Or were you looking for something fairly safe?

Ignorance can have something to do with your will-ingness to take risks. If you tend to be a conservative investor, you probably already know enough to avoid invest-ments you don't understand. But if you become interested in one investment category and begin to study and comprehend it, a new door may open for you. Suddenly you understand the nature of the risk in small stocks and find that it isn't as frightening as it was when you didn't really understand it. Conversely, if you think you're a high flyer and jump into commodities (See how this subject of commodities keeps coming up? Are you catching on yet?) without understand-ing what that market is all about, hopefully it won't take you too long or cost you too much to figure it out. Flying high in a carefully designed aircraft is one thing; jumping out of that plane with no parachute is something very different.

In the end there is no point in trying to fool yourself or others about all this; nobody else really cares, and it is the quality of *your* life that's at stake. Figure out what sort of per-son you are, then be at peace with it. If you're comfortable with a conservative approach to investing, don't berate your-self because everybody, including your mailman—oops, sorry, letter carrier—is riding high on some hot little stock. Take pleasure instead in your ability to sleep very well.

EMOTIONS AND INVESTING

Some of the best professional investors we know are the ones who have managed as much as possible to remove emotion from the investment process. They aren't much fun, but they're good investors. There are several emotions that most investors encounter, and it's important that you be aware of your own susceptibility to them. The most natural one, of course, is pure *greed*. You will almost certainly come across ideas or opportunities that seem as though they will result in big gains fast. The desire for those potential gains can blind you to the possible losses. Combat greed by keeping in mind the simple maxim: If it looks too good to be true, it probably is.

Another controlling emotion is *fear*. Too often investors focus on short-term results to confirm that their investment judgment is sound. This anxious investor moves much too quickly to dump a stock that stumbles for a quarter or two. If you are investing for the long run, give your investments time to work. If you find yourself too anxious, you should adjust your portfolio to bring that anxiety level down to manageable levels.

A third emotional hurdle facing you as an investor is the tendency to project the future from your most recent experience. If your portfolio performs spectacularly this year, you want that performance to continue next year. When it doesn't, you'll be disappointed and tempted to change your approach to investing. On the other hand, if your portfolio performs poorly this year, you'll feel that you have made a serious mistake and begin adjusting your investment program to try to get better performance, perhaps raising the risk to an unacceptable level and causing even bigger problems. This weakness for "straight-line projection" of the future is why we think one of the worst things that can happen is for you to win big the first time you play the commodities markets.

Of course we can't and probably don't want to become automatons. Rather, accept the fact that emotions will be part of your investment approach and be prepared to recognize and deal with them. A little greed and a little anxiety will keep you on your toes. A lot of either will result in catastrophe.

How Much Time Do You Have?

Now let's go back to the subject of time again—specifically, how much of it you have to devote to your investments *each week*. Tending to an investment portfolio is a lot like gardening. Most small gardens don't require much attention, and large ones require more. But they both require some. The difference between investing and gardening, at least up north where we live, is that gardening is a seasonal thing while investing is a year-round undertaking. If you have either accidentally or purposely set up a portfolio that requires ten hours of attention each week, but you have only two to give to it, you will get into trouble. And you must give your time willingly. If you get up resentfully on Saturday mornings and trudge upstairs after breakfast to your desk to review the new issue of *Barron's* when you'd rather be at your daughter's soccer game or off the coast trying to catch a tuna, you are flashing yourself a warning that you're in over your head. The flood of money into mutual funds in recent years is the result, at least in part, of hundreds of thousands of busy people deciding they are better doctors, executives, or parents than they are investment managers. Don't be ashamed to admit it. Set up a portfolio—or turn it over to someone else—that frees you to do the things which are really important to you.

Here is something else to think about: Assuming you have the time to run your own investment portfolio, or at least parts of it, you now need to ask yourself how much money you are willing to spend—invest, really—in running your portfolio. Forget for the moment the outside costs that come with investing—mostly the fees you're going to be charged for buying or selling securities. We'll get to those next. Right now we are thinking about the newsletters, the databases, the computer software, and all the other things that purport to make investing easier. You don't *need* any of them, yet they can be helpful if you have the time and money to devote to learning how to use them. You just have to remember that a dollar spent—sorry, invested—in computer software is a dollar that isn't invested in a stock or bond. If you use that computer software to evaluate stocks faster than you can do it otherwise, it may be worth the price. But do you really need to evaluate that many stocks that fast? Why?

Our advice is to start your investment program with a yellow legal pad, a No. 2 Dixon Ticonderoga pencil, and a subscription to *Barron's*. Add the other stuff when you feel it becomes helpful and you have the time to really use it. We'll look at some other sources of information and help in subsequent chapters.

TAXES AREN'T YOUR ONLY PROBLEM

We have already seen how taxes can knock the wind out of a good investment, reducing a healthy and robust 12% gain to a sickly, sniveling 8% return with just a flourish of a Form 1040. Well, your problems aren't over yet. Depending on what you invest in, how often you do it, and with whom, *transaction costs* are going to take another big bite out of your money. Fortunately, unless you're some kind of crazed day trader with a compulsion to place buy and sell orders every few minutes, transaction costs won't be as onerous as taxes. But one of the particularly annoying aspects of many investments is that you pay to buy *and* to sell, whether or not the investment was profitable. At least Uncle Sam recognizes transaction fees as raising the cost basis of your investments, that baseline from which profits and losses are measured.

There are things you can do, of course, to minimize transaction costs. The easiest is to adopt a buy-and-hold strategy in which you simply don't trade very often. That's an especially good way to reduce costs when investing in stocks because you minimize both transaction costs and the tax bite, which occur only when the stocks are sold at a profit. Thus, your capital can compound for years without having to pay either taxes or sales commissions. But as we warned you in the introduction to this book, make investment decisions on investment criteria, not because of taxes or other factors. You'll see later why that buy-and-hold approach has investment risks that may more than offset the cost savings.

Another way to save some money on transaction costs is to work through a discount broker rather than a full-service broker. It's something we certainly recommend, although it isn't without trade-offs. Full-service brokers, especially those employed by big Wall Street firms, do have access to the small armies of securities analysts employed by those firms. Those analysts are supposed to be diligently studying profit-and-loss statements and balance sheets, interviewing corporate managers, and weighing the investment potential of one company and industry against another. At least that's how the full-service broker is going to describe the process to you. If you are a big enough player, you will be put on the mailing list to receive some of the research reports that are churned out by all those analysts. And your full-service broker, when he doesn't have a better client to call, will hound you with the latest "buy" ratings put out by the analysts over the firm's "hoot 'n holler" intercom linkup during the course of the day.

That kind of information can be useful as long as you understand where everybody fits into the grand scheme of things. First, everybody employed by the brokerage house is there to help the firm get your money, along with lots of other money. Second, many securities analysts do good work and try to present a fair picture of the investment potential of the companies they cover. But being a lowly individual investor, you can't sit down and talk directly to the analyst. When he isn't doing his research, he is meeting with bigger, more lucrative clients to give them his additional insights into what is going on so that they can buy or sell something before you do.

What's more, the analyst is constantly looking over his shoulder at the firm's investment bankers, who are busily trying to suck money out of the companies the analyst covers by offering to peddle a new issue of the company's stock, restructure the company's balance sheet, or perform any other service that the bankers can dream up. Analysts who make the investment bankers' jobs more difficult by warning investors to stay away from that dog of a company tend to worry about where they'll find another job. It's easier to concentrate their efforts on finding nice things to say about a company. So when it comes to taking brokerage house research advice, keep in mind the phrase "Damned by faint praise."

You also need to remember that most brokerage firms really thrive on institutional business. Your account is just a dab of gravy on the main course. But in recent years the institutional business has become increasingly competitive. Wall Street firms are being pressed by the big pension and mutual funds to cut their fees to the bare bones. The firms are therefore trying to make up some of that lost profit from the last remaining suckers—the individual investors. They will charge you a fee for setting up an account and for closing it. You will even be charged for having stock certificates sent to you.

Then there is your broker—or your "account executive," as he or she probably prefers to be called. More than anyone else at the brokerage firm, this executive is a salesperson first, last, and always. He probably doesn't have the educational background or experience to evaluate what the analysts tell him. Indeed, he may not even understand it. What you hear from him about a certain company may have little relationship to what the analyst said or thinks. He doesn't have the financial incentive to watch carefully over your investment program, either. Indeed, his incentive is to persuade you to trade more often while your objective is to minimize the amount of trading you do. Remember, the broker isn't your friend. If you let him make your decisions for you, you will get what you deserve. If his firm's research reports seem useful to you or if you treat his advice merely as a source of ideas that you investigate further before making your own decisions, fine, it's your money. But at least figure out the minimum size of account you need to get that kind of service. Do the rest of your trading through a discount broker. You won't get any research reports, but you won't be bothered by lots of phone calls, either.

Having said that, make sure your discount broker is *really* a discount broker. Generally speaking, there are three levels of discount brokers that want your business. The "deep discounter" is the cheapest of all. It's no-frills service, but executions of trading orders are generally fast and accurate. The next level consists of discount brokers who operate as regional firms or through banks. Bank brokers can be useful if you want the convenience of automatic fund transfers between your bank and brokerage accounts, but you usually pay for that convenience through higher commissions.

Finally, there are the big nationally advertised discounters, the best known of which is Charles Schwab. They have offices in most big cities and a nationwide reputation (built up through expensive advertising) that attract many individual investors who find something fuzzy and warm about dealing with such firms. They pay for that feeling, believe us. Commissions at Schwab can be more than double what you pay at a deep discounter.

Discounters don't all operate alike. Some charge commissions based on the value of the transaction. There you would pay the same commission for selling 100 shares of a $50 stock as you would selling 1,000 shares of a $5 stock. Others base their commissions on the number of shares traded. Selling 1,000 shares of that $5 stock will cost you a lot more than selling 100 shares of the $50 stock. If you like playing among the emerging growth companies, the value guys are your best bet. But if you're trading big blue chips, you probably will get the better deal among the brokers charging on the basis of the number of shares traded.

In any case, do a little telephone work before establishing an account. Most firms will be happy to send you the schedule of commissions they charge, and once they're in hand, you can set up a few hypothetical trades to figure out which one best suits your needs and style. If you go with a Charles Schwab, make it a point to visit the nearest office. You're paying for the sofas, the electronic quote board, and the coffee, so you might as well enjoy them. Don't bother visiting your local deep discounter—if indeed he even has an office anywhere near your home. Deep discounters tend to be in older, somewhat dowdy office buildings. They won't have a nice lounge with an electronic tape running. You won't be encouraged to stick around and chat with anyone. They're in the business of making money by processing lots of trades quickly and efficiently, and anything that distracts them from that goal is costing them— and you—money.

Lately, discounters have begun offering their services by computer, some of them doing business only in that manner. The fees tend to be lower because the firm can employ fewer people to handle customers' orders. They are fine if you already have a personal computer and other equipment (such as a modem) needed to avail yourself of these services. But it isn't worthwhile buying a computer solely to trade stocks electronically. Use the phone and save a bundle.

There is one important part of the financial markets in which discount brokers find it tough to take on the full-service firms: bonds. If, like so many individual investors, you want to own a chunk of bonds in your portfolio, you probably will find the commissions at full-service brokers to be close to those charged by discount firms, especially as the size of your transaction grows. But nobody—we mean nobody—beats Uncle Sam's deal on Treasury bonds: When you buy directly from the nearest Federal Reserve Bank or from the Treasury Department in Washington, they are commission free.

Mutual funds are a way to reduce transaction costs and to relieve some of the burden of actively managing some parts of your portfolio. Don't dismiss them as only for wimp investors who can't make their own decisions. A diversified portfolio will contain a number of investments that you can't or shouldn't be making on your own. It isn't easy, for example, for the individual investor to purchase stocks in many foreign markets. If you want foreign stocks in your portfolio—and you probably will when you finish this book—using a no-load mutual fund for that portion of your portfolio is efficient and sensible. And you certainly will want a money market fund in which to temporarily park cash awaiting a more lucrative home. If you choose, you can even construct an entire portfolio around various mutual funds. Such a portfolio is far from maintenance free, but it can probably run longer without attention than a portfolio of individual stocks and bonds.

If you use a mutual fund or funds, however, steer clear of funds with loads, or sales charges. They are the ones your broker will try to palm off on you. The load doesn't guarantee any better performance and, in fact, sets a hurdle that the fund must cross before you earn anything. They aren't for intelligent investors.

Many wealthy investors, frightened of making their own investment decisions or simply without the time to tend a portfolio, use money management firms. There is nothing inherently wrong with them and a lot that is right. The best of the firms will provide their clients with well-structured, diversified investment portfolios that are tended carefully. They also will hold their clients' hands, massage their egos, and otherwise reassure them. But at what a price! Two or more percent of your money goes to pay the annual management fee—unlike the one-time-only sales fee on a load mutual fund. And the best firms don't want to talk to you unless you're forking over $1,000,000 or more. Money management firms are for people who need stroking and reassurance and have the money to pay for it. Probably the ultimate manifestation of this genre of investment programs is the "private bank," an expensive form of money management that usually provides subpar performance. They are for the people more worried about losing money than making it.

We won't waste your time here with a lecture on transaction costs involved in other investments. If you ever bought a house, you know full well just how many people come out of the lawyer's office woodwork with their palms extended at the typical real estate closing. The scene is repeated in most commercial real estate transactions. The same is true for other types of investments, and we'll deal with those as they arise.

THE HIDDEN COSTS OF SMALL STOCKS

A word about hidden transaction costs in buying stocks. If you are trading stocks on the New York Stock Exchange, you can be fairly certain—fairly, not completely—that you are getting the best price available at the moment the transaction takes place. That's because the vast majority of trades occur when buyer meets seller at the same price. If you want to sell a stock at 35¼, you are likely to be paired, either electronically or by floor brokers at the New York Stock Exchange, with someone looking to buy at 35¼. The few trades that aren't matched are funneled to the NYSE specialist whose job it is to maintain an orderly market in that particular stock. The specialist will buy or sell your stock, keeping the difference between the bid and asked price as his compensation for assuming the risk that the stock price will move against him before he can get rid of it.

Not so in the so-called over-the-counter (really over-the-telephone-and-computer) market. In this market there's a practice called "payment for order flow." Your stockbroker may have an arrangement with an over-the-counter dealer under which your broker receives a payment for funneling your orders through that dealer. Clearly, that's an additional cost to the dealer. We suspect that some dealers, maybe many, recoup that extra cost—we think of it as a kickback—somewhere other than in their profit margins. One easy method is simply by increasing the bid and asked prices for those stocks. If that's the case, guess who's paying it? Right. You. And just because you trade an exchange-listed stock doesn't mean you're entirely immune to this phenomenon. As much as 10% of the trading volume of exchange-listed stocks takes place over the counter. Big institutional traders know this and won't stand for the possible extra costs, so we'll let you guess again whose trade of an exchange-listed stock is most likely to take place over the counter. Right, again.

Unless and until this potential abuse is banned by the regulatory authorities, you can fight it by ordering your broker to execute over-the-counter transactions on NASDAQ's Small Order Execution System and to buy or sell exchange-listed stocks on the exchange.

STRATEGIES FOR GETTING WET

At this point you should know what your investment objectives are, how long you have to reach them, and how much risk you are willing to take to get there. If you have concluded that your objectives aren't very big, are a long way off, and you're really not willing to take much risk to reach them, well, you have wasted the money you spent to buy this book and the time it took you to read this far. Salvage what you can. Get a little box, put this book in it, wrap it in some nice paper, and give it to somebody as a birthday present (assuming you haven't spilled coffee on more than a few pages).

But if you are intent on pushing a bit to meet some lofty goals, it's time to get wet. Whether you are starting with a little or a lot, we figure that you are committed to a lifetime investment program in which you will periodically have more money, probably the result of diligent savings, to invest. So we're here to sell you now on the concept of dollar cost averaging. It's an amazingly simple idea that accomplishes what should be your main goal: getting started. That's because it eliminates the most worrisome aspect of investing: timing the markets. For most people timing the market just doesn't work. The natural temptation is to be lured into the markets when everyone is ebullient, the economy is rebounding, and stock prices are rocketing higher. But you, being a smart investor, know better than to do that. You'll wait for a pullback before you jump into the market. You bide your time and miss, say, a 3% run-up in prices in two weeks. Then the happy mood that dominated the market disappears, and prices drop 2% in three days. Is this the pullback you were waiting for? If so, you lost 1% by waiting. Or is this the start of something much bigger, a major correction or even a bear market? Prices continue to fall, down 10% in a month, 20% in three months. Now is the time to buy, you say. But wait a minute. What if this keeps going down even further? You don't want to lose 10% on your money. So you wait for the rebound, and the cycle starts all over again. Your money sits in a savings account, you fret all the time, and millions of other investors make money—and lose some, too—on their way to meeting their investment goals.

With dollar cost averaging you automatically time the market correctly. By committing yourself to invest a fixed amount of money periodically, preferably monthly or quarterly, you automatically buy more of a given investment when its price is lower (and when you should, despite your emotions, be buying) and less when its price is higher (when, again despite your emotions, you shouldn't be buying much). A typical plan might call for you to invest $500 a month. The low cost of getting started with a mutual fund makes the funds good candidates for the early stages of this kind of program; you can switch over to individual stocks when you've

Figure 1.4 How Dollar Cost Averaging Works

By putting $500 a quarter into AT&T, no matter what the stock is doing, you buy more shares at lower prices, fewer shares at higher prices.

Date	Price	Shares purchased without exceeding $500
3/31/95	51.750	9
6/30/95	53.000	9
9/30/95	65.750	7
12/31/95	64.750	7
3/31/96	61.125	8
6/30/96	62.000	8
9/30/96	52.250	9
12/31/96	43.375	11
3/31/97	34.875	14
6/30/97	35.063	14
9/30/97	44.250	11
12/31/97	61.313	8

In the three years shown in this example, a total of 115 shares are purchased at an average price of $49.96 a share.

accumulated enough money to make the transaction costs of trading a smaller percentage of the total investment. Some investment managers counsel making your automatic investment annually, but we don't think anyone putting up more money on an annual basis is really an investor. What the hell were you doing with the money all year anyway?

Dollar cost averaging is, of course, tailor-made for the investor without a large lump sum available to invest. A variant, called value averaging, is better suited to the investor who has a grubstake with which to work or is inclined to be a little more aggressive. Instead of putting in a fixed amount of money each period, the value averaging investor commits to increasing the value of his investments by a set amount each period. Let's say you commit to increase the value of your portfolio by $2,000 each quarter. The original $2,000 will then become $4,000 three months later. If your portfolio rises $500 in that time, you have to put in $1,500 of new money to hit the target. The $4,000 is then due to become $6,000 at the end of the third quarter. If by some lucky stroke the stocks in the portfolio have gained enough to total $6,100, you don't put in anything. In fact, you can take out $100. But if the portfolio has fallen from $4,000 to $3,000, you owe the kitty $3,000 of new money to hit the target. It's easy to see why value averaging requires a pool of capital with which to smooth out fluctuations in the portfolio's value. The approach also requires more attention and incurs higher transaction costs, but over time it should produce modestly better results than dollar cost averaging.

In all fairness, it must be said that for the investor with a substantial amount of capital to put to work—whether from an inheritance or merely the result of pooling the remains of many unrelated investments that didn't work—neither dollar cost averaging nor value averaging is theoretically the most lucrative way to invest that money for the long haul. Studies have shown that, over sufficient time, the best returns are obtained by putting the full sum to work in the market as soon as possible, even if you wind up buying at a high point in the stock market cycle. Over the long haul, the returns available from being fully invested outweigh the immediate losses if the market tanks. We don't dispute the accuracy of those studies, but they don't take into account investor psychology. We'd rather see you move slowly into a long-term investing program that you can live with than watch you flee the markets in dismay after your $800,000 inheritance turns into $600,000 in a four-month bear market that begins the day after you commit it all.

If you do grit your teeth and take the plunge with a large chunk of cash, you have two choices. The simplest, and one that conservative investors often pursue, is "buy and hold." It's self-explanatory. You buy a broad-based portfolio of stocks and perhaps other assets and sit back. As time goes by, most of them will gain in value. One day you will wake up and find you have arrived at the investment objective you set for yourself years ago. Maybe. Maybe not. The trouble with a buy-and-hold strategy lies in the tendency of riskier assets to produce greater returns—again, over the long haul—than more conservative assets. We'll go over asset allocation schemes in the next chapter, but we assume here that you set up your buy-and-hold portfolio with assets in a range of risk that you find comfortable, such as half in relatively conservative assets and half in riskier assets. You may be comfortable with that balance now, but what will that portfolio look like in ten years? The conservative assets will probably have grown slowly, as expected, perhaps doubling in price. The riskier assets, though, may have tripled or even quadrupled. While you were sleeping for ten years, your comfortable portfolio has mutated into a highly risky one. That's okay if you, along with it, have mutated into a risk-taking investor. But it could present you with a nasty surprise one day if your taste for risk hasn't changed.

Figure 1.5 Dollar Cost Averaging versus Lump-Sum Purchases

A lump-sum purchase
produces a higher return
if the stock rises

	Buy $500 a month of Gillette stock for 36 months	Lump-sum purchase of $18,000 at $37.438 a share
Start:	Dec. 31, 1994	Dec. 31, 1994
Stop:	Dec. 31, 1997	Dec. 31, 1997
Total Shares Purchased:	293	480
Average Cost Per Share:	$57.64	$37.44
Total Cost of Shares:	$16,888.50	$17,970.00
Market Value 12/31/97:	$29,829.94	$48,210.00
Gross Profit:	$12,941.44 or 72.5%	$30,240.00 or 168.3%

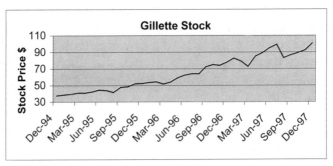

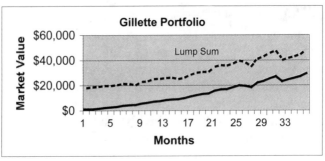

Figure 1.5 *continued*

Dollar cost averaging
produces a higher return
if the stock declines

	Buy $500 a month of Sybase stock for 36 months	Lump-sum purchase of $18,000 at $37.438 a share
Start:	Dec. 31, 1994	Dec. 31, 1994
Stop:	Dec. 31, 1997	Dec. 31, 1997
Total Shares Purchased:	815	346
Average Cost Per Share:	$21.49	$52.00
Total Cost of Shares:	$17,518.02	$17,992.00
Market Value 12/31/97:	$10,849.69	$4,606.13
Gross Loss:	-$6,668.33	-$13,385.88
	or -38.1%	or -74.4%

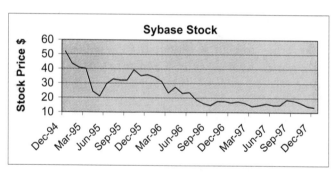

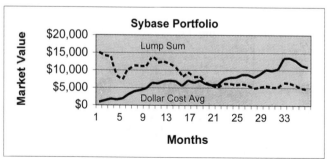

The alternative is a constantly rebalanced portfolio. In this approach you make your initial investments based on your risk tolerance. Then you keep a close eye on your portfolio and periodically, perhaps quarterly or semiannually, rebalance it by selling risky assets that appreciated to bring that portion of your portfolio down to its original size, or adding to conservative assets that haven't grown very fast. Sure, your transaction costs are higher, but your portfolio isn't undergoing some Jekyll and Hyde transformation that will scare you witless years from now.

Of course there isn't any reason you can't blend these approaches to meet your investment needs. A buy-and-hold strategy is fine for junior's college fund that consists mostly of short-term and intermediate bonds. We certainly hope you have the resources to devote a constant stream of new money to your investment program, through either dollar cost or value averaging. And any good investor will track a portfolio, adjusting it to reflect his changing needs or his increasing or decreasing tolerance for risk. What all this really amounts to is diversity and asset allocation, the subject of the next chapter.

Before you move on, though, we want to emphasize this particular point: For a truly successful investment program, you need to monitor your real rate of return. Of course, you say. But the fact is, only the most conscientious investors keep close track of how much money they spend in the process of investing. The rest go through life assuming that their investments are earning the dollar amounts by which their stocks have increased or the interest payments coming to them from their bond holdings. But in order to know an investment's real rate of return and to measure it against other alternative investments or methods of investing, you must include *all* costs that went into your investment—not only broker commissions but also the costs of the books and periodicals you buy to get ideas and the taxes you

Figure 1.6 What You See Isn't What You Get

The Real Return on 100 Shares of a Top-Performing Stock.

At first glance, stock market profits can look great:

Buy 100 shares of Microsoft on Dec. 31, 1996, at $82.625 a share:	$8,625.00
Sell 100 shares on Jan. 31, 1998, at $149.188 each:	$14,918.80
Gross return:	$6,293.80
	or
0.0025 1252.76 280.3125	72.97%

But to calculate your real return you must:

Subtract commissions to buy and sell ($30 total from a discount broker), leaving:	$6,263.80
Subtract capital gains taxes on adjusted gross (20%, or $1,252.76 in this case), leaving:	$5,011.04
Subtract the effect of inflation on your initial investment (assuming inflation is running at about 3% annually, it would have lowered the value of your initial $8,625 investment by 3.03%, or $280, over the 13 months you held the stock), leaving a net gain of:	$4,731.04
	or
	54.85%
	(50.6% annualized)

Now that's still a great return, but significantly less than what you first thought. And if this were your only stock purchase, you would also want to deduct from your profit the other expenses that went into making the investment, including your subscription to *Barron's*, the safe-deposit box where you kept the stock certificate, the yellow legal pad, and the No. 2 pencil that you used to calculate all this.

owe on your profits. If you spend $600 this year on comput-
er software and databases, and the resulting investment nets
you $1,000, you haven't done very well. The only way we
know to be sure you are tracking your portfolio's performance properly is to keep meticulous records. We can't put a
value on the time you spend managing your investments. But
rest assured you will know whether it's worth it or not, and
either you will derive much pleasure from the process, or you
will wind up changing your portfolio to require less of your
time.

SOURCES OF INFORMATION

By reading *Barron's* regularly, you will find answers to many
of the questions you have. There is no better periodical from
which to absorb the "feel" of the investment process. Still,
most *Barron's* articles are topical in nature, so you'll have to
read a lot of them to glean the fundamentals. If that's what
you are looking for, there are some additional publications
that focus directly on these matters.

Most big brokerage and accounting firms, mutual
funds, and money managers have materials available free of
charge that explain financial planning. These materials usually offer tables and charts that will help you set up your own
income statement, balance sheet, and investment goals.

Two of the most detailed treatments of the subject of
financial planning and investing are books prepared by the
money management firm of Bailard, Biehl & Kaiser in San
Mateo, California: *How to Set and Achieve Your Financial
Goals* and *How to Be a Successful Investor* are both published by Dow Jones–Irwin.

Investors who get serious about their portfolios can
do no better than spending $49 for a membership in the

American Association of Individual Investors. Membership includes an annual subscription to the AAII Journal, a monthly publication that delves into all aspects of the investment world, as well as *The Individual Investor's Guide to No-Load Mutual Funds.* The AAII can be reached at 625 North Michigan Avenue, Chicago, Illinois 60611. The web site is at www.aaii.com.

The novice investor who would like to move slowly might consider joining a local investment club. Most such clubs pool a small amount of money, which the members jointly decide how to invest. Members share the homework chores involved in searching for the right investment. The emphasis is heavily on stocks. The National Association of Investors Corporation at P.O. Box 220, Royal Oak, Michigan 48068-0220 can put you in touch with clubs in your area. The web site is at www.better-investing.org. You can also join the association for $39 annually and receive a year's subscription to its *Better Investing* magazine. The magazine isn't as sophisticated as the *AAII Journal,* but it usually contains a detailed analysis of one company as a possible investment and provides a form that you can fill out to guide you through your own analysis of stocks.

2
Asset Allocation

Spreading the Risk,
Reaping the Reward

"Sorry, we've already 'seized the moment' with another brokerage firm."

Asset allocation can be as simple or as complex as you want to make it. Either way, the sole aim of the asset allocation process is to maximize returns while minimizing risk. It is accomplished through diversification, which is nothing more than spreading your money among different kinds of investments. Deciding how much of your assets to put in each investment category is the allocation process. And lest you not take this process seriously, you should know that most money managers consider asset allocation far more important in reaping eventual rewards than the selection of individual stocks and bonds. If the time available to devote to your investments is limited, then asset allocation is where you should devote it. Someone else can pick the individual stocks and bonds that go into your portfolio.

The process can be amazingly simple as long as you understand the goal. Studies have shown that five randomly selected stocks can significantly reduce the risks that would be inherent in owning a single stock. As long as they were randomly selected, those five stocks would tend to exhibit different growth rates, be in different industries, respond differently to changing variables such as interest rates, and be treated differently by the investment community as a whole. When one stock was in decline, for whatever reasons, another one would be rising. In the end, the portfolio won't do better than the single best-performing stock in the portfolio, but it won't do as badly as the worst-performing stock, either. And you don't know at the outset which of the five stocks will fall into either of those two categories. That's the value of diversification.

But a word of caution: Just because a little diversification is good for your portfolio doesn't mean a lot of diversification is even better. As with virtually everything else, you can have too much of this good thing. The result will be a mishmash of every possible investment, ranging from three-month Treasury bills to complex options and futures strategies to a portfolio of foreign stocks protected by currency hedges. The best solution for the average investor lies somewhere between the randomly selected five-stock portfolio and the hydra-headed monster that some people construct. Chances are good that the ideal solution for you is a lot closer to the small portfolio than it is to the monster.

But before you start thinking about how to set up an asset allocation scheme, you have to think about how your assets are already allocated. Like it or not, your entire life to date has been an unconscious and ever-changing asset allocation program. The biggest decision you probably made was to become a real estate investor. A goodly piece of change resides along with you in your house or condominium, for better or worse. Your cars, too, represent a decision to spend money on a depreciating asset rather than an appreciating one. And if you have worked at one place very long, you may have considerable assets tied up in profit sharing or 401k plans as well as Individual Retirement Accounts if you were smart enough to take advantage of them when you were eligible. All these assets should be taken into account as you construct your investment plan. You will want to ask yourself if you really want to skew your total portfolio even more heavily toward real estate than it already is. And how is the money in your profit-sharing plan invested? If it's in a fixed-income investment, such as a guaranteed investment contract, or GIC, you might want to designate that money as your long-term income-producing resource while you put new funds into something likely to grow faster, albeit with greater risk. If you're unlucky enough to participate in one of the crummy 401k plans in which your only choice is the stock of your company, you should find some other ways to diversify your retirement portfolio.

To do an especially good job of diversifying, you need to consider other assets, too. Not to be morbid about it, but many of us stand to inherit some kind of estate from our parents. While you don't own any of those assets yet, you should have a fairly good idea of what they are and adjust your own portfolio accordingly. If, for instance, your parents are very conservative investors and have a lot of their money tied up in savings accounts or Treasury bonds, you should feel at least a little freer to take some risks with your own portfolio, skewing it more heavily toward stocks than you might otherwise. Do your in-laws own a big house as well as a vacation house? Assuming you and their son or daughter are still on good terms, that's a big chunk of real estate that will probably one day come your way, depending on how many siblings your spouse has. You might want to trim your real estate investments in favor of something else, such as stocks or bonds. Much of your knowledge about such potential assets will depend on how freely you and your family discuss financial matters. Some families are reluctant to bring up these topics, and that's fine. But on the whole, the more you know about the financial position of everyone around you, the better you'll be able to make intelligent decisions for the future.

Once you have a feel for the pool of assets under your control or available to you long-term, you can begin the allocation process following the same approach that many professional money managers use. That approach takes place at three levels. The first level is *strategic asset allocation.* That's the process by which you determine your willingness to take risks to achieve defined investment goals over time. We explored it in the first chapter. Your conclusions about yourself and your goals will help you construct a portfolio that is aimed at reaching your goals without giving you high blood pressure or a heart attack.

The second level is called *dynamic rebalancing.* That's just a fancy name for readjusting your portfolio from time to time to keep its relative risk at a predetermined level. We discussed that, too, in the first chapter when we demonstrated the dangers of a buy-and-hold strategy that gets out of kilter over the years, becoming more risky than you might like. You should think of this second stage of asset allocation as keeping your portfolio running on the track that you laid down in making your strategic decisions.

The third level is called *tactical asset allocation.* The pros use it as a market timing tool, judging the relative values of the various assets in which they invest and moving funds from what they believe are high-priced assets to what they hope are low-priced assets. If it works, they realize the dream of every investor: buying low and selling high. They tend to use computer models to make those decisions, and how they do it is beyond the scope of this book. But don't worry. You can still adapt the concept to your own circumstances. In its simplest form we can call the decision to sell a stock in your portfolio that has appreciated 60% in two months and put the profits somewhere else a tactical asset allocation decision. And while we certainly don't favor the wholesale shifting of assets from one type of investment to another in an effort to catch the next big run-up in some market, we do think it's a good idea to favor the underdog, putting more emphasis on underpriced assets and pulling money out of high- or overpriced investments. But you don't need computers and software to figure out if the stock market is overvalued or if bond prices have a better chance of heading up than down. We'll discuss those subjects in the upcoming relevant chapters.

To be successful, an asset allocation strategy must put an investor into two or more assets that have as little relationship to one another as possible. That way if one asset is hit by a disaster, the remaining asset classes are likely to be fairly immune to a similar collapse. Let's take the simplest asset allocation that investors might choose: a portfolio of big, blue chip stocks and a handful of 10-year Treasury bonds. As we all know, the stock market goes through cycles, and few, if any, stocks are immune to those cycles. When the inevitable temporary downturn (what the pros call a "correction") or bear market (a drop of 20% or more from the high point) comes along, our hypothetical investor's stock portfolio is going to suffer a decline. What happens to the Treasury bonds when stocks are declining? They could very well rise in price if the stock market decline is part of an economic slowdown that caused interest rates to fall. There is a chance that bond prices could fall along with the stocks. But regardless of what happened to the bond prices, the interest income would still keep coming in, as it was intended to, thus smoothing some of the loss from the stock portfolio. Besides, unless our hypothetical investor panicked, the stock portfolio loss would be only a paper loss. In time, those paper losses will likely disappear, given that stock prices eventually rebound. Just be aware that there can be such a thing as a prolonged bear market or, even more frustrating, a long stretch of stagnation. (See Figure 2.1.)

For most individual investors the menu of assets from which to construct a diversified investment portfolio looks

Figure 2.1 Returns from Various Investment Classes 1970-1997

Year	U.S. Stocks	International Stocks	Cash Equivalent	Real Estate	U.S. Bonds
1970	3.9%	-11.6%	6.6%	10.8%	14%*
1971	14.3%	27.4%*	4.4%	9.2%	13.2%
1972	19.0%	26.2%*	4.0%	7.5%	5.7%
1973	-14.7%	-13.6%	6.9%	7.5%*	4.2%
1974	-26.5%	-24.6%	7.9%*	7.2%	4.0%
1975	37.2%	39.3%*	5.9%	5.7%	6.1%
1976	23.9%*	-2.1%	5.0%	9.3%	13.6%
1977	-7.2%	18.8%*	5.2%	10.5%	1.0%
1978	6.6%	27.1%*	7.1%	16.1%	-0.5%
1979	18.6%	10.4%	9.8%	20.5%*	3.4%
1980	32.5%*	24.6%	11.3%	18.1%	-0.4%
1981	-4.9%	-1.4%	14.1%	16.6%*	7.7%
1982	21.5%*	0.1%	10.9%	9.4%	33.5%
1983	22.6%	26.4%*	8.6%	13.1%	4.8%
1984	6.3%	6.1%	9.6%	13.8%	14.2%*
1985	31.7%	57.6%*	7.5%	11.2%	27.1%
1986	18.7%	56.3%*	6.1%	8.3%	18.6%
1987	5.3%	20.2%*	5.8%	8.0%	-0.8%
1988	16.6%	25.9%*	6.8%	9.6%	7.2%
1989	31.7%	19.6%	8.2%	7.8%	16.2%
1990	-3.1%	-12.8%	7.5%	2.3%	8.3%*
1991	30.5%*	15.8%	5.4%	-5.6%	17.5%
1992	7.6%	-5.8%	3.5%	-4.3%	7.7%*
1993	10.1%	39.4%*	3.0%	1.2%	12.8%
1994	1.3%	3.6%	4.3%	6.3%*	-5.6%
1995	37.6%*	14.1%	5.4%	7.5%	23.0%
1996	23%*	11.5%	5.0%	10.3%	1.4%
1997	33.4%*	3.9%	5.1%	11.2%	10.5%
Average Annual Return	13.0%	12.7%	6.8%	8.8%	9.3%

Source:

    Bailard, Biehl & Kaiser, using these data sources: U.S. stocks: S&P 500;
    U.S. bonds: Shearson Lehman Govt./Corp. Bond Index;
    International: Morgan Stanley Capital International EAFE Stock Market Index;
    Cash: 91-day Treasury Bill offering; Real Estate: Various sources.

* Indicates the class with the best total return in any given year (total return includes reinvested dividends or interest, if any).

fairly limited: stocks, bonds, real estate, and gold. Because houses and gold are both used as protection against high inflation (but houses are more versatile, providing shelter and tax advantages that gold doesn't), the list can really be narrowed to three. An investor who owns a house, a portfolio of stocks, and some Treasury bonds has, in our view, achieved a basic diversification.

But it isn't as easy as it seems. The asset category known as "stocks" isn't some homogeneous group from which you pick 10 or 15 for your portfolio. Rather, stocks can be divided into at least three distinct types of investments: large company stocks, small company stocks, and foreign company stocks. Large stocks don't always move in the same direction at the same time as small stocks. Foreign stocks usually don't track the performance of either small or large U.S. stocks. Indeed, foreign stocks also can be subdivided into various performance and risk categories, the most obvious being stocks in the major industrialized nations, such as Japan, Germany, and Great Britain, and stocks of companies in emerging markets, such as Taiwan and Mexico. So, by selecting among large and small U.S. stocks and issues traded in established and emerging foreign markets, an investor can construct a stock portfolio that provides significant diversification by itself.

The same is true of bonds. Treasury bonds—the world's safest investment—don't behave exactly like corporate bonds, particularly lower-rated corporate bonds. And neither performs in lockstep with foreign bonds, whether government or corporate issues. Municipal bonds are another breed in and of themselves because their tax-free status appeals to a different kind of investor than any of the others. Also, there is the matter of "duration," or the time until a bond matures. Thirty-year Treasury bonds don't act like one-year Treasury bills. So, again, the careful investor could put together a broadly diversified portfolio of nothing but bonds.

Ditto for real estate. If you want to explore investing in real estate beyond owning your home, you can choose from residential or commercial property. Residential real estate ranges from owning a few homes that you rent out to a small apartment building to investing in a syndicate building or buying a high-rise condominium or apartment tower. Commercial real estate? A single office building, a strip mall, or a major multiuse complex all behave differently from one another. There is also the opportunity to diversify geographically; similar kinds of real estate behave differently in various parts of the country.

Thus we see that within any one broad asset class, the elements move in somewhat different ways, allowing an investor to construct a diversified portfolio consisting solely of stocks, bonds, or real estate. But the picture gets much more interesting when elements of two or more broad asset classes are mixed together. The extreme might be a portfolio consisting of U.S. Treasury bonds and foreign stocks. Studies have shown that the movements of these two asset categories have practically no bearing on each other. Another extreme would be a portfolio of U.S. Treasury bonds and ownership of several single-family dwellings. Because both are affected by inflation, but in different ways (inflation tends to raise the value of the property while lowering the value of the long-term bonds), their moves are related but in different directions.

Don't misunderstand: Portfolios consisting solely of Treasury bonds and foreign stocks, or bonds and houses, are not necessarily desirable. They are just highly diversified. A big bunch of foreign stocks is likely to be much more risky than most investors would like. Further, as we will see in the chapter on foreign investing, they aren't easy or cheap to buy. Transaction costs and currency risks can be a deadly combination in the foreign stock arena. Transaction costs and other expenses make real estate expensive to buy, too. A better portfolio would be one that included some exposure to foreign stocks, perhaps through a mutual fund, some Treasuries, some U.S. stocks (both large and small), and a house (that's your real estate component and inflation hedge). This isn't such a difficult portfolio for an ambitious and conscientious investor to set up.

RANKING THE RISKS

To set up an asset allocation system you obviously have to have a sense of the risks involved in the various investment categories you will be using. Those risks can't always be quantified, unfortunately, but we can make some general assumptions about risks that can serve as a guide as you go about setting up an investment portfolio.

A note of caution, however. Virtually all the investment categories we discuss throughout this book have legitimate uses. Stocks and bonds enable companies to raise much-needed capital. Real estate offers us all places to live and work. And commodity futures allow producers and users of those items to reduce their business risks. But when used unwisely, these same investments can be highly dangerous to your financial health. We hope the fact that you're reading this book is an indication of your intent to use these investment vehicles properly. If you don't and get hurt, just remember whose fault it is.

Here is our general ranking of the various investment vehicles from least risky to most risky, with some comments on each category:

TREASURY BONDS. Held to maturity, there is probably nothing safer. The U.S. government can bring virtually any resources to bear (including its unique ability to print money) to ensure that you are paid the interest and principle you are owed. Trading bonds can be risky, however, because you are betting on the direction of interest rates. We don't know any experts who can forecast rates correctly on a consistent basis. If you must speculate on the direction of interest rates, remember that longer-term bonds of any type respond more sharply to changes in interest rates than do shorter-term bonds.

AGENCY BONDS. Issued by government agencies, these bonds aren't necessarily backed by the full faith and credit of the United States. While there really isn't any default risk, you can't count on the maturity dates because they may be redeemed early.

CORPORATE BONDS. If you choose to own highly rated corporate bonds, there is little risk that you won't get what is owed you. But if you move down the rating scale in an attempt to earn more interest, beware. Risks of defaults grow. There's a reason the lowest-rated bonds are termed "junk."

MUNICIPAL BONDS. The tax-free nature of these bonds is alluring to many investors. Defaults are fairly rare, so if you hold a muni bond to maturity, you are probably okay. But ratings count, and ratings agencies downgrade muni bonds more often than you might think. If you need to sell a muni bond before maturity, you could take quite a hit if it has been downgraded since you bought it.

ZERO-COUPON BONDS. These bonds don't pay periodic interest, although you are taxed as if they did. Their appeal is that a small investment now can lock in a big return several years from now. The danger is that zeroes are highly sensitive to changes in interest rates. If you have to sell before maturity, you could lose a lot of capital.

BLUE CHIP STOCKS. Carefully selected growth stocks usually provide better long-term returns than most bonds. But bear in mind that any company in which you own stock is subject to problems, ranging from unexpected competition to plain old bad management. In the short run, even the bluest of blue chips can take an alarming dive. Cyclical stocks are great on the way up but can hammer you hard on the way down.

REAL ESTATE. It's difficult to assess the risks in real estate. Homeowners who once thought house prices could go nowhere but up have had a rude awakening in recent years. Still, you have to live somewhere, and the government makes home ownership very attractive: Mortgage interest is deductible from income taxes, and profits on your house are tax free. Commercial real estate is another matter, though. If you can catch it just before a boom, great. But if you climb aboard just ahead of a bust, you're going to feel some pain.

SMALL COMPANY STOCKS. All other things being equal, stocks of small companies tend to fluctuate in price more sharply than stocks of large companies. Small companies often have a chance to grow much faster than their big brethren, but they're also more vulnerable to changes in demand for their products or services.

FOREIGN STOCKS. Not only do you face all the challenges you have in the United States of picking the right stock, but with many foreign stocks you must also consider factors such as political upset and the risk that changing currency values can hurt your share price even if the price itself rises.

COLLECTIBLES. From an investment standpoint, it's very seldom that you will make much of a profit from art, antiques, baseball cards, or any of the other various things that people collect. It happens just often enough to warrant splashy coverage in the media, which lures in a fresh bunch of suckers who think they can do it, too. You're better off buying a lottery ticket. If you buy a piece of art, do it because you like the art, not to get rich.

COMMODITIES. Unless you are in the business of producing or using large quantities of oil, gold, wheat, or any other commodity, you're just gambling when you venture into the futures markets. The chances of losing—and losing big—are enormous. Ditto with options if you use them to speculate on stocks or whatever. However, there are option strategies that actually reduce some of the market risk inherent in, say, stocks. But you have to know what you are doing, and until you do, consider it risky.

MAKING ASSET ALLOCATION WORK FOR YOU

Now let's walk through a few easy exercises in asset allocation, using various assumptions and examining the rationale for a particular allocation. These are by no means asset allocation models you should follow. They are intended to help you think about the components of your own program and tailor them to meet your carefully thought out needs.

DINKs

We will start with a really easy one. Assume you and your spouse are both 35 years old, have secure jobs that pay well, and elected long ago not to have kids. You're the classic DINKs (double income, no kids). For our purposes you are renting and don't plan to buy a house. Having come only recently to the belief that you should invest for your retirement, you have tamed your formerly profligate spending habits and figure you can invest $300 a month. Your employers both contribute annually to profit-sharing plans that are beginning to look like real money—about $100,000 in each plan. You realize you have many years for the higher risks of stock investing to be smoothed out before you need your nest egg. What do you do?

First, get those 401k or similar defined-contribution retirement accounts to work harder if your company gives you any choice at all. If you can tap into a growth stock fund (typically smaller, more risky stocks), put a large chunk—say, 75%—of your 401k account there. If you have some means within your profit-sharing plan for investing in foreign stocks, the remaining 25% of your funds can go there. If not, bet the ranch on the growth stocks. The $300 you are putting aside monthly can go to one of two places: a money market account or a blue chip stock fund—preferably an index fund that tracks the Standard & Poor's 500-stock index or Dow Jones Industrial Average—where it will reside until it adds up to enough to start making some stock purchases of your own, say $12,000 or $15,000. If you don't think you're going to want to take the time and invest the energy needed to research and track individual stocks, divide the money instead between a large-cap index fund and an aggressive small-stock growth fund. Avoid income-producing investments such as bonds; you have enough income and don't need to be paying Uncle Sam taxes on interest payments.

Here's what a potential portfolio for novice DINK investors might look like:

The 401k Accounts

Small, risky growth stocks	$150,000
Foreign stocks	50,000

New Money to Be Invested

Large Stock Index Fund	$150 per month
Small-stock aggressive growth	$150 per month

That's a volatile mixture, and the values can shift suddenly. If those movements are apt to keep you awake at night, you need to change the complexion of your portfolio so that it is a little more conservative. One way to do that is to lighten up on the small stocks, especially in the aggressive growth fund. Foreign stocks can be volatile, too, particularly since they are subject not only to the ups and downs typical of any stock but also because they face currency risks should the dollar move the wrong way against other currencies. Most 401k plans offer some kind of bond fund or fixed-income alternative to stocks. Be aware, though, that bond funds aren't bonds: The value of the fund tends to fluctuate with the direction of interest rates. Those moves won't be as extreme as what you would experience in the stock market, but you could find that your bond fund loses 10% of its value in some situations. A money market fund or guaranteed investment contract (GIC) can offer more stability and contribute to sound sleep. So the nervous DINKs portfolio might look like this:

The 401k Accounts

Fixed income	$100,000
Large-stock index fund	75,000
Small-stock growth fund	25,000

New Money to Be Invested

Small-stock aggressive growth fund	$300 per month

Some of the volatility that can frighten novice investors has been removed from the portfolio. You could carry this process to an extreme, of course, and come up with a portfolio of nothing but safe, fixed-income investments. That would indeed by a "sleep well" portfolio, at least for the next five years or so. At the end of that time, however, an alert investor who compared the returns from this kind of portfolio with one that had been invested in stocks for the same period would probably end up kicking himself.

An Older Couple

Now let's look at an older couple with more resources. We'll make them 45 years old, again with good incomes and 401k plans valued at $300,000 each, a house, and $1,000 a month to invest. We will also give them a $300,000 grubstake, perhaps an inheritance, that they need to invest. At their age they still have plenty of time before retirement to enjoy the fruits of the stock market, but they may still feel cautious.

The 401(k) Accounts	
Small-stock portfolio	$200,000
Foreign-stock portfolio	50,000
Large-stock portfolio	250,000
Fixed-income portfolio	100,000
The Inheritance	
Large-stock index fund	$150,000
Aggressive growth stock fund	50,000
Ten-year Treasury bonds	100,000
New Money to Invest	
For the index fund	$500 a month
For the aggressive growth fund	$500 a month

This is not a particularly risky portfolio when you break down the asset categories:

High Risk	Moderate Risk	Low Risk
Small and foreign stocks $300,000 33.3%	Large stocks $400,000 44.4%	Fixed Income $200,000 22.2%

And remember that we haven't even considered the couple's house, which is their primary inflation hedge. We regard a house in which you live a fairly low risk investment, particularly given the tax-advantaged leverage it provides. If it were valued at $300,000 in this case, the total portfolio value would be $1.2 million, and the percentages would look like this:

High Risk	25.0%
Moderate Risk	33.3%
Low Risk	41.6%

If they could sleep at night, we would step up the high-risk component while bringing down the low-risk allocation. After all, if our couple plans to retire at age 65, they have 20 more years to recover from any big downswings in the stock market.

What would change if our 45-year-old couple had a teenager two years away from college, with college likely to cost an estimated $20,000 for each of four years? The ideal asset allocation given our couple's risk tolerance would call for a proportional reduction of assets in each category amounting to $80,000. Use that money to buy eight Treasury bonds ($10,000 each), two of which mature at the beginning of each college year. A riskier but probably more rewarding approach would be to hold steady, peeling $20,000 each year off the bond portion of the portfolio as tuition bills came due. But, again, that depends on your tolerance for risk.

Ready to Retire

Finally, let's look at the situation facing a 65-year-old couple on the verge of retirement. Their home is paid for, they will have a modest income in retirement, albeit not enough to maintain their current standard of living (they like to eat out and travel) or to continue making regular investments, and they have an investment portfolio of $800,000. What to do?

If they want to maintain their current standard of living, they must generate more income. Treasury bonds are the easy answer because they are safe and the transaction costs are low. Theoretically, the entire $800,000 could be put into a bond portfolio to produce maximum additional income. Maturities should be staggered between 5 and 12 years to mitigate the "reinvestment risks" should interest rates decline at some point during that period. Our couple would have virtually risk-free assured income that would continue for the foreseeable future.

But consider that at age 65 our couple probably has, on average, 20 years ahead of them. If they invested $200,000 of their $800,000 nest egg in blue chip stocks, the potential 8% to 10% annual gain over time would certainly outdo the 6% or so income from their bonds; yet their portfolio would still be conservative by any measure, considering that they own their house. We would recommend that $400,000 go into stocks if they could stand the market fluctuations.

Of course, life is never this simple. Given the evidence we've all seen in the past several years, there isn't any such thing as a truly secure job. Both our DINKs and our older couple should squirrel away a few months of operating expenses so they won't have to dip into their investment program right away if the unthinkable happens and they are laid off. And companies everywhere are cutting health care costs by reducing retiree health benefits. Our couple verging on retirement should have ready access to some cash to cover unexpected medical emergencies. If our retirees are thinking about leaving some of their wealth to their children (in an ordered financial house there is a will), they might consider taking a riskier approach to investing. Given their total assets, it's unlikely they will exhaust their funds, and the kids will appreciate (we hope) the improved performance in what will ultimately become their portfolio.

THE REBALANCING ACT

The hypothetical portfolios just outlined represent the first stage of the asset allocation process in which you make fundamental decisions about your goals and your willingness to take some risks to achieve them. The second stage involves rebalancing those portfolios from time to time—at least annually. Let's look at what might happen to our three couples over time if they did no rebalancing.

Since our cautious DINKs were the ones who didn't particularly like to take risks, we will examine their portfolios 10 years down the road. The $100,000 fixed-income component has become $179,085 (compounding at a generous 6% after taxes). The blue chip portion of their plan has grown to $194,533 (at an average 10% per year). And the small-stock fund now stands at $77,648. But look at that $300 a month invested in the aggressive small-stock growth fund. It would total well in excess of $90,000 at the end of 10 years, assuming a 12% annual return on small stocks. Keep in mind that we're not making allowances for the monthly investable portion to grow along with our couples' incomes. If they increased their monthly investments by $100 a month each year, they would skew their portfolio much more heavily toward the more risky end of the spectrum. However, we also aren't making any allowances for any further company contributions to the retirement plans, which would push the total portfolio back toward the conservative end of the spectrum. In any case, in terms of percentage allocation among risky, moderately risky, and conservative assets, here's the picture at the beginning and end of 10 years:

	Risky	Moderately Risky	Conservative
Beginning:	12.5%	37.5%	50.0%
End:	31.0%	36.0%	33.0%

As we can see, the portfolio has taken a decided tilt away from conservative and toward risky. It is hoped such returns will convince our cautious couple that it's worth taking a little more risk than they were willing to do 10 years ago. Maybe they learned to live with the risk and even enjoy those extra returns. But if not, they are overdue for rebalancing. The plan would be to sell some of those risky assets and put the proceeds back into the conservative side of the portfolio, achieving the initial balance as closely as possible. Had they been doing that annually, their portfolio would never have gotten so far out of kilter (and perhaps they would not have had as graphic a lesson in the potential rewards that accompany risk). The same would be true of our middle-aged couple. As the high-risk portion of their portfolio began to outrun the low-risk portion, they would probably want to take some of the profits out of the high-risk instruments and put them in the moderate category.

Now think about our couple on the verge of retirement. Let's assume they took our advice and put $200,000 of their $800,000 nest egg in blue chip stocks. In years in which the stock portfolio performed well, they could rebalance by simply selling enough shares to lower the value of their stock holdings back to $200,000. In years in which the overall value of the portfolio dropped below $200,000, they could either leave it alone, waiting for it to rebound, or do some value averaging by taking whatever is necessary from their maturing bonds that year to boost the total stock portion to $200,000. Either way, in the long run they would probably come out better than if all their savings were held in bonds.

There is also another reason to rebalance diversified portfolios. Different investment vehicles come into and fall out of favor over a period of time. If you as an investor don't make the effort to readjust your portfolio, you'll always be carrying too much of yesterday's hot investment and not enough of tomorrow's favored vehicle. We realize that, taken to an extreme, this aspect of portfolio rebalancing amounts to market timing, which is and probably should be anathema to many conservative investors. But a judicious rebalancing strategy will give the alert investor at least a modest leg up on those who buy and hold until rigor mortis sets in or who otherwise ignore the dynamics of markets.

TILTING THE BALANCE

If we haven't said it enough, we'll say it again: Market timing is dangerous. Attempting to figure out when the stock market is on the verge of a massive rally or a prolonged decline seldom profits even the professional investor, who has all day and lots of resources at his or her command. We can assure you that you probably will fail miserably and be sorry that you tried.

Tactical asset allocation, on the other hand, needn't involve the rapid movement of funds among various markets. Instead, if you want to test your ability to decipher the economy and assess the investment markets, you can, with a little homework, make an educated guess about where the various investment markets stand in their periodic cycles. Then you can "tilt" your portfolio slightly toward the under-valued markets and away from the overvalued ones. If you are right, you will add an extra bit of return to your portfolio that over the years will add substantially to your total wealth. If you are wrong, you will wind up a little behind where you would have been otherwise, but you probably will under-stand the markets better, which has its own long-run benefit.

How do you determine which way to tilt? We said it would take some homework, and we can't provide enough details in this book to do the subject justice. But the thrust of your homework is to determine among the categories of investments in your portfolio which ones have been enjoying a sustained rise, which ones have languished, and which ones have been in a prolonged decline. With a little knowledge of historical values in those markets, you should be able to pick which ones are far enough out of kilter to warrant either buy-ing or avoiding.

Let's consider the stock market. Since 1926 the aver-age compound annual return for the 500 stocks in the Standard & Poor's index, including reinvested dividends, has been 10.3%. Since 1950 the compound annual return has averaged 12.3%. And in the 10 years from 1987 through 1997 the average annual compound return was a stunning 18.6%. But can you expect those kinds of returns to continue? Probably not. It's far more likely that stock price apprecia-tion will begin returning to its historic norm. It will take time, of course, and there may still be some years of 20%-plus returns—offset by an occasional 10% loss. You just have to remember that a period of three years of 20% annual gains simply can't sustain itself. Tactical asset allocation suggests that after three such years—1995, 1996, and 1997—there may be other places to put some of your investment money that haven't surged quite as much or perhaps have even gone down.

Now consider the historic returns for small stocks. Since 1926 small stocks have returned an average of 12% per year. Since 1950, though, the return has been 14.4% annually. And in the past decade small stocks have produced annual gains averaging 14.8%. That kind of return suggests that small stocks haven't gotten nearly as far ahead of themselves as have their big brothers in the S&P 500. So perhaps they are likely to perform better (performance is relative—it may just mean they won't fall as far) than big stocks.

Bonds? The average yield on Treasury bonds looking back 100 years is about 5%. Rates on long-term bonds have been dropping substantially for the past decade from more than 14%, a trend that suggests bonds have been marching back toward their historical average yield. As we write this, the yield on the 30-year bond is hovering near 6% even as unemployment in this country stands at an astoundingly low 4.9%, a level that many economists predict will result sooner or later in rising inflation.

If you have the guts to play this game, the places to be in the opening months of 1998 were Japan and Southeast Asia. Japan had been enduring a grueling bear market for years, and many of the "Asian Tiger" countries had been undergoing a tremendous crisis of confidence, reflected in plunging currency values and stock markets. Yet no one can reasonably suggest that either Japan or the Tigers are going to go into such an eclipse that someday they won't once again be wonderful places to invest. If as you read this you see a similar situation in the world, get cracking.

SALVAGING THE WRECKAGE

If you are trying to salvage the wreckage of a previous investment program that didn't work, your asset allocation job may be a little more difficult than if you are new to investing. The first step is to figure out why the previous program didn't work. "What program?" you may ask. That's precisely the point. Most initial attempts at investing don't work because the investor approaches it all willy-nilly, with no set objectives (except to make a lot of money) and no guiding disciplines. Professional money managers called in to rescue such investors tell us what they often find in a crashed portfolio is simply a bunch of broker suggestions for whatever seemed hot at the moment. The investor's tax returns are filled with long-term losses and short-term gains on stock sales (it should be exactly the opposite: short-term losses and long-term gains) and contain few other investments designed to moderate risk or meet short-term goals. Often the investor doesn't have a clue about her own net worth or about how her expenditures match her income. People like that need a financial planner—not a money manager—who can help them get control of their financial lives.

In any event, reshaping an existing portfolio can be painful and expensive. Once you have gone through the first steps of setting up a long-term investment portfolio—determining your objectives and your tolerance for risk—you must rid your portfolio of things that don't fit your new approach to investing. That may mean selling previous investments at a loss, something many investors are loath to do. But the alternative—keeping a highly risky or a poorly performing investment in your portfolio—will only cost you in the long run. It will cost you money if it's a poor-performing investment, or anxiety if it is too risky for your new approach. More important, hanging on to an inappropriate investment costs the one thing you can't replace: time. The longer you sit with the wrong investment, the less time you have to enjoy the fruits of the right investment.

Disposing of the bad parts of your old portfolio should leave you with a pool of capital ready to be put to work. Before you do that, however, there's one last thing to get rid of: the advisers who got you into the lousy investments in the first place. Clearly your broker, your brother-in-law, or whoever advised you to make those investments either didn't know what he or she was talking about or at least didn't understand and appreciate your own financial situation. Dump these advisers (we don't mean divorce your spouse to get rid of your brother-in-law; just quit heeding his advice), acknowledge that you are responsible for whatever becomes of your financial future, and begin over again with a systematic approach to investing.

SUGGESTED READING

Some of the larger mutual fund companies, such as Fidelity, Vanguard, and T. Rowe Price, offer assistance in developing an asset allocation plan. Their materials, naturally, are skewed toward their own funds, but the principles they apply are valid. They have many asset allocation models, and you might find one that closely resembles your own circumstances.

There are many books about the overall process of financial planning that contain ideas for asset allocation, but among the more enjoyable are three by Andrew Tobias: *The Only Investment Guide You'll Ever Need, The Only Other Investment Guide You'll Ever Need* (he lied), and *Money Angles*. There is some repetition among the three, and it's probably correct that the only one you'll ever need is the first. But the books are fun and, more to the point, probably available free in your library.

3

Stocks

The Investors' Playground

GATE 20A

FLIGHT 2003

BOSTON TO NY

DEPA... ...

ARR. ...

20A

Cable

"At this point we would like to begin boarding all passengers who are beating the Dow by 20% to 35%"

Our fathers are both retired, and they do a bit of investing. Neither one of them will have anything to do with the stock market. "I just don't understand it," explains one. "Too risky for me," says the other.

Far be it from us to urge our own fathers to do something they aren't comfortable with. Indeed, they are practicing exactly what this book preaches, which is basically to know your tolerance for risk and invest accordingly. Nor could we argue successfully with their observations that companies must constantly struggle to survive against all sorts of adversities—foreign competition, new technology, government restrictions, consumer whims, and the ups and downs of the economic cycle. Furthermore, they note with unassailable common sense, stock prices all too often rise for no apparent reason, then plunge for some equally invisible reason.

Frightening, isn't it?

But if there is any fun in investing, chances are you will find it in the stock market. The nightly TV news doesn't mention the price of the Treasury's 30-year bond or the median price of commercial office towers because such information is boooorrrrrrinng. But the Dow Jones Industrial Average gets its daily due simply because so many people are fascinated by the workings of the stock market. For the active investor, the stock market is a vast playground where he and millions of others engage in a constant game of "Find the Next Winner."

For the winners do very well indeed. Decade in and decade out, stocks offer the largest total returns of any asset class. Sure, they may be outshone by bonds one year, real estate the next, and even gold once in a while. But over ten-year spans stocks are consistent performers. The good news is that if you play the game long enough, using reasonable strategies, the odds are substantial that you will be among the winners. The key is not to bet on just one horse.

THE MENU, PLEASE

Diversification within an asset class can be just as important as overall diversification in a portfolio. Nowhere is this statement more true than in stocks. Consider that in 1983, as the personal computer industry was accelerating at a frantic pace, there were 57 disk-drive makers vying for a share of that burgeoning business; today there are 3. The right pick would have made you rich, but putting your entire nest egg into one of the 54 losers wouldn't have left you with even an omelet. There are dozens of so-called biotech firms out there today, each the result of what seems to the company's officers to be a great idea—if they can only persuade investors to give the company enough money to bring the idea to fruition. How many do you think will be around a decade from now?

The menu of stocks from which an investor can choose is huge. The New York Stock Exchange lists some 3,500 issues, another 800 or so are traded on the American Stock Exchange, and the rapidly growing NASDAQ system carries 6,000 stocks. Several thousand more small or thinly traded stocks are listed in the "pink sheets," which is jargon for small, thinly traded stocks whose prices used to be published on pink paper. The entire menu is constantly growing as more companies choose to sell shares to raise capital. And that's just in the United States. Most other industrialized nations have their own stock markets, with hundreds or thousands of listed stocks, and many less developed nations are trying to spur economic growth by setting up stock markets. Even Vietnam has an embryonic stock market.

Indeed, one of the problems that many investors—particularly new ones—have with stocks is the difficulty of getting their hands around so huge a universe. Some money managers try to make sense of it by subdividing stocks into various categories. Size, or market capitalization (share price multiplied by number of shares outstanding), is one way they classify stocks, resulting in what we call the Goldilocks assortment: "big" stocks, "little" stocks, and "middle-sized" stocks (known as "large caps," "small caps," and "mid caps"). Others prefer to categorize stocks as "growth" or "cyclical," the difference being the relative sensitivity of share prices to the economic cycle. There are defensive stocks, which are popular during times of market turmoil, and hot stocks, which thrill-seekers grab for a fast ride, hoping they can jump off before the crash. There are stocks that act like bonds. (There are also bonds that act like stocks, but we will deal with them in the next chapter.) In short, even with categories, the stock market is still awfully confusing. How does an investor make sense of this mess?

MOTHER KNOWS BEST

You can start with two pieces of wisdom from great thinkers of the past: "Know thyself," counseled the Delphic oracle. "Do your homework," said Mother.

You will get tired of reading this, but we must keep stressing that you need to know your own tolerance for risk. That's especially true if you want to play in the stock market. If the thought of a 10% decline in the value of your portfolio brings on nausea, you probably should join our fathers on the permanent sidelines. Many analysts and professional investors look for—indeed, hope for—a 10% "correction" (a decline in stock prices) every so often simply because it gives them a chance to buy stocks more cheaply. If you are unnerved by the market's occasional dips, you might want to steer yourself toward large, well-researched stocks that you can easily monitor and that tend to be a little less volatile. But if you are intent on maximum growth in your stock portfolio and risk be damned, you can find the thrills you're seeking among small-growth stocks.

Professional money managers often specialize in one type or class of stock, for various reasons. They may be utterly convinced that their specialty is unquestionably the best way to make money in the stock market (don't ask; they can't explain why other, equally smart money managers, studying the same data, came to another, very different conclusion). Marketing is the more likely reason for this specialization. Investors, both individual and institutional, usually look for a money manager with a certain investment "style," be it small-cap growth or large-cap cyclical. By taking a rigid approach to investing—their charter often purposely restricts them to only certain types of stocks—these specialist money managers hope to attract investors looking for that particular style.

That approach is fine for the money managers and huge institutional investors, but not necessarily for an individual investor. Instead of casting yourself in the role of the money manager, take the part of the money manager's client. More often than not, these big investors hire several different money managers, each with a different style. That way they achieve diversity while their portfolios are still being overseen by those they hope are among the best money managers in each category. You, too, will probably want to seek a similarly eclectic approach in your investment program. Unless you are very confident that a specific approach is the best way to make money, and you have mastered the intricacies of this investment style, it's much better to follow a broader path, nibbling a little something from each platter on the banquet table.

ECONOMICS FOR IDIOTS

In any event, you'll need to do some research and to understand the nature of the risks you're taking before plunging headlong into the stock market. Your most basic research should be aimed at understanding the economic environment in which you're investing. But don't worry, it won't take long. This isn't a primer on economics, so if you need a dose of the dismal science, you'll have to go elsewhere. It's sufficient for our purposes to know whether the economy is growing, contracting, or staying about the same. The economy tends to move in cycles of varying lengths, and the stock market tends to rise and fall in similar cycles (ignoring, for the time being, the cycles within cycles) about six to nine months ahead (hence the inclusion of stock prices in the government Index of Leading Economic Indicators, a forecasting tool you might start keeping an eye on). It may seem stupid to look at the economy now since the stock market has long ago moved in anticipation of what is happening in the economy today. But, in fact, the stock market's daily ups and downs can confuse people about what is going on now, never mind what will happen next. Watching the economy in connection with some broader measures of the market—the 200-day moving average in each week's issue of *Barron's*, for instance—can help you keep your bearings. And you should know at any given moment what the Federal Reserve is doing with the nation's money supply. Monetary policy doesn't change frequently, and it's a good indicator of where the Fed is trying (albeit not always successfully) to take the economy. If the Fed is pumping money into the economy, there's a good chance the bulls will be running. If it's draining money out, watch out for bears.

As you read your daily newspaper, you will inevitably come across one economist or another making some pronouncement about what is going on in the economy and what it means for the future. And if you read a newspaper two days in a row, you'll probably find that the interpretation and forecast of the economy by yesterday's economist was entirely different from today's. Welcome to the world of high-paid economic analysis. Seldom in the history of the world have there been people who devoted more time and effort to their calling with less success (if success is defined as predicting the economy's move accurately; being paid a high salary is another matter) than economists. Certainly there are some good ones. Some of the best are the ones who don't just make pronouncements but put their (and your) money behind their predictions. Overall, however, the record of economists has been about as dismal as their science. Consider two studies that looked at what would have hap-

Figure 3.1 Stock Prices Predict the Economy

Stock prices tend to move up and down ahead of similar moves in the economy. In this chart the Dow Jones Industrial Average tends to hit a peak and begin falling some months before the onset of an economic recession.

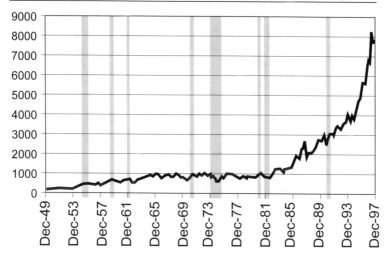

Source: National Bureau of Economic Research

▨ Recession

pened to investors who followed the advice of some of the nation's best-known economists: One showed that an investor would have fared better simply by flipping a coin, the other that an investor betting *against* the economists would have done far better than an investor taking their advice. Peter Lynch, probably the world's best-known stock picker, has this to say about economics and the stock market: "If you spend more than 14 minutes a year on economics, you've wasted 12."

HOW'S THE MARKET DOIN'?

The second level of research concerns the overall health of the stock market itself. Individual stocks tend, to a varying degree, to move with the ups and downs of the market. Indeed, some studies indicate that 85% of the gain or loss in a single stock is explained by overall market action, not by anything pertaining to the stock itself. We want to be very clear: This is not an argument for market timing—that is, playing the game of moving your portfolio fully into stocks just before a bull market move begins and pulling it all out of stocks just as the bear market begins. That's a fool's game, both because you will be wrong most of the time and because it runs up a lot of expensive commissions, which benefits brokers and not you. Instead, this is an argument for knowing which kinds of stocks do well under varying market conditions and understanding how the market moves.

How do you take the temperature of the stock market? There are many ways, and none of them are foolproof. We tend to favor simple methods over more complex ones, and the simplest of all is to measure the level of the stock market against an easily available historical benchmark, the price-earnings ratio. The price-earnings ratio, known as P-E, of the market is found by taking the past 12 months' per-share earnings of all the stocks in some market gauge, such as the Dow Jones Industrial Average or Standard & Poor's 500-stock index, and dividing that number into the index itself. Say the Dow industrials closed at 7000 and the earnings-per-share of the 30 component stocks during the past four quarters totaled $375. The market P-E would be 18.67. Historically, the price-earnings ratio of the market has averaged about 15. If the P-E is significantly above that level, the market is considered pricey and vulnerable to a correction. Significantly below it, and stocks are thought to be a bargain.

Don't worry about having to calculate the market P-E; *Barron's* publishes P-Es each week for the Dow industrials and its offshoots, the Dow Jones Transportation and Utility averages, as well as the S&P 500 and the S&P Industrial Index of 400 companies.

But even such simple and popular indicators have their failings. For one thing, as an investor you're interested in *future* earnings, not *past* earnings. Why do you care what stocks earned last year? You need to know what they will earn this year and the next. Stock market strategists are always willing to forecast earnings for the overall market for the next year, but they seldom get it right. And while it's true that the market tends to return to the average P-E (otherwise, it wouldn't be the average, would it?), that can happen through changes in earnings, prices, or some combination of the two. If the market P-E is above average, investors look for earnings to rise or, failing that, prices to fall to bring the P-E back to normal.

The P-E ratio purports to measure whether the market is *over*valued or *under*valued. Another simple measure of value that is often cited by money managers is the *dividend yield* of the stock market. That is the percentage of the market investment that you get back each year through the payment of regular dividends. Instead of adding up the earnings of the 30 stocks in the Dow, add up the annual dividend payments, then divide that number *by,* not into, the index. If the Dow closed at 7200 and the total dividends added up to $225, the dividend yield would be 3.13% ($100 divided by 7200). The higher the stock prices go without a corresponding increase in dividends, the lower the dividend yield. Since the 1960s, many market experts have argued that a dividend yield of less than 3% signaled a dangerously high market. Again, you can relax. *Barron's* will do the work for you each week.

The problem with using the dividend yield as a guide to stock market valuation is the same one we had with the

P-E ratio: You can't predict what will happen to bring an out-of-whack yield back to average. If the yield is too low, will it climb through increased dividend payouts or by stock prices falling? If it's too high, will it fall because dividends will be cut or stock prices will climb? Another problem: The yield measure doesn't take into account the vast number of rapidly growing companies that don't pay dividends but instead reinvest that money in further growth.

Value isn't the only way to measure the market's health, inasmuch as an overvalued market can become extremely overvalued and go on to become ridiculously overvalued. If you bail out when it is just modestly overvalued and it goes to ridiculous extremes, you have missed a good part of the return available from stocks. That's why some market experts swear by sentiment indicators—basically, evidence of how other investors feel about the stock market. Sentiment can be measured many ways, but the point to remember is that it is a *contrary* indicator. That is, the better other investors feel about stocks, the worse the market is likely to do; the worse they feel, the better stocks are likely to do. This seemingly paradoxical measure has its roots in the presumption that if people feel good about the stock market, they already have acted on those feelings and are fully invested in stocks. Once they are fully invested, they have no more money in reserve with which to buy more stocks, so prices stop rising. And since good news alone can't generate any more money for investment, good news will have little further impact on stock prices. But *bad* news can quickly persuade those investors that they have made a colossal mistake and should bolt for the exit. So, lots of good feelings about stocks leaves the market poised at the head of a one-way street—down.

Of course, the converse is also presumed to be true: If people hate the stock market, they don't own stocks. Thus, bad news can't drive stock prices down. But good news has the potential of persuading gloomy investors that they have made a mistake and that stocks are the place to be after all. As they pile into the market, prices zoom higher. Once you grasp the logic behind sentiment indicators, they tend to make some sense. But as with the other indicators we have examined, there isn't much precision about sentiment. Gloomy investors can become despondent or even hostile, and ebullient investors can turn downright rabid in their desire to own stocks.

Finally, there are professional investors who argue that the only way to invest in the stock market is to follow the trend, or the overall direction in which the market is headed. "Don't fight the tape" is their rallying cry, referring to the stream of transaction data spewed out by exchanges and NASDAQ. The trend they really are talking about, though, tends to be some averaged value for the stock market, say a 50-day or 200-day moving average of the market's closing price. Let's say the average closing price for the Dow Jones Industrial Average for the past 200 trading sessions is 6850 (it's in *Barron's*). If the Dow closes today above 6850, the trend is up, signaling trend-following investors to buy or hold stocks. But if it closes below the 6850 level, the trend is down, and such an investor would want to lighten up on stock holdings. This is a potentially interesting measurement as long as the daily close is substantially higher than or lower than whatever moving average you have chosen. But what happens when the daily close hovers very near the average? One day you're selling, the next you're buying. Confusion reigns until the daily close moves decisively away from the average; then it confounds you by quickly moving back to the average.

You can make the job of measuring the market's health as complex as you like, especially if you delve deeply into what is known as "technical investing." Most stock market technicians believe that stock prices are determined

Figure 3.2 Paving the Market's Bumpy Road

The erratic daily fluctuations in the stock market often obscure the over-all direction. A "moving average" smooths out the bumps and jiggles, revealing the market's true trend. One frequently used moving average is for 200 days, because that is about one calendar year of trading days. The 30-day average gives a short-term view.

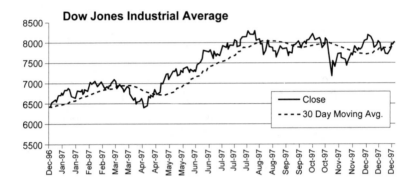

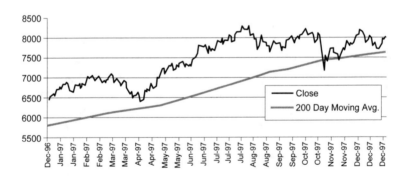

solely by the interaction of supply and demand factors, which in turn are governed by both rational and irrational decisions by investors. They contend that although there will always be minor fluctuations in the market, stock prices tend to move in long-term trends, and changes in those trends are caused by shifts in supply and demand. They say these shifts become apparent sooner or later in charts of stock price movements. Thus, technical analysts make their living by looking for historical patterns in stock prices and the economy. Then they compare what's going on in the economy and market today with their vast catalog of previous patterns to see which ones most closely match. From that they predict the likely course of stock prices. In its most basic form, technical analysis of the market can overlap with so-called fundamental analysis. The price-earnings ratio, for instance, is a valued tool of both fundamental and technical analysts. Sentiment, on the other hand, tends to be more of a technical tool. Among the many other factors that technical analysts examine are such things as momentum, the speed at which stock prices are rising or falling; volume, or the number of shares changing hands each day; and market breadth, which is measured by comparing the number of individual stocks that are rising in price to the number falling. All those factors are then applied to the charts of price activity to determine whether stocks are in a positive trend (a bull market) or a negative trend (a bear market).

We aren't technical analysts, and to be honest, we are dubious about some of its more extreme forms. However, it should be clear to anyone that the supply of stock in the market (holders who are ready to sell) and demand for shares (investors ready to buy) have a lot to do with price movements, though probably not everything. The important thing to remember about technical analysis is that a lot of people believe it works. Therefore, it can affect stock prices. We'll

CHARTING FOR THE BEGINNERS

The granddaddy of technical analysts was Charles Dow, the founder of Dow Jones & Co. and the editor of *The Wall Street Journal*. He theorized that there are three major movements at work in the stock market at any given time: daily fluctuations, secondary movements lasting anywhere from two weeks to a month, and primary, or

Figure 3.3 Charting in a Nutshell

Technical analysts look for a stock's "support" and "resistance" levels, hoping for a "breakout" that carries the stock price higher, as we see in this example of General Electric's stock price. The support price is a low price that usually draws in investors looking for value. The resistance price is the level at which investors tend to sell the stock to take their profits.

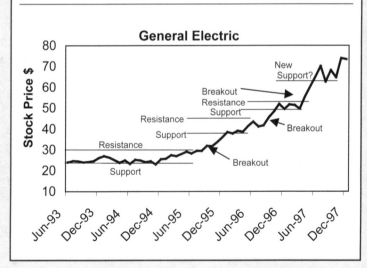

long-term, trends. The first two are important only insofar as they help establish the direction of the primary trend. At its simplest, Dow's theory maintains that a positive primary trend is in place as long as each low in the secondary movements is higher than the previous low and each high in the secondary movements is higher than the previous high. The trend reverses when the secondary moves fail to go higher than the previous high and fall lower than the previous low. And while the Dow Jones Industrial Average is the main barometer, the Dow theory—so named by his followers, not by Mr. Dow himself—holds that trends in the DJIA must be confirmed by a similar trend in the Dow Jones Transportation Average before it can be known with any certainty that a new trend is indeed in place.

Charting can also be used to judge the price direction of individual stocks by looking at *support* and *resistance* levels on a chart of the individual stock's price movements. A support level occurs when the price of a stock reaches a low enough level to attract bargain hunters, who see uncommon value in the stock at that price. A resistance level occurs when the stock price becomes high enough to prompt many investors to sell the stock and realize their gains. Stocks tend to trade between support and resistance levels in what analysts call a *trading range*. Technical analysts watch for stocks that exceed either their resistance or support levels. When that happens, it's a *breakout* that establishes a trend for that stock, either down, if the stock falls below its support level, or up, if it surpasses its resistance level.

Figure 3.4 The Dow Theory, Illustrated

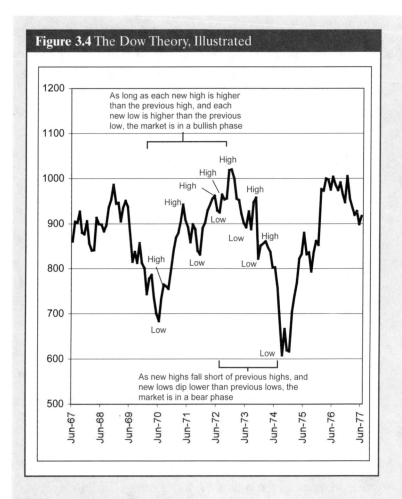

discuss it further as we examine when and how investors decide to buy or sell a stock.

We hope that you can see more clearly now why we are such advocates of the dollar-cost-averaging method of buying stocks that was explained in the first chapter. If you buy a fixed dollar amount of stocks each month, regardless of P-E ratios, dividend yields, sentiment figures, or head-and-shoulder patterns on a price chart, you will wind up buying more shares of stock when prices are low (when you should be buying them) and fewer shares when prices are high (when you shouldn't be buying).

DON'T BE SCARED, BE SMART

Any investor worthy of the name should understand the nature of the risks in an investment vehicle. It so happens that stocks have more than their fair share of risks, and you should know about them. We aren't telling you this to scare you away from stocks. Rather, we feel that an informed investor is a better investor and one who will keep his head when all around him are losing theirs. The risks in buying a stock or stocks can be listed from the broadest to the narrowest.

At the top of the list is *economic risk,* the danger that slower economic growth will cause investments to fall in price. As we will see, shares of emerging growth companies often require a vigorous economy to sustain the rapid earnings gains that investors expect of them. And cyclical companies, with their huge capital investments in plant and equipment, can't cut costs fast enough to make up for a declining economy, so the value of their shares is almost certain to fall when times get tough.

Interest rate risk is broad-scale, too. Rising interest rates can hurt stocks in several ways, not the least of which is that higher rates make it more difficult for companies to grow and increase their profits. Rising rates also attract money away from the stock market and into investments, such as bonds, that investors perceive as being "safer." Because stock dividends seldom keep pace with interest rates, stocks become less attractive.

Next comes *market risk,* the chance that the overall market may hit an air pocket and take a sickening dive, carrying your portfolio with it. We have just examined some of the ways you can attempt to measure the likelihood of such a risk, but as we pointed out, none are fail-safe. Take consolation in the fact that the stock market has tended to move higher over time, the fits and starts and big drops notwithstanding. We can presume that as long as the American economy remains market-oriented and operating in a democratically controlled political environment, the market's overall advance will continue.

The risks that are specific to the company whose stock you own are usually called *business risks.* These are the toughest ones for an investor to sort out because the potential risks come from every direction. Is management competent? Is the technology the best available? Is the product a fad? Do competitors have big advantages of one sort or another, such as cheaper labor? Those are just a few of the possible concerns; if you think hard about it, the list of questions becomes nearly endless. Unfortunately, you won't ever be able to answer them all with any degree of certainty. If you could, there would be no risk in making the investment. But you should, in most instances, be able to answer enough of them that you can make your decision without feeling you are doing nothing more than rolling dice in a craps game. If you can't, don't buy the stock.

At the lower end of the risk spectrum comes what we call the *financial risk* a company faces. This is fairly simple to analyze by examining the company's financial statements. This isn't a book about accounting methods, but it isn't hard to determine if a company has a burdensome load of debt on its balance sheet. If so, has that debt load been increasing or decreasing over the past year or so?

Finally, there is *information risk,* the chance that some piece of damaging information about the company will come out that causes the stock price to plunge. Fortunately, the United States has some of the world's most stringent disclosure laws. The Securities and Exchange Commission, which regulates such matters, goes to great lengths to ensure that companies keep investors and potential investors well informed. None of this precludes a company in which you've bought stock from announcing some horrible news, but you will find out about it at around the same time other investors do. You should realize, though, that full disclosure tends to apply to larger companies more than smaller ones. Larger companies tend to get much more scrutiny from securities analysts and the news media than smaller companies.

Another difference between big and little stocks that you should know about is liquidity because it presents a risk when investing among smaller issues. Liquidity is a fancy term for how quickly you can buy or sell something—especially sell it—without a big change in price. Thousands of shares of the biggest stocks change hands each day. If for some reason you decide suddenly that you want to get rid of 1,000 shares of DuPont, you needn't worry. Just make a quick call to your broker ordering the sale of your DuPont at the market price, and presto, it's done. Not so with many issues traded over the counter. There are many days when not a single share of some small companies changes hands. Should you want to sell 1,000 shares of MicrobioTech Synergy Corp.

(we made this up; don't go looking for it), it could require a few days for your broker to unload it, and she might have to keep cutting your asking price to do it. The lack of liquidity in small stocks is one reason that big institutional investors don't own a lot of small stocks. These huge institutions throw around millions of dollars each day, and there simply isn't enough liquidity among small stocks to sop up that kind of money.

Now that you understand the nature of some of the risks facing the stock investor (and if you haven't gotten scared and stuffed your investment kitty back under the mattress), we'll examine the various categories of stocks with an eye toward their suitability to different kinds of investment portfolios. While we aren't trying to scare you, we owe it to you to spell out what can go wrong with the various types of stocks. Once you start dealing with investment professionals, they will go out of their way to tell you about the rewards of each category, but they will be far less eager to tell you about the risks. We want you to go into the game adequately armed to defend yourself.

BLACK AND BLUE CHIPS

Let's start with the stocks that are perceived to be the least risky—the so-called blue chips. For those of you who know better than to waste your time and money in a casino, the name "blue chips" comes from the variously colored chips issued to gamblers in casinos, the blue chip being the most valuable. Blue chip stocks tend to be the biggest companies. They count among their number the 30 stocks that comprise the Dow Jones Industrial Average, some of which have experienced tremendous price drops that left investors stupefied.

You must remember above all that nobody makes any guarantees about the price behavior of *any* stock, regardless of how big or how blue. Which brings us to Big Blue, International Business Machines Corp., which in the first edition of this book was our example of what can go wrong with a seemingly safe stock.

For many years IBM was the paragon of stocks. The company skillfully managed the transition from mechanical business machines to electronic computers. Its products set the standards for the computer industry. Its sales force was the envy of every other company. Its management ranks were the prime recruiting ground for the rest of corporate America. And its stock price and dividend steadily climbed,

Figure 3.5 Big Blue's Big Fall—and Bigger Rise

Stock performance of International Business Machines since 12/31/90.

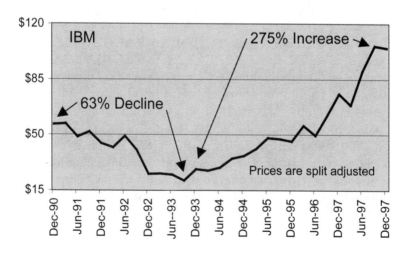

transforming many investors into millionaires over the years. There were few professional or individual investors who didn't have a dollop of IBM in their portfolios.

Then it all went to hell. While this mighty colossus was building ever-more-powerful, ever-faster mainframe computers, Steven Jobs was laboring away in a garage creating a computer that could literally sit on a desktop. And it wasn't long afterward that William Gates started designing software to make those new little personal computers work faster and better. In less than a decade, the mainframe computer became a has-been, useful only in a limited number of applications. Even the personal computer became a commodity product. The real growth in technology lay in the design of the microprocessors and software that made the little computers so powerful. But investors were so convinced nothing could shake Big Blue that they failed to recognize what was happening to their favorite company. When the stock price fell below $100 a share in late 1989, thousands of investors snapped it up, crowing about what a bargain IBM was under $100. By 1993 the stock was touching $40, and few investors were talking about IBM stock as anything but a dog.

That's where the story ended in our first edition. But instead of continuing to wither, IBM hired a new chairman, Louis V. Gerstner, Jr., in 1993 and set itself on a comeback course. Since then, revenue per employee is up 58% and growing, and nearly two-thirds of its $76 billion in annual revenue comes from outside its mainframe business. In addition, the company has generated enough cash to pump $16.5 billion into buying back its own stock, which has quadrupled and set a new 10-year high in 1997. No wonder the IBM board signed Gerstner up for a new five-year contract that awards him options for two million shares of stock.

So, a happy ending after all? Not so fast. The story is continuing, as it does for all companies and all stocks. While Gerstner describes the new culture at IBM as "one of restless self-renewal," he admits to a nagging fear: "I do worry that we sort of get complacent again. But I don't think anybody is going to get complacent around here as long as I am here, including me." IBM's new strategy of promoting "solutions" to customers' problems requires the company's many units to work together. That, Gerstner acknowledges, "will be a continuing challenge for us, but I think we are getting better."

Although few stocks have undergone the stem-to-stern transformation that IBM underwent in the past few years, other blue chip stocks have also taken their lumps. General Motors was battered badly in 1992 as it became increasingly apparent that the company had been terribly mismanaged for more than a decade. GM's 40% stock slide from 1989 into 1992 also culminated in an entirely new management team being brought in by GM's activist board to replace the executives who nearly drove the company into bankruptcy. After halting the bleeding in 1993 and 1994, their focus was to clean up the balance sheet. In GM's North American unit, whose profligate spending was the cause of much of the company's problems, executives slashed supply costs and became more disciplined about spending on redesigning vehicles. In its struggle to survive, GM couldn't afford billions for new vehicles and new engines, so it made marketing hay out of its long line of reasonably priced, no-frills vehicles, becoming in its way the Wal-Mart of the auto industry.

Since its low point in 1992, GM's stock has climbed more than 60%. But this story, like IBM's, isn't over. GM is still far behind industry standards for efficiency and new-product development. Its market share in the United States is hovering around 33%, the lowest it has been in decades.

There are plenty of other black and blue chip stories, among them Sears (a 63% decline from 1987 through 1990, followed by a 197% jump over the next seven years), Citibank (down 76% from 1989 through 1991, then up 1565% through the third quarter of 1997), and, more recently, AT&T (down 47% from the third quarter of 1995 to the first quarter of 1997, up 27% through the third quarter of 1997). But if ever there was a tribute to the principle of diversification, it is the fact that in early 1993 the Dow Jones Industrial Average—with IBM, GM, Sears, and Westinghouse of its 30 stocks battered and bleeding—nevertheless could climb to new record highs.

As the Dow's performance suggests, there are plenty of big, well-known, and well-managed companies deserving of blue chip status and investor attention. Among the other Dow industrial stocks, General Electric and Hewlett Packard seem best suited to represent blue chips as an investment category. Both companies are well managed, with top-of-the-line products and services, and are closely covered by small armies of securities analysts and by the business press. Of course, their prices reflect the esteem in which they are held. The lesson in all this is simply that even in the largest, seemingly safest stocks, investors have to play heads-up ball. The smartest investors clearly saw signs of trouble in IBM and began unloading it long before the vast majority caught on. Unless things have changed dramatically since we wrote this book, you can probably buy Coca-Cola or GE shares with some feeling of safety. Their dividends are probably going to rise over time, as will the price of their stocks. You just want to be sure that if one day GE or Coca-Cola stumbles, you are among the savvy investors who saw what tripped them up when it happened, not one or two or ten years later.

GROWN-UP GROWTH STOCKS

Money managers tend to divide big stocks, including blue chip issues, into two distinctive categories that are worth thinking about: growth stocks and cyclical stocks. Many companies exhibit some of the traits of both. But if we had to choose one, we'd spend most of our time and money playing in the growth stock arena. The companies are well known, their activities are closely monitored by the news media and securities analysts, many pay dividends, and it's always easy to buy or sell their shares.

Definitions of growth stocks tend to vary from one investor to another, but the underlying idea is always the same: a company that because of the product or service it offers tends to grow at a steady and somewhat predictable rate, virtually independent of the economic cycle. Through much of the 1980s and into the 1990s the premier growth stocks were in such industries as food, tobacco, beverages (both with and without alcohol), and pharmaceuticals. It was widely believed that regardless of what the economy was doing, consumers would stuff their faces, puff their butts, swill their beer, and take some drugs. (Unfortunately for investors, we're only concerned with sales of legal drugs; the other kind may be more profitable for somebody, but a bad bet in that market could result in a real killing.) Because the growth of such companies appeared so predictable, and profit margins on such products as cereal, cigarettes, beer, and tranquilizers were so high, investors fell in serious love with the stocks. And as is always the case, the newly smitten lover fails at first to see the warts.

In the case of the food and beverage companies, greed among corporate executives was overtaken by the often underrated common sense of the American consumer. Kellogg's, Quaker Oats, Coca-Cola, and Pepsico spent huge

sums to market what was essentially baked grains and fla-
vored water in one form or another. Consumers didn't have
to be geniuses to figure out that they were paying a lot more
for the advertising of the cereal and the soft drinks than they
were paying for the consumables themselves. That realization became increasingly important as a new mood of financial restraint settled over the nation in the early 1990s following the financial excesses of the previous decade. Generic
cereals and soft drinks began springing up, offering shoppers
a better deal. The resulting pressure on sales and profit margins at the big brand-name cereal and soft drink makers
undercut their reputation as predictable growth companies.
Without either the growth or the predictability, investors no
longer were willing to pay a premium to own the stocks.
Coca-Cola rebounded more quickly than the others as the
mid-1990s bull market favored big stocks with brand-name
franchises. But by 1997 it, too, was cautioning investors that
its growth wasn't unlimited.

Drug stocks also suffered from their own earlier success. The Clinton administration, wrestling with the problem
of rising health costs in America, set its sights squarely on the
pharmaceutical firms. Fortunately, government controls
weren't enacted, but the revolution of containing health care
costs continued on its own, without Washington's meddling.
As a result, the drug business became less predictable in
terms of profit margins and steady growth of sales and earnings.

Meanwhile, tobacco companies ran into a firestorm
of litigation by cancer victims and their families. It got so bad
that the tobacco companies secretly huddled with state and
federal officials, along with public health advocates, to hammer out an agreement in which they would shell out $368.5
billion over 25 years to help curb underage smoking and to
issue warning labels declaring cigarettes addictive. In return,
the tobacco companies would receive extensive liability pro-

tection. But as we write, the agreement is under fire for being too lenient on the tobacco companies. At the very least, the amount they must pay for legal protection is bound to go up.

It isn't that food, soft drinks, pharmaceuticals, and tobacco weren't legitimate growth stocks. For a period of time they clearly satisfied the requirements of steady and predictable growth. But like anything else, they couldn't go up forever. The investors who recognized the potential for sustained growth in these companies 15 years ago were well rewarded for their insight. The investor who bought the stocks a couple of years ago because they had performed so well in the past and because everybody else seemed to own them has been handed his head on a plate.

There was another reason the big growth stocks performed well, and it had little to do with their underlying businesses. Instead, it was the result of an investment technique called "indexing." Indexing stemmed from the growing realization among investors that they were paying good money to portfolio managers who were consistently failing to do better than the overall market, as measured by such barometers as Standard & Poor's 500-stock index. In fact, once fees and transaction costs were taken into account, the money managers were found to be doing very poorly. The result was the creation of "index funds," which are nothing more than investment vehicles designed to mimic the behavior of a popular index like the S&P 500. Since they don't require close attention as "actively managed" portfolios do, management fees were very low. Because they don't involve a lot of trading, transactions costs were low, too. And because they mimicked the ups and downs of the broad market, the investor never underperforms the market. Of course, he doesn't outperform, either, but he wasn't having much luck at that in any case. It just so happens that the S&P 500, the most popular of the broad market measures for indexers, contains a lot of big growth stocks, so those stocks were automatically purchased for inclusion in index funds. Nobody knows how much additional buying of those stocks occurred because of index funds, but it was substantial and clearly helped pump up, and hold up, their prices.

We have seen how different growth industries lost some of their growth characteristics. That's something you should be wary of if you want to invest in growth stocks. But at the same time, if you're shopping for growth stocks, don't make the mistake of confining yourself only to the stocks of companies in industries that are growing steadily. The retailing business, for instance, is hardly a growth industry. Margins are often razor thin, and sales frequently ebb and flow with the rising and falling of the economic tide. Yet within that often beleaguered business are two of the most vital growth stocks in recent memory: Wal-Mart and Home Depot. By paying careful attention to their customers' needs and by nurturing and training their workers, these two companies have turned the business of selling toilet paper and hardware upside down. Once again, the price of their stocks climbed sky-high in recognition of their stunning success. As we wrote the first edition, however, the bloom seemed to be fading from both roses. Though neither has a serious competitor, it was simply inevitable that their stunning growth would slow at some point. But their stocks broke out of their holding pattern in 1997 and started climbing again, testimony that the two retailers had mastered their earlier growth spurts and figured out how to manage at the behemoth level.

It's fun to find winners like these and climb aboard for a gloriously profitable ride. But keep your eyes open for whatever it is that will bring the train to a screeching halt. You want to get off before that happens.

A final word on growth stocks: Just because sales and earnings seem to be growing at a steady rate, don't think the stock price will perform with equal discipline. Everybody wants to own a winning stock, and the rush to buy shares of

Figure 3.6 Growth Stocks Don't Grow Forever

As these 10-year charts of Wal-Mart and Home Depot show, go-go growth stocks tend to run out of gas eventually. In these cases, the companies took notice and made adjustments to their operations. After a while, profit growth resumed, and their stock prices started moving up again. One test of a company's management is its ability to handle situations such as these.

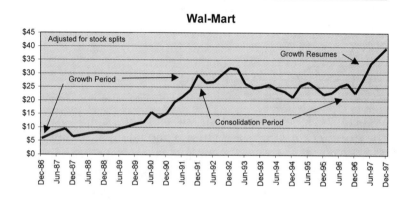

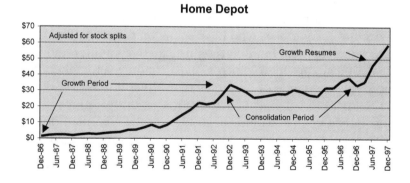

growth companies often drives stock prices to incredibly high levels. Can any company grow fast enough and steadily enough to warrant a price-earnings ratio of more than 100? Not for long. Any such stock is virtually certain to come down to a more reasonable, although still high, level. There is uncommon value in predictable and steady growth, but exercise some common sense and forgo paying ridiculously high prices for these characteristics. As Mother said, "Do your homework."

LET'S GO CYCLING

Cyclical stocks are called that for one very simple reason: The prices of the stocks tend to rise and fall in harmony with the ups and downs of the economic cycle. If the economy is emerging from a recession, cyclical stock prices are virtually certain to be on the rise. If the economy is headed into recession, cyclical stock prices are falling. It follows then that if you can just predict the economic cycle, you'll be a millionaire in short order.

Dream on. As we pointed out earlier, there are dozens of economists who have spent years getting Ph.Ds in the subject, then building sophisticated computer models that are supposed to mirror the economy and take into account thousands of variables that affect it. And we don't know one who has called the turns in the economy right more than chance would suggest. Even the chairman of the Federal Reserve, the one economist who can do anything about the economy, can't always get it right, so how do you figure you can?

The point is that there isn't a simple way to know when to buy or sell cyclical stocks. The economy is a vast and complex mechanism that we're still far from understanding, much less controlling. What's more, through the magic of the market, cyclical stocks tend to rise *ahead* of a recovery, not during it. You can, of course, buy cyclical stocks and hold them, hoping eventually to ride them higher in one of their cyclical bursts. But while you are doing that, others will be minting money in growth stocks and any of a dozen or so more lucrative investments.

Companies in cyclical industries make their money on volume, not price. Industries such as steel, aluminum, paper, automobiles, and airlines are intensely competitive and require huge investments in factories or airplanes. If those factories sit idle or those airplane seats fly empty, the companies lose vast amounts of money. If we, the consumers, aren't buying cars, then General Motors and Ford shut their plants and cancel their orders for steel and aluminum. That means Bethlehem Steel and Aluminum Co. of America shutter their plants, too. And even when demand picks up, they aren't always able to raise prices to make up for the earlier losses because the pressure of competition is too great. Thus it stands to reason that only through the full use of their factories or airplanes will these companies profit.

If you feel compelled to have a few of America's basic industries in your portfolio, that's fine. There is a lot of money to be made in the run-ups that cyclical stocks enjoy from time to time. But cyclical stocks require discipline and, we're sad to say, market timing. Try to choose the best company within any industry and buy the stock amidst the gloom and doom of a recession, not in the middle of an ebullient economic expansion. Be prepared to sit with your choice until times get better. Finally, don't be greedy. Cyclical stocks have a nasty way of taking investors on round trips. You want a one-way ticket. Get out of the stocks as soon as you sense the improving mood, either in yourself or others, that accompanies an economic recovery.

RIDING THE SMALL-GROWTH-STOCK ROCKETS

This is it, the place you want to play if you are really intent on making big bucks in the stock market—and if you are prepared to lose big bucks in the stock market. The object of the game: Find a company with a unique product or service that is growing at an unsustainable pace, buy the stock cheap, ride

Figure 3.7 Small Stocks Give Investors a Rougher Ride Than Big Stocks

This chart compares the performance of the Dow Jones Industrial Average, comprising 30 big stocks, with the Russell index of 2,000 small stocks. The market for small issues is far more volatile. Over extended periods in the past, small stocks have tended to produce higher returns than big stocks. But this bit of market lore didn't hold true in the decade ending in 1997.

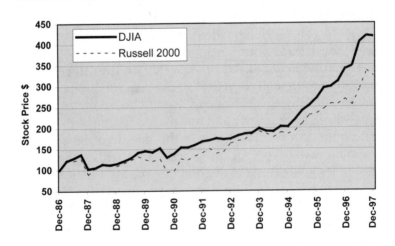

it high, then bail out and go find another company that will let you do it all over again. Good luck. You're up against Wall Street's best.

The excitement of small stocks lies in the pace of the action, the skill of the players, and the enormous risks and rewards. Things move awfully fast here. Money managers specializing in small-growth stocks seldom hold the stocks more than a year and sometimes only for a few days. A stock can drop by half or double in price in a single day's trading. The players are hotshot money managers looking to make their names and fortunes with 30%, 40%, or 50% annual gains. The risks are obviously high for anyone playing in this market, but you're coming to it with some built-in disadvantages. You have to play with your own money, not other people's like the money managers do. You probably have a job, while their job *is* playing the market. And they have relationships with big Wall Street brokerage firms that reduce their transaction costs far below yours.

Still want to play?

If you have a normal tolerance for risk, you probably should join the action with at least a part of your portfolio, keeping in mind some advantages you have that the pros don't. You don't have to own any of these stocks at any given time; the pros are paid to invest money in small stocks, and they have to do it in good times or bad. You don't have to make 30% or 40% returns on your portfolio of small stocks; the pros don't, either, but if they don't, they won't be pros very long. You can afford to take a longer-term view, holding a small stock until it becomes a medium-sized stock if you wish; by the nature of their jobs, pros are forced to sell when a company's pace of growth slows and look for another risky stock to buy as a replacement.

To understand the process of selecting small-growth stocks, you have to understand the process by which a company grows. Most new companies are started by someone with an idea and a small pool of money, either his own or borrowed. The new company gets launched and usually fails utterly within a year or so. The few that survive go on to the next step in which they find a bigger pile of capital, often from venture capital sources that, in exchange for the capital, are given partial ownership in and control of the fledgling concern. As growth accelerates, management builds a track record. At the same time the need for capital grows, too. It is at this stage of aggressive growth that the company sells stock for the first time in an *initial public offering*. (We'll look at IPOs shortly.) Once the stock is sold, the company is off and running, promoting its product or service and expanding as rapidly as possible. If it is able to continue to grow at a rapid and somewhat predictable rate, the company will start to attract the attention of investors looking for just that combination—fast and predictable growth. As more investors pile into the stock, its price soars. Eventually, of course, the growth rate must slow. Any company growing at 50% per year would soon be gargantuan. As the company matures and the growth slows, the "hot money" investors sell the stock and go shopping for another, more youthful, and faster-growing stock. A different kind of investor takes their place—one who hangs in as long as the company continues to produce predictable growth and the price of its stock can continue to rise, albeit not nearly as fast as it once did.

The difficulties of picking small-growth stocks may seem overwhelming. Chief among them is the lack of information about many small companies. Newspapers seldom report on small companies, and the big Wall Street firms tend to ignore them. It is typical for a company like General Electric to have some 40 to 50 securities analysts keeping watch over it. But many small companies have no analysts watching them. Even when a company becomes well known among the cognoscenti of small-stock investors, it may be followed only by a handful of analysts at regional or specialty

" OH, YEAH · THE DISNEY PEOPLE TOOK OVER HERE IN JUNE OF '95."

brokerage firms that follow specific industries. Yet it is the very lack of information that contributes to the volatility of small stocks and makes them so attractive to risk-taking investors, who feel they have a chance of seeing something in a small company that no one else sees. It's also what makes a publication like *Barron's* so valuable.

Many professional money managers make a big deal about the fact that they sit down and talk to management of a small company before buying stock in it. You probably can't do that unless you intend to invest $100,000 or so in the stock. But don't conclude that access to management is something special. Anybody who thinks the managers of a company growing 30% or more a year have some grand strategic vision are sadly mistaken. These guys are sitting aboard a rocket, and they're hanging on for dear life. They are so busy putting out fires and solving the everyday problems of a rapidly growing business that they don't have time to have any grand visions. If they're succeeding at solving most of the problems, you won't hear much about the company; you'll just watch sales continue to rise. If they're not succeeding, you and the professional money manager will probably take the same bath. This doesn't mean, by the way, that management isn't absolutely crucial to the success of a small firm. It is. Small companies typically don't have the depth of management that big companies enjoy, and the loss of a key executive can spell doom for a small concern.

The pros often are so committed to investing only in skyrocketing companies that they have little tolerance for an occasional minor slip-up. You, on the other hand, can afford to be more patient. Often when a small-growth company comes up short a penny or two of what money managers expected in quarterly results, the pros will dump the stock. It isn't unheard of for a small stock to drop 30% to 40% in one day on an earnings disappointment. If you're following that company as a potential buy, or even if you already own it, such debacles can present wonderful opportunities to put the stock into your portfolio or add to your current holdings. Just be sure the slip-up was minor and not a prelude to disaster. The stock won't recover very fast, so you have time to do your homework.

Not surprisingly, the valuation criteria of small-growth stocks is different from other stocks. Since you are buying future earnings when you buy a stock, you can expect a company that produces 40% gains in annual earnings to carry a higher price tag than one that produces 10% gains. That's why you'll find the price-earnings ratios of small-growth companies somewhere up in the stratosphere. It isn't unusual to see these stocks carrying P-Es of 50 or higher, compared with 18 to 20 for the typical large-growth stock. Some professional managers argue that the rapid growth of small firms prevents them from operating efficiently and producing the best possible earnings. Under those circumstances they think that a better valuation measure is the price of a share divided into total per-share revenue. For most companies that figure would be around 1 to 1.5, while the fastest growing small companies may have a ratio of 5 or higher.

More than any other category of stocks, small-growth stocks are vulnerable to fads. If one company launches a product or service that looks as if it will work, other entrepreneurs (that's what they call themselves; we call them copycats) will launch a similar company. If the first company's stock is hot, a bunch of investors who missed the first opportunity will be panting to buy stock in the second, third, fourth, or tenth company to jump into the business. Video stores and bagel shops both mushroomed overnight in this fashion. The smart investors are the ones who get in on the process early and get out early, because fads are based on nothing more than the "greater fool" theory: I'll be foolish and buy it today on the assumption that I can sell it to a greater fool tomorrow. The fad lasts until it becomes clear that not all these companies are well managed and the competition in the new arena is getting fierce. Then all the investors who turned out to be the greatest fools head for the door at the same time, and the house of cards comes tumbling down. Back come the really smart investors, picking through the rubble, looking for the stock of the company that does it best.

Small-growth stocks are not for everyone, and we recognize that. But for those willing to take a bigger-than-average risk with part of a portfolio, the excitement and challenge of small stocks is unparalleled in the investment world. If you are reluctant to dive in, get wet slowly. Invest in a small-growth-stock mutual fund and track what the managers are buying and selling. Look for potential investing

Figure 3.8 Prospectus Mandatorius

Researching a stock—before you buy it—should include reading the offering prospectus. It is among the most important documents for investors deciding whether to buy a stock. In these examples, note the prominent advisories to heed the sections on "Risk Factors."

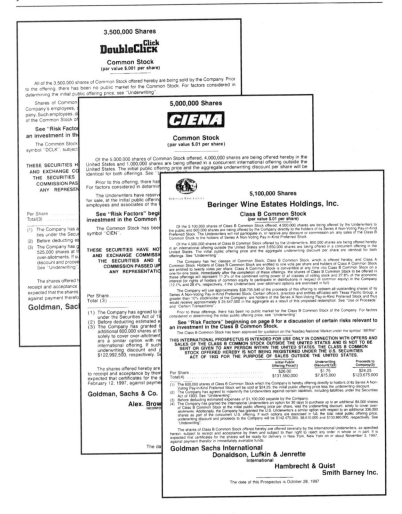

ideas in *Barron's*. Then call the company for copies of the annual and quarterly reports, the proxy statement, and a prospectus. Think about the product or service that is being offered. What are the business risks the company faces? After a while we think you'll begin to feel more confident about making a decision to buy a few small-growth stocks. Our only caveat is to be particularly wary of small companies with no product or revenues, only an idea. The biotech industry is rife with these long shots. If they ever come up with a product that works, you'll still have a chance to invest. Let somebody else take the really big risks.

INITIAL PUBLIC OFFERINGS

Here lies danger. In tracing the growth of a company from start-up to maturity, we noted above that there comes a time when the management of a company needs to sell stock to raise capital. There's a strong temptation among investors to "get in on the ground floor."

Resist it.

Initial public offerings, or IPOs, are for the pros and other sophisticated investors. You'll see why after we show you how the process works. Once a company has progressed to the stage that it must seek capital from the public, the management typically calls in an investment banking firm to handle the transaction. The bankers research the company, prepare documentation on its past performance, and attempt to get a feel for what investors will pay to own the stock of the fledgling company. Along with a gravy train of lawyers, they help the company prepare what may be the most important document for the investing public: the prospectus. In it, the company's financial history is disclosed, its managers profiled, and, critical to the potential investor, the risks it faces are detailed. Once the prospectus is ready, the bankers start beating the drum to attract buyers. "Road shows" are booked and staged, featuring presentations about the company's product and service, and putting top management on display for securities analysts and big institutional investors who get to ask any questions they want. The whole thing is designed to whet the appetite of potential big investors. When the actual sale of the stock is held, the investment bankers, often acting together with other firms in a syndicate, set the price and then buy the stock directly from the company. They then turn around and sell the new shares to other investors.

The key to the process clearly lies with the investment bankers' reading of how valuable the stock will be in the public market. If they think the new company can be a raging success, the investment bankers will earmark lots of the stock for their favorite clients (not you) and will even keep a portion of the new offering for themselves in anticipation of a big price increase. If they aren't so sure about the new company's prospects, they won't hold any of the new stock any longer than they must to find buyers. Often those buyers are less-favored clients (again, not you). If the bankers have succeeded in making some buyers eager to buy the stock, the price of the shares naturally will rise, at least for the first few days. That will usually be your first opportunity to buy the stock, and if you move quickly, you'll be the patsy riding it back down to the level at which it should have sold in the first place. One study showed that buyers who purchased an initial public offering at the closing price on its first day of trading (when it would first be available to most of us) earned about 2% annually on the investment, less than you could make by keeping your money in a bank account.

That's why we recommend that you take part in the initial public offering process vicariously. Request the prospectus of a company that will soon be going public. Study it, then watch the price move when the stock is finally sold. Wait a few weeks or even months for the price to settle down or to establish a solid pattern of gains. Then and only then do you want to own the stock. Anything else is being greedy. Sooner or later, greed always gets punished in the stock market.

VALUE IS ANOTHER NAME FOR CHEAP

We have just taken a look at small-growth-stock investing, where investors buy high and sell higher. Now let's look at the other end of the spectrum, value investing, or buying low and selling not quite as low. There is little about value investing that is glamorous, macho, or romantic. It's a plodding discipline that sometimes takes years to pay off. It usually involves stocks in boring industries, and it requires more than a little homework. Yet for those willing to abide by its disciplines, value investing can be very lucrative over the long run.

The heart of value investing is finding stocks in companies that are unloved, unwatched, or unknown, yet are sound investments. The assumption is that eventually other investors will reach the same conclusion and buy the stock from you at a higher price than you paid for it. The danger, of course, is that a stock price is low because the company is going nowhere now and never will. Buy that stock, and you'll be buying low and selling lower, not exactly a formula for investment success.

A key difference between the small-growth-stock investor and the value investor is that the value investor doesn't care what stage of development a company is in. Value plays can be found among giant, mature companies or small, obscure firms. Often the value investor will be looking for the jewels hidden among the debris of a wrecked industry. The pounding taken by the banking industry a few years ago, for example, presented value investors with a smorgasbord of potential investments, including J. P. Morgan, one of the world's largest and soundest banks. Emotional investors fleeing the problems of the industry dumped bank stocks indiscriminately, lumping Morgan in the same basket as banks that were near failure. It didn't take the value boys long to discover J. P. Morgan stock among the ruins.

Figure 3.9 Finding a Value Play

Sometimes, stocks are unjustifiably hammered when investors go gunning for others in the same industry. The Asian financial crisis of 1997–98 is an example. Stocks of big U.S. banks were dragged down because investors were worried about exposure to bad loans in Asia. Among those hit was Banc One, a big bank, to be sure, but which had little to no Asian loan exposure. As a result, there emerged periods in which Banc One shares were substantially undervalued—and ripe for a play by a value investor.

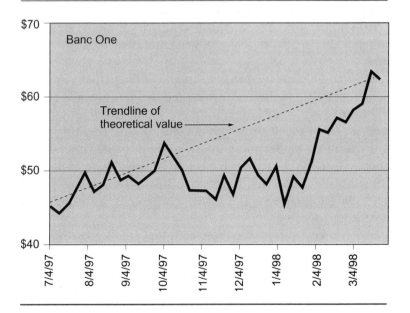

Value investors don't often go for home runs. They assume they can find stocks that are undervalued by the market for some reason right now but that have the potential to return to some "fair" value eventually. That fair value might not be particularly high, it's just higher than it is when Mr. Value Investor buys the stock. The most common measure of value used by these investors is the price-earnings ratio. Some have a discipline that doesn't allow them to even consider owning a stock unless its P-E is below 10. And then the company has to have a viable product or service, good management, and low debt. Others look for companies that have assets which aren't being fully valued by the market. An example would be a forest products concern with vast timber holdings that have, over a period of years, appreciated in value but are on the company's books at the original purchase price of 20 years ago.

Value investing requires discipline and patience along with some knowledge of securities analysis. But we think it's a valuable offset to the frantic pace of small-growth-stock investing in a diversified portfolio. You will have to go beyond the simplistic lesson in securities analysis that we present here, but investing the time to do that will pay rewards in other stock market arenas, too.

DEFENSIVE STOCKS

This is a catchall category of stocks for chickens. Many of them can be considered growth companies that aren't growing. Their appeal is to the worried investor who wants something that won't go down with the rest of the market in times of economic turmoil. Unfortunately, such stocks probably won't go up with the rest of the market, either. The best examples may be some of the food companies that make

A SHORT—VERY SHORT—COURSE IN SECURITIES ANALYSIS

It doesn't take an MBA to do fundamental securities analysis. All you have to know is which questions to ask and where to get the answers. The questions are easy: Can the company pay its bills? Is it financially sound? The answers are easily found by performing some quick and simple math on the company's balance sheet. (A well-managed company with nothing to hide will probably have done this for you in its latest financial report.)

First, you want to know if the company can pay its bills. You can establish that by matching current assets with current liabilities on the balance sheet. That is called the "quick ratio." The assets you want to use are listed as "cash and marketable securities." If those assets are approximately equal to liabilities, that is, the ratio is 1 to 1, go to the next step. If cash exceeds liabilities, keep going. If liabilities exceed cash, find another stock.

Second, you want to know how deeply in debt the company is by measuring long-term debt against total capital, the aptly named "debt to capital ratio." Remember, the money the company borrowed is part of its working capital, so add long-term debt and total common stock outstanding (multiply the number of shares outstanding by the price per share) to arrive at the total capital. Divide long-term debt by total capital and, presto, you have the percentage of total capital that is represented by debt. Some industries typically operate with more debt than others, but if the debt ratio is more than 25%, consider searching elsewhere unless you know the industry and are comfortable with higher levels of debt.

You can carry this process much further, getting deeper and deeper into the complexities of accounting and analysis. If you're interested in doing that, you should start with some basic books, working your way up eventually to the all-time classic mentioned in the Suggested Reading section of this chapter, Benjamin Graham's and David Dodd's *Security Analysis*.

what we think of as commodity food products. People have to eat regardless of the condition of the economy, but there is only so much oatmeal a person can stand. Oatmeal consumption tends to run along a fairly flat line. It did enjoy a brief heyday, however, when a medical report suggested that increased consumption of oatmeal might help prevent colon cancer. But, as we said, there is only so much oatmeal a person can stand.

A subcategory of the defensive stock group is the "income issue," a stock that pays unusually high dividends. The best of all possible worlds would be a stock that would rise in price each year while still paying a dividend of, say, 10%. Don't bother looking for one; they don't exist. Utility companies have a reputation for paying high dividends, but that may change as the business of delivering energy becomes less regulated and more competitive. Meanwhile, the high-dividend-paying utilities tend to be confined to certain geographical regions; they have little prospect of growing any faster than the regions they serve. Also, many state governments still have a say in pricing. The state utility commission, often made up of hack politicians who mutate into minor demagogues, in some cases can even tell the utility how much money it will be allowed to make. Because utilities typically have very high capital costs for their generation and distribution systems, they have to provide some incentive for investors to buy their stock. Frequently, the incentive is a high dividend.

Companies other than utilities sometimes pay high dividends, too. But often the high rate doesn't last very long and is the result not of a deliberately generous dividend policy but of a stock price which has sunk to the point that the dividend yield has risen substantially by default. IBM is a case in point. Briefly the dividend yield on a share of IBM stock was 10%. The price had fallen so far that what once was a 2.5% dividend, back in August 1987 when the stock reached its high of nearly $175, had more than tripled by the time the stock had collapsed to $50 a share. Needless to say, it didn't take IBM directors long to correct that situation. They slashed the dividend by 55%.

If you detect a little cynicism about defensive stocks, you're right. We figure you are in the stock market to see your portfolio grow, not stay the same. If it's income you want, buy a bond. That's why they exist.

WHAT'S SO SPECIAL ABOUT SPECIAL SITUATIONS?

Here is another catchall category, sometimes called the "businessman's special." These are the stocks of companies that aren't easily classified among the other categories. For some reason somebody expects the stock to do well even if it has been a laggard for years. Sometimes the reason is that the old management has gotten the boot and the new chiefs have plans to turn the company around. If they succeed, the stock will indeed soar. If they fail, the stock goes back into the trash can. It's awfully difficult to call the outcome in such a situation, but the winners tend to win big. The losers don't get beaten too badly because the stock usually was priced low enough that it won't sink a lot lower.

Mergers and buyouts offer another special situation. They were at the heart of the raging bull market in stocks that preceded the Crash of 1987. Investors then were actually looking to buy shares of poorly run companies on the theory that some other company would want to buy up the assets, throw out the old managers, and run the company better. That happened frequently enough to make the strategy profitable for some savvy investors (or those with inside tips on what was going to happen, a thoroughly illegal way to invest). Of course, when no other company came along in this corporate variation of the greater fool theory mentioned above, those savvy investors took a round trip back to where they started. The dumb investors, the ones who couldn't stand the pressure and decided to buy after the stock had climbed 60%, took the one-way ride to immense losses.

Special situations aren't for everyone. If you think a new management can work wonders on an ailing company, you'd better have the skills to judge just how sick the company is. That means you'll have to learn a lot more about securities analysis and accounting than you will pick up in this book. And he who gambles on a potential merger or buyout to bail him out of a sick stock is just that—a gambler.

THE STOCK PICKING PROCESS

Now that you have a general overview of the types of stocks that are out there, it's time to think about how to pick the stocks you want to buy. We would argue the first step should be to read what the professional investors are thinking. In their interviews with *Barron's* editors, professionals are asked which stocks they own and why they bought them. While *Barron's* is in effect vouching for these pros by giving them lots of space on its pages, remember that they already own the stock and wouldn't mind if you bought it, too, because that makes the price go up. Don't worry, you aren't being played for a sucker. As we've pointed out, your investment discipline and time horizon are probably far different from those of the professional money manager, who usually is intent on the best possible quarterly results in order to keep current clients and attract more. However, you can't just go out and buy willy-nilly whatever stocks a pro mentions. You have to do your homework to ensure that the pro knows what he or she is talking about. (Would you be flabbergasted to find out that some—not necessarily those in *Barron's*—don't?) Most important, be certain that the stock really does suit your own investment style and needs.

Professional money managers often use "screens" as a first step in the stock-picking process. Basically, they program a computer to sort through the thousands of stocks on the New York Stock Exchange and NASDAQ, eliminating all those that do not meet some predetermined criteria, such as a specified annual rate of earnings growth, a certain dividend yield, or even a certain size based on market capitalization or sales. When the computer is finished chewing up all the data, it spits out a list of a few hundred stocks. This is the menu from which the money manager begins to pick seriously. Some companies can be eliminated quickly, while others require detailed research. Eventually the list is winnowed to 20 or 30 stocks, and the final selection is made from among them, sometimes on nothing more than a gut response by the manager.

You can do the same thing even if you don't own so much as a hand calculator. It's just that your initial screening criteria need to be somewhat broader. Let's say you want to set up the value side of your stock portfolio. Get out this week's issue of *Barron's,* turn to the stock tables, and start running your finger down the P-E column. Every time you come to a P-E of, say, 10 or less (this is a fairly stringent requirement; we don't want you simply to be copying the stock tables on your yellow legal pad), write down the name of the company (if you can figure it out from the abbreviation you're given; if not, write down the stock symbol), its closing price, and the 52-week high and low. If it pays a dividend, write down the yield, too. After two hours, at best, you will have an initial screen of value stocks you may want to own. You might take a second cut at the list by eliminating

Figure 3.10 A Wealth of Informaion

Barron's stock tables not only provide a detailed weekly summary of trading activity, but also show the latest per share earnings, with a year-earlier comparison, and the most recent dividend payment.

NEW YORK STOCK EXCHANGE COMPOSITE LIST

Mkt. Sym	52-Wk High	52-Wk Low	Name	Tick Sym	Div Amt	Vol 100's	Yld	P/E	Week's High	Week's Low	Week's Last	Net Chg.	EARNINGS Latest Full Year	EARNINGS This Year	EARNINGS Next Year	DIVIDENDS Latest divs.	DIVIDENDS Record date	DIVIDENDS Pay date
	27 1/2	25 7/8	SantndrFnl prE		2.14	282	7.9	...	27	26 5/8	27	+3/16	... ...	...	...	.53 1/8	3-16-98	3-31-98
n	27	24 3/8	SantndrFnl pfG		2.03	397	7.6	...	26 11/16	26 3/8	26 9/16	−1/16	... ...	...	...	.5078	3-16-98	3-31-98
	26 9/16	25 1/2	SantndrOv pfB		2.18	1605	8.4	...	26	25 13/16	25 27/32	−1/16	... ...	...	...	q.54 3/8	3-15	3-31
	26 1/2	25	SantndrOv pfD		2.00	378	7.8	...	25 7/8	25 9/16	25 9/16	−1/16	... ...	...	..	q.50	3-15	3-31
n	25 5/8	24 1/8	SantandrFin		51p	598	...	...	25	24 3/4	24 13/16	−1/16	... ...	...	...	....	....	....
	63 5/8	39	SaraLee	SLE	.92	68369	1.5	dd	60 1/8	56 3/4	59 13/16	−9/16	06/97 1.98	2.25	2.55	**q.23**	**6-1**	**7-1**
	19 3/4	15 1/8	SaulCtrs	BFS	1.56	1178	8.5	29	18 5/8	17 15/16	18 3/8	...	... ...	...	...	q.39	4-16	4-30
	25 7/8	24 1/2	SavnhEP pfB		1.66	11	6.5	...	25 3/8	25 5/16	25 3/8	+1/16	... ...	...	...	**q.41½**	**6-30**	**7-15**
	30 1/8	25 7/16	Sbarro	SBA	.81j	4222	...	16	29 1/2	28 1/16	29 1/8	+9/16	12/97 1.87	2.03	2.05	.27	12-18-97	1-2-98
	31 3/8	23 7/8	SCANA	SCG	1.54	8204	5.2	14	30 1/8	28 9/16	29 13/16	+3/8	12/97 1.90	2.11	2.21	**q.38½**	**6-10**	**7-1**
	30 3/4	21 3/8	Scania A	SCVA	.69e	5	3.0	...	23 1/8	23 1/8	23 1/8	−7/16	... ...	...	...	.5846	4-27-98	5-14-98
	31	21 1/2	Scania B	SCVB	.69e	7	3.0	...	23 3/16	23 1/8	23 3/16	−3/8	... ...	...	...	.5846	4-27-98	5-14-98
	16 5/8	7 3/4	Schawk A	SGK	.26	841	1.6	18	16 3/8	15 5/8	16 1/8	−3/8	12/97 .55	.69	.82	q.06½	3-17	3-31
n	25	20 1/2	ScheinPharm	SHP		3338	...	...	24 15/16	22 7/8	24 13/16	+1 1/2	... ...	...	...	....	....	....
▲	77 1/2	45 3/4	Scherer	SHR		14574	...	26	77 1/2	72 1/2	73 9/16	−2 3/16	03/97 2.32	2.41	2.72	....	....	....
s	86	39 9/16	ScheringPl	SGP	.88f	80126	1.1	39	81 1/8	75 7/8	80 1/8	−1 1/8	12/97 1.95	2.30	2.67	**q.22**	**5-8**	**5-29**
s	94 7/16	53 1/2	♣ Schlumbgr	SLB	.75	138218	.9	31	86 3/4	75 1/2	85 9/16	+7 13/16	12/97 2.52	3.06	3.74	q.18 3/4	6-2	7-10
s	44 1/4	22 1/2	SchwabC	SCH	.16	47999	.4	36	35 7/8	32 3/4	35 9/16	+1 1/8	12/97 1.05	1.21	1.48	q.04	5-13	5-27
	44 1/2	31 7/8	ShwtzMaud	SWM	.60	2801	1.8	12	33 5/8	32 7/8	33 9/16	+7/16	12/97 2.82	2.67	3.20	q.15	2-9	3-9
	26	17	SciGameHldg	SG		2159	...	37	23 1/8	22 1/16	22 1/2	−3/4	12/97 1.71	1.73	1.94	....	....	....
	26 1/8	14	♣ SciAtlanta	SFA	.06	58305	.2	28	24 1/2	21 7/16	24 1/4	+1 1/16	06/97 .78	.86	1.11	q.01½	3-10	3-25
	66	38 7/8	Scor ADR	SCO	1.74e	73	2.8	...	63	59 11/16	61 3/4	−2 3/4	... ...	...	...	1.4478	6-4-97	6-25-97
	30 3/4	23 1/4	♣ Scotsman	SCT	.10	601	.4	16	28 5/8	27 1/2	28 1/2	+3/8	12/97 1.76	1.89	2.27	q.02½	3-31	4-15
	4 11/16	1 7/8	♣ ScotLiqdGld	SGD	.10e	326	3.6	7	2 15/16	2 3/4	2 3/4	−1/8	... ...	...	...	.10	2-24-98	3-2-98
n	38 1/2	27 1/8	ScottPwr ADS	SPI	.56p	206	...	...	37	36 1/8	36 3/4	−1/4	... ...	...	...	.56¼	12-30-97	3-16-98
	38 1/4	25	ScottsCo	SMG		3235	...	34	37 3/8	35 3/4	36 11/16	−5/8	09/97 .99	1.61	1.90	....	....	....
	58 1/2	36 9/16	ScrippsEW	SSP	.52	1520	.9	31	58	55 5/16	58	+9/16	12/97 1.67	1.78	2.02	q.13	2-27	3-10
	16 7/8	12 1/2	ScddrGlblFd	LBF	1.50a	919	10.5	...	14 5/16	14	14 1/4	−3/8	... ...	...	...	q.37½	4-20	4-30
	15	8 11/16	ScudAsiaFd	SAF	.44e	2876	4.2	...	10 9/16	10 1/8	10 1/2	−5/16	... ...	...	...	.44	12-31-97	1-13-98
s	21 5/8	11 5/16	ScudNewEur	NEF	2.20e	2784	10.7	...	20 9/16	18 7/8	20 9/16	+1/16	... ...	...	...	2.27	12-31-97	1-13-98
s	19 1/2	9 3/16	ScddrSpnFd	IBF	2.68e	1691	14.5	...	18 11/16	17 1/2	18 1/2	+1/16	... ...	...	...	2.675	12-31-97	1-13-98
x	39 1/8	16 1/8	SeaCont A	SCRA	.77	5133	2.0	18	38	35 1/16	37 13/16	+1 1/2	12/97 2.02	2.95	3.70	q.19¼	5-5	5-20

any stock that doesn't pay a dividend or any stock near its 52-week low (figuring something is wrong with the company, and it could easily go lower).

You can do the same thing for the growth part of your portfolio by picking stocks with P-Es of more than 35. That screen would give you a list of stocks that other investors are betting will grow very fast. Of course, you might catch one or two disasters in your net, stocks whose prices have plunged on some recent bad news that both inflates the P-E and makes the past 12-month earnings irrelevant. Don't worry, you will weed them out before you are finished.

As you might imagine, a computer linked to a database would speed this process immensely. There are many such databases available and software to do screens for any number of variables. More are being released all the time. (*Barron's* has a feature that reviews these programs and database services. We suggest reading about them for a while before you buy, to increase your chances of picking a program that suits you.) You just have to decide how much money you want to invest in the process of investing compared to money actually put to work in the market.

Another, more interesting way to do a screen is simply to get into the habit of sizing up any company with which you have dealings for its investment potential. Fidelity's Peter Lynch made a big deal of this technique in his two books. If he stayed at a motel he liked during his many research trips, he'd study up on the stock. If the financial performance looked good, the debt level wasn't too high, and the growth rate seemed sustainable, he'd buy the stock. When it works, this technique can work well. As inveterate home tinkerers we remember our first visit to a Home Depot store. Accustomed to surly and ill-informed salesclerks, meager inventories of shoddy products, and relatively high prices at the do-it-yourself stores we had been shopping at for years, we suddenly found ourselves in Home Handyman's Heaven. The prices were great, the selection immense, and, best of all, we could talk to a salesclerk who knew right where the item we wanted was shelved. They'd even thread pipe for you while you waited. Regretfully, we were so caught up in the thrill of it all that we forgot to buy the stock.

Of course, that strategy has its limitations. We don't, for instance, deal with the major defense contractors often enough to know how well their jets and submarines perform. And we aren't in a position to judge how skillfully biotech companies splice their genes. The most worrisome part of this strategy, though, is that we run across a lot more companies whose stock we wouldn't dare own than ones that intrigue us. There's an awful lot of shoddy products and poor service out there.

One of the most challenging intellectual exercises that an investor can put himself through is to think of what we call Big Trends. We always find it useful to read *Barron's* annual Roundtable, the discussion each January among several very prominent money managers who offer their opinions about what's going on in the world. These investors are good because they often discern Big Trends before anyone else. The consumer fascination with what we call "designer coffee" was one Big Trend that suggested itself to these guys a while back. An even bigger trend has been suggested by thoughtful analysts looking at demographic data who see an aging population that needs fewer new houses and more long-term, in-home medical care. Not all Big Trends suggest stocks to buy. They can also steer you away from potential traps. Among the Big Trends mentioned in the 1997 Roundtable were the increasing consumption and declining supply of nonferrous metals such as lead and zinc; the increasing demand for financial services by aging Americans, who tend to buy less and save more; the technological innovations in action sports such as snowboarding, skiing, and in-line skating; and, finally, the rising demand for long-term-care insurance, spurred partly by legislation allowing tax deductions and penalty-free IRA withdrawals to pay the premiums.

Then there's the hot-tip-at-the-bar method of selecting stocks. Everybody you talk to seems to have some tip on a little-known stock that is about to take off. It doesn't hurt to listen, but check them out before you buy. It's amazing the number of otherwise cautious people who get caught up in tip fever and drop $10,000 on an investment about which they know essentially nothing. We aren't worried about you. It's all those other saps that do foolish things like that. Right?

However you do your initial screening, at some point you will have in front of you a list of potential stocks to buy. Now it's time to write or call the companies for the necessary documentation to do your more rigorous homework. The annual report, the last year's quarterly reports, the proxy statement, and, if one is available, a prospectus are the core of your research documents. A value investor will be looking for such things as low debt and for the reason that the stock is priced so low. A growth investor will be looking for consistent yearly and quarterly gains in sales and profits. We can't offer you a specific formula for finally settling on which stock to buy. There won't be any sign that flashes on. Rather, the process consists of winnowing until just one stock remains. You will still feel uncertain, and that's fine. There isn't any certainty in buying a stock. But you can be confident that you have reduced the risk as far as you can and that this stock suits your needs. Call your broker and buy it.

KEEPING TRACK

Once you own a stock or a few stocks, the investment process has just begun. Now you must monitor your choices. That doesn't mean you call your broker each day at 4:02 P.M. to see how it did. You don't even have to check it daily. But it would be a good idea to get a feel for how your stock moves in relation to the overall stock market. If the Dow Industrials were up a little at the end of the week, what was your stock or your portfolio doing in the same period? Obviously you will watch for news about the companies in your portfolio. If you own the stock of a company like General Motors, there will be plenty to read, but most of the news will have little if any discernible effect on the stock's price. GM stock will rise and fall on the prospects for automobile sales and the outlook for earnings. Unless the chairman is bounced, as he was in 1992, executive changes at a company like GM will be of minor consequence. And there isn't any need to do in-depth product research, such as reading the car buff magazines. They focus on performance minutiae of cars that don't matter to the vast majority of consumers.

But what if you bought MicrobioTech stock? Chances are you won't read anything about it in the daily press unless it is either rocketing higher or falling through the floor. The only regular information about the company will come through the documents it sends you. Pay attention to them. They could save you a lot of money in the long run. Quarterly reports aren't known for forthcoming candor, but you should study each one you receive to make sure nothing has changed significantly for the worse in the balance sheet, that sales and earnings aren't collapsing, and that there have been no significant management changes. The annual report should provide a more through discussion of the company's operations for the past year and some kind of outlook for the coming year. The public relations guys probably wrote it, and their job is to make the company look as attractive as they legally can. Watch for "fudge" phrases that, translated into real English, mean trouble. "Earnings are expected to continue under pressure" probably means "We're having a hell of a hard time making any money." And watch the footnotes. That's the only place where all sorts of little surprises, like major lawsuits, are reported. The hope among the PR flacks who wrote the report is that you can't find your bifocals when you sit down to read it. Don't simply scan the report and look at the pictures. *Study it.* If management hasn't done it for you, make a few quick calculations—debt to capital, price-earnings, dividend yield—to make sure the company's finances haven't deteriorated and that the stock price is moving in the right direction.

Along with your annual report you will probably receive your proxy statement for the annual meeting. Investors often toss the densely worded proxy statements in the garbage, but they can be valuable guides to what is going on within a company. You need to study your proxy just as carefully as you do the annual report, especially since the Securities and Exchange Commission mandated improvements in the amount of information contained in proxies. Among the many things an investor can monitor through proxy statements is how executive pay at the company compares with stockholders' returns. Remember, as a stockholder you own a piece of the company, and no matter how full of themselves the executives get (which is very full, believe us), they are, in fact, your employees. If the stock price is falling while executive pay is rising, you should take a closer look at the stock. Also pay attention to how the executives are paid. You and your fellow shareholders hired these guys to make money for you via a rising stock price. A large part of their pay should be tied to that stock price. Otherwise, they are likely to be more interested in earning money for themselves and less interested in earning it for you. The board's compensation committee is supposed to explain to you in the proxy how it determined the payments to the top executives. Be sure the board members have a logical reason for their compensation decisions other than "Joe is a great guy, and he hired us for these cushy board jobs, so we think we ought to pay him a lot." Take a look, too, at how much company stock the executives and directors own. They ought to shoulder some of the risk by owning more than a token amount of the stock. Finally, watch out for a change of auditor. Management has a way of looking for another auditor when the one already on board doesn't agree with the company's accounting procedures. Management may be trying to sneak something through.

All the while you are monitoring your existing portfolio, you also have to keep searching for new candidates to buy, either as more money becomes available to you through savings or when you decide to sell one of your current stocks for whatever reason. Running a stock portfolio is a never-ending job. A portfolio made up of large-cap growth stocks isn't as demanding of your time as a handful of small-growth stocks or cyclical issues, but they both require some tending.

SAYING GOOD-BYE
IS HARD TO DO

As difficult as it is to know when to buy a stock, it's harder still to know when to sell one. Ironically, most investors have a more difficult time bringing themselves to sell a losing stock than to sell a winner. Like it or not, we all have something more than money tied up in a stock. To a certain extent our ego is on the line, too. We don't like to admit we've made a mistake, and selling a stock at a loss is like admitting you screwed up. The temptation is to wait, figuring that if you wait long enough, your original judgment that led you to buy the stock will be proved correct. Meanwhile, you sit with a loser while all around you other investors are making money. A professional money manager has a few advantages over you when it comes to the selling process. First, it isn't his money at stake, so he will be quicker to take a loss. Second, his ego, like yours, is at stake. The difference is that his clients get a statement each quarter showing what stocks are in their portfolios. The egotistical money manager doesn't want them to know he was dumb enough to buy a loser like Rack 'N' Ruin Corp., so he sells it before the quarter ends. The process is called "window dressing," and we've yet to find a money manager who admits he does it. But it's more than a coincidence that stocks which fell sharply during any given quarter tend to drop again just before the quarter ends. In any event, to counter the natural tendency to stay with a losing stock, keep in mind one of the oldest pieces of advice on Wall Street concerning when to sell: "Cut your losses and let your winners run."

Certainly, you should never get into an investment without thinking about how and when you are going to get out. After all, you bought the stock with the idea that it will accomplish some goal over time. If it becomes evident that it won't reach the goal—or, on the other hand, when it does indeed reach it—you must figure out what to do. If you are holding the stock of a small-growth company whose business is based on the skills of three people and two of them suddenly leave, you don't want to hang around to see if the remaining guy can shoulder the entire load. But sell signals are seldom so clear-cut. What if the stock drops 10% for no apparent reason? Do you want out then? What about a 20% gain? Is that enough to make you happy? Will you kick yourself if it rises another 40% after you've sold? Some money managers impose stringent sell disciplines on their portfolios, automatically dumping a stock if it gains, say, 30%. Then they'll wait 30 days before looking at that same stock again. If nothing has changed, they'll buy it back. Sometimes they wind up owning the same stock three or four times. Others sell only when they have something better to buy. They rank their stockholdings in order of their expectations, then try to find a stock they don't own that is more attractive than the bottom stock in their portfolio.

Valuation techniques can help trigger a sell decision. Suppose you studied a stock and found that it regularly sported a P-E of 20 to 25. Being smart, you bought it when the P-E was 18. Now it's 30. Has something changed in the company's operations to suggest that it now deserves to be valued more highly than it was when you bought it? If so, hang on to it. But if you can't find any reason that convinces you the company's fundamentals have changed, maybe it's time to lock in some profits and find another, cheaper candidate for your portfolio.

Technical analysis can also bring some discipline to the selling process. If your stock is falling on lighter-than-normal volume, technical analysis might suggest that nothing is wrong and you can afford to sit tight. But if the price is dropping and trading volume is rising, perhaps you want to think twice about how attractive your stock is.

We think such disciplines are fine but are no substitute for thinking. Adjust your targets to allow for things like a minor screw-up by management or, in the other direction, unexpected demand for a company's product that sends the stock price rocketing higher than you thought possible. Put each stock's movement into the broader context of where the economy and the stock market seem to be headed.

There may occasionally come a time when you simply need to raise some cash quickly. If you have been tending your portfolio properly, you should know which stocks are ripe for sale. Keep in mind, though, that if you are selling for some reason other than that a stock has reached the point when it should be sold, other considerations might enter the decision, such as taxes. All things being equal, it's better to sell a loser than a winner. Uncle Sam shares some of the loss with you, and your winner stays in the portfolio where you assume it will continue to provide a stellar performance.

Finally, in both your buying and selling don't make the common mistake of thinking you have to either be in or out of a stock. Start out cautiously, buying 100 shares of a stock. If you feel comfortable with it a few months from now, buy some more, especially if the price has fallen. If it rises 45% over the next year and pays a three-for-two stock split, sell 100 shares—investing the proceeds in some other stock—and keep the rest of it until a better reason to sell comes along or until this cycle repeats itself yet again.

RAISING THE RISKS

There are some techniques that investors can use to increase their gains in a winning stock, and we will mention some of them in the futures and options chapter. But two methods are so tempting—and your broker will try to persuade you to use them—that we should discuss them right now. The first is using a margin account. Buying on margin means using borrowed funds to purchase stocks. Your broker will be delighted to set up a margin account for you, provided you can meet the minimum funding requirements (those minimums are designed to keep small investors from getting in way over their heads). In any event, you are expected to provide a down payment of your own money, and your broker will lend you more money, all of which is used to buy stock. Your intention, of course, is to buy a lot more shares than you otherwise could have of a stock that is going to rise sharply. When it rises, you sell it, pay off your loan from the broker, and pocket the rest of the profits. Here is how you want it to happen: You put up $10,000, and your broker lends you $10,000. With your total $20,000 in hand, you buy 200 shares of Cheap Inc. at $100 a share. Sure enough, just as you figured, Cheap stock soars to $150 a share. You sell your 200 shares for $30,000, pay off the broker's $10,000 loan, and walk away with $20,000 (before you-know-who gets his cut next April 15). You have used *leverage* to turn your initial $10,000 stake into $20,000. Had you not had your broker's loan, your $10,000 investment would have bought you 100 shares of Cheap, and you would have ended up with only $15,000, not $20,000. Marvelous, isn't it?

But what happens if, in making your buy decision, you missed some salient little fact about Cheap that results in its stock price going not to $150 a share but to $50 a share. Your $20,000 margined investment becomes a $10,000 investment. Of course, you still owe the broker $10,000. You walk away from this one with a $10,000 loss. And either way you paid interest on your margin loan while it was outstanding, not to mention your broker's commission both when you bought and sold. (See how these guys make money coming and going? We're telling you, they're not your friends.)

The second technique we need to discuss involves not borrowed money but borrowed stock. It's called *short selling* and relies on your ability to spot not an undervalued stock but an overvalued one. In short selling you borrow shares from your broker (don't worry, if he doesn't have them, he'll find them) and sell them right away on the assumption that everybody else is soon going to see the stock's fatal flaw and dump it, forcing the price way down. When the price has tumbled, you buy enough shares to pay back your broker (known as "short covering") and pocket the difference between the high price at which you sold the borrowed shares and the low price at which you bought their replacements. Let's walk through a typical short sale: You see that the price of a stock you have been watching has climbed to $100 a share even though, in your opinion, the company's executives are a bunch of yo-yos. Figuring that everybody else will soon see the executives for the clowns they are, you borrow 100 shares from your broker and sell them immediately, pocketing $10,000. Sure enough, the chairman makes a series of harebrained decisions, and the stock price drops to $50 a share, at which point you buy 100 shares for $5,000. You return the 100 shares to your broker and keep the other $5,000.

But—aren't there a lot of buts in this business?—what happens if you misjudged the chairman? What if his decisions turn out to be brilliant and everybody flocks to buy the stock, driving it up to $150 a share? You have to shell out $15,000 to cover your short position. You're now $5,000 in the hole. And the really big problem is that you never know how high the shares you shorted can go. Many short sellers lose money not by being dead wrong but by being so far ahead of the crowd that it takes a long while for their viewpoint to prevail. Meanwhile, a general market updraft could carry the stock's price higher and higher, with the short sellers losing money all the way. At least when you buy a stock outright you know exactly how much your maximum loss will be—the price of the stock. With short sellers, the sky is the limit for losses.

We don't subscribe to the argument that short selling is somehow despicable, un-American, or worse. It is a legitimate investment technique, which *Barron's* recognizes by including short-sale recommendations in money-manager interviews and the like. But short selling is extra risky and therefore demands extra homework before you do it and extra diligence in monitoring the position after you have done it. Unless you are willing and able to pay these dues, give short shrift to short selling.

The point is, leverage exaggerates reward, but it also exaggerates losses. Assuming your goal is to build wealth, we don't see the point in adding more risk to what is already a somewhat risky business. If you insist, we can't stop you. But go in with your eyes open.

MITIGATING RISK

You may be interested in some techniques meant to take a little of the risk out of stocks. One is to use *limit orders* when buying stock rather than the more common *market orders.* When you place an order with your broker to buy or sell a stock, it's usually a market order—that is, it will be executed as quickly as possible at whatever price is available in the market. Your broker can tell you what the price is at the moment you enter your order; in the biggest, heavily traded stocks, your execution price will be very close to the price he quotes you. But when you're buying or selling a smaller, less-traded stock or when the overall market is in the throes of an occasional upset, the difference between the price when you place your order and the price at which your order is executed can vary substantially. Those swings can be prevented by placing a limit order instead that specifies the maximum price you're willing to pay or, if you're selling, the minimum price you'll accept for your shares.

A variant of the limit order is the *stop loss* order. It basically is an order to your broker to sell a stock if the price declines to a specified level. The idea is to protect you from a sharp decline in the price of a stock by getting rid of it before your losses mount. You can also use it to keep from taking a round trip with a stock you own. As the price climbs, for example, you can set progressively higher stop loss orders that, should the stock suffer a reversal, will get you out of the shares before you lose all your gains. Say you buy a stock at $50 a share. You might set a stop loss order at $40 a share to minimize potential losses. If the stock climbs to $75, you would want to raise your stop limit order to perhaps $60 a share, potentially locking in a $10 gain if the stock enters a prolonged slump that eventually takes it all the way back to $50 a share. The danger is setting your stop loss order too close to the current price and being forced to sell on a minor setback rather than on a full-scale retreat. Also, a stop loss order isn't a guarantee that your stock will be sold at the price you set. A stop loss order becomes a market order when your target price is reached. That means the shares will be sold as soon as possible at whatever price can be obtained. If the stock is in a free fall, that might be substantially below your target. As we said, nothing is guaranteed in the stock market.

One final word of advice concerns *dividend reinvestment plans*. Not all companies pay dividends, and not all of those that do offer dividend reinvestment plans. But if you own stock in a company that provides this service, make use of it. You still pay income taxes on the dividends of the company, but the reinvestment plans use your dividends to automatically buy more of the company's stock. Some companies even offer a small discount on stock bought through dividend reinvestment plans, and most of them charge no commission or other fee. It's a form of dollar cost averaging that also reduces acquisition costs. The smart investor will take advantage of these plans.

SUGGESTED READING

Bookstore and library shelves are bending under the weight of all the beat-the-market books that have been written, most of them by "experts" with some "proven system" for beating the market. If you find an author whose investment philosophy is especially convincing or blends with your own, fine. But visit your local library before buying any of these tomes with perfectly good, investable money.

In the interest of keeping investing fun and not turning it into work, we'll highly recommend only a few books:

One Up on Wall Street and *Beating the Street* by the Magellan Fund's legendary manager Peter Lynch are fun and easy to read, and make it sound oh-so-simple. You won't become the next Peter Lynch by reading these books, but you will garner some insights into the investment process.

For those of you with a mathematical or conceptual bent—or if you just need to know more about securities analysis and how to do it—there is Benjamin Graham and David Dodd's *Security Analysis*. It is the classic work on the subject, and the words "Graham and Dodd" are synonymous on Wall Street with value-oriented investing. The two original authors updated it four times since it was first published in 1934. A fifth edition is now out, written by three Graham and Dodd disciples, all professorial types, which means it's well on the dry side. The original Graham and Dodd approach still prevails, however, and it is almost the opposite of the "efficient market theory" espoused by many academics. That theory says stock prices are highly rational and that superior investment performance is largely a matter of luck. To the contrary, "Markets are wrong most of the time," says one of the fifth edition coauthors. Adds another: "Prices tend to orbit the central value. It is sort of a gravitational force that causes the price and value to coincide every now and then."

Security Analysis is heavy going, but you'll know a lot more about evaluating both stocks and bonds when you're finished. If you finish.

4

Bonds

The Secure in Securities

"Thanks for having me on, Hal, and giving me an opportunity to talk about the pulsating world of long-term bonds."

Many investors think of bonds in terms of safety and income. They are right, up to a point. There are bonds that are extremely safe, and there are bonds providing steady, reliable income to millions of people. But the realm of bonds includes a lot more than Treasury bonds, which lend an aura of super-safety to the entire bond market, and municipal issues, which wealthy investors use to thumb their noses at the tax man. Lurking out there waiting for the unwary investor are collateralized mortgage obligations, callable corporates, munis that aren't bonds, and, most notorious of all, junk bonds. We even are including in this menagerie preferred stocks, because more often than not investors acquire them for income as they would a bond. The point is, the generic investment class known as bonds includes a vast array of instruments with varying degrees of risk and reward that can make an investor's life complicated. But used correctly, bonds can be the second most important part of a lifetime portfolio, after stocks.

When we write about bonds in a general sense, we mean the range of *fixed-income* instruments that includes not only bonds, which technically are debt securities with maturities of 10 years or more, but also their shorter-lived brothers and cousins, right down to 90-day certificates of deposit and even 30-day commercial paper. All of them are loans of your money to the issuing entity—be it Uncle Sam or General Motors Acceptance Corp.—and they all have a fixed life, whether 30 days or 30 years. Most of what we'll consider in this chapter are *negotiable securities*, which are instruments such as bonds that can be bought and sold in a secondary market, much as stocks are. There are some fixed-income investments that are *non-negotiable*, such as savings accounts, which can't be sold.

The investors who regard bonds as a source of steady, predictable income are individuals. Few professional money managers think of them that way. Instead, they use bonds much as they use stocks, trading in and out in an effort to get the maximum possible returns through the combination of income and capital appreciation. When their trading strategies work, they can work very well indeed, producing returns as high as 30% or 40% in a good year. Of course, their strategies don't always work, and they can have a lousy year, posting net losses occasionally. This is a safe and stable investment? Sneer not, for you, too, might want to step in and do a little trading from time to time. Many investors let the fact that bonds have a definite maturity date lull them into holding on to an investment that they should sell so they can buy something more lucrative.

When buying bonds, we urge you to keep in mind the same guideline that applies to buying stocks: Have at least some idea about when and how you want to get out of the investment. Trading bonds is a little more difficult than trading stocks. Most bond prices aren't quoted regularly in newspapers, and most bond trading is done over the counter rather than on an exchange like the New York Stock Exchange. Still, once you know a little about how bonds are valued and have found a reliable broker, trading bonds need be no more intimidating than trading stocks.

On the whole, bonds are simpler to understand than stocks. Probably the most difficult concept to grasp is the inverse relationship of bond prices and yields. As a bond's price *falls* the bond's yield *rises.* Conversely, when a bond's price *rises,* its yield *falls.* Here is how it works. We'll start with a $1,000 bond with a nominal or coupon yield of 8% and a maturity of 10 years that sells at par. All that means is that you fork over $1,000 (the par value of the bond) and receive in exchange a promise that you will be paid $80 per year (the 8% yield) for 10 years (the maturity). At the end of 10 years you get your $1,000 back. Now assume that something happens to lower the price of the bond—never mind what. As we'll soon see, there are lots of things that could have such an effect. In any case, the price of the bond that you paid $1,000 to buy is now at $960. If someone bought it from you at that price, they would still receive the same $80 annually that you were promised. But since they paid less to obtain that promise, their yield will be higher. Just divide the $80-per-year payments by the $960 purchase price to see that the yield now is 8.33%. Suppose the bond price rises instead, to $1,050. The purchaser receives the same $80-a-year payout, but because he paid more than you did to get it, his yield is lower than yours. Again, divide the $80 payment by the purchase price of $1,050 to see that the yield now is 7.62%. Bonds selling at less than their par value are called *discounted bonds,* and those selling at prices above their par value are called *premium* bonds.

Not all new fixed-income securities come to market at par, which is the term for face value. For instance, Treasury bills, which mature in 3, 6, or 12 months, are sold at discount. That simply means you pay less than the $10,000 face value for a bill. When the bill matures, you receive the full $10,000. You earn the difference between what you paid for the bill, say $9,800, and the $10,000 you get at maturity.

We saw in the preceding chapter how difficult it is to assess the risk in any given stock and to predict how it will perform. With bonds, though, it is only a slight oversimplification to say you can judge the relative risk of one bond compared to another by looking at their yields. The higher the yield, the higher the risk. That is why you must guard against becoming a yield junkie, forever searching for an extra tad of return. In addition, certain agencies grade bonds according to their relative risk, and their ratings are another indicator. As for keeping tab on the economy, there are really only two factors you need to monitor closely: the direction of interest rates and inflation.

There, now, isn't that easy?

Most of this chapter will be aimed at providing an understanding of those very basic concepts of risk and reward in bonds, plus fleshing out some of those oversimplified places. (See Figure 4.2.)

Do you remember that at the outset of this book we said time is your friend and can help reduce risks? While this maxim is generally true, it doesn't work that way in bonds. When you buy a bond—that is, make a loan—the risk increases with time that you won't be paid back; or if you are, the risk is greater that the money you receive will have lost some of its value due to inflation. Take the case of a large company that has been in business for years, has recently posted healthy quarterly profits, and has a balance sheet that is in good shape. You really don't have to worry much that the company will collapse in the next 30, 60, or 90 days. You can also assume that inflation isn't going to erode much of the dollar's value before the end of next month. Thus, you (or, more likely, your money market fund) can confidently purchase the company's short-term commercial paper. But

Figure 4.1 Rising Rates Take a Toll on Bond Performance

An illustration of how total returns on Treasury bonds would be affected over the course of a year if interest rates rise one or two percentage points. These examples reflect interest payments as well as price changes; investors holding bonds to maturity would not be affected by the price changes.

	If Interest Rates Remain Unchanged	If Rates Rise One Percentage Point	If Rates Rise Two Percentage Points
3-year Treasury	4.22%	2.58%	0.97%
10-year Treasury	6.10	-0.23	-6.05
30-year Treasury	7.04	-3.99	-13.12
30-year zero coupon bond	7.27	-18.65	-38.22

Figure 4.2 Maturity and Yield

Normally, the longer the maturity of a fixed-income security, the higher the yield.

Treasury Security	Yield
30-day T-bill	3.158%
6-month T-bill	3.277
12-month T-bill	3.517
2-year T-note	4.141
3-year T-note	4.423
5-year T-note	5.139
7-year T-note	5.493
10-year T-note	5.846
30-year T-bond	6.728

what will happen to our safe, sound company over the next 30 years? The corporate graveyard is full of companies that 30 years ago were enjoying enormous prestige and profits. And what of inflation in the next 30 years? We don't know anyone who accurately predicts inflation two years ahead, so we certainly aren't willing to trust any 30-year forecasts. That explains why the yield on a 30-year bond is substantially higher than on 30-day commercial paper. It's also the main reason that the interest you earn on a five-year certificate of deposit is higher than what you earn on a daily passbook savings account.

This is probably the time and place to bring up one of bond investors' favorite evaluation tools, the *yield curve*. It is simply a graphic plotting of the relationship between the maturity and yield of similarly graded bonds. More often than not, you will see the yield curve plotted to show Treasury bond maturities and yields, though any series of bonds can be used to draw a curve. As you might expect, given the relative risks of long-term bonds versus short-term issues, the yield curve normally slopes upward. That is, as the maturities extend further and further into the future, the yields rise higher and higher. The value of the yield curve lies in its ability to show graphically what investors (lenders) and borrowers *expect* interest rates to do. If investors expect interest rates to rise in the future from present levels, they will want to keep money in short-term instruments to avoid getting locked into low-yielding long-term bonds. But borrowers, who tend to act in direct opposition to investors, will try to extend the maturity of their debts to take advantage of low interest charges. Their combined actions push short-term rates lower and long-term rates higher, thus *steepening* the yield curve. But suppose investors and borrowers expect interest rates to fall, not rise. Then investors try to buy longer-term bonds to lock in the relatively high interest rates currently available. Borrowers, on the other hand, try to

Figure 4.3 As the Yield Curves

Three variations on the "yield curve"—plotting yields on the *y* axis and maturities on the *x* axis.

The Yield Curve

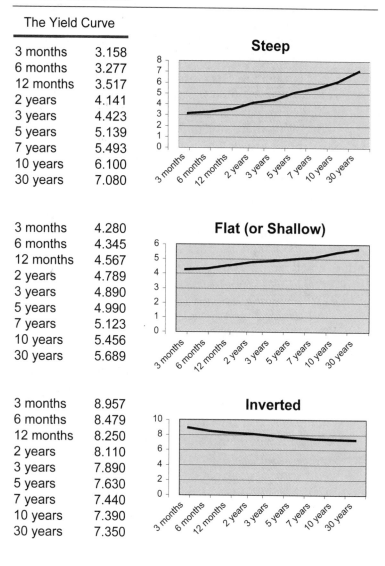

3 months	3.158
6 months	3.277
12 months	3.517
2 years	4.141
3 years	4.423
5 years	5.139
7 years	5.493
10 years	6.100
30 years	7.080

3 months	4.280
6 months	4.345
12 months	4.567
2 years	4.789
3 years	4.890
5 years	4.990
7 years	5.123
10 years	5.456
30 years	5.689

3 months	8.957
6 months	8.479
12 months	8.250
2 years	8.110
3 years	7.890
5 years	7.630
7 years	7.440
10 years	7.390
30 years	7.350

move into short-term loans to await the fall in long-term rates. Those combined actions push short-term rates higher and long-term rates lower. The yield curve tends to *flatten*. In extreme cases, it actually *inverts*. In that situation, yields on the short-term end of the curve are higher than on the long-term end. Basically, the yield curve gives you a rough approximation of what others in the fixed-income market expect interest rates to do and therefore is worth watching.

Inflation is by far the biggest risk facing the bond investor, and as we have seen, that risk rises with the maturity of a bond. But there are other, more subtle risks that a bond buyer must also keep in mind. Closely linked to the inflation risk is *interest rate risk*. Suppose you buy a bond that is paying 6% interest; subsequently, interest rates in general rise. At that point other investors will be able to buy equally rated bonds that pay more interest than yours. If you continue to hold your bond, you will miss out on the better yields that are available to other investors. But if you sell your bond, you will have to take less than you paid for it. Unless you offer it at a discount, why would anyone buy a bond yielding 6% when they can buy one yielding 8% for the same price? Interest rates tend to rise in times of rising inflation, hence the close connection between inflation risk and interest rate risk.

The combination of inflation and interest rate risk results in greater volatility in long-term bond prices than in short-term bond prices, an important point to keep in mind. Let's assume that you own two bonds, both of which yield 7%. One bond is a 30-year issue, the other is a 10-year issue. What happens if interest rates rise by one percentage point? The price of your 30-year bond drops 11.3%, but the price of your 10-year bond falls only 6.8%. Of course, if rates fall, the long-term bond gains more in price, too. The point is, if you don't like price fluctuations, stick to shorter-term bonds.

Another broad risk facing the bond investor is *market risk*. As with almost everything else, bonds respond to supply and demand. If more people want to own them, the prices of bonds rise. If fewer people want them, the price falls. And if there are lots of bonds on the market, their price will be lower than if there are only a few issues for sale. You can see these market forces at work. Every so often, for instance, the U.S. Treasury debates whether it should continue issuing large amounts of 30-year bonds to fund the government. Every time word of such a debate leaks out, the prices of 30-year Treasury bonds spurt a little higher. The reason? If there are going to be fewer 30-year Treasuries in the future, the existing supply just became more valuable. During international crises the prices of Treasury bonds also tend to climb. Regarded as one of the world's safest investments, more people want to own U.S. Treasuries in times of crisis. When the trouble passes, the bonds tend to slip back to their pre-crisis prices. Conversely, as the mergers and buyouts craze of the 1980s began to wane, prices of the junk bonds that were used to finance many of those deals collapsed. With all the questions surrounding the ability of the merged companies to compete or even survive, no one wanted to own their bonds. Eventually, prices reached such a low point that some investors considered them a relatively safe bet. But junk bonds remain anathema to most investors.

Somewhat related to all the above is *reinvestment risk*. Many bonds, especially those offered by corporations and municipalities, have *call provisions* that give the issuer the right to call, or redeem, the bonds before maturity. Typically, that would happen if, a few years after the company or sewer district had issued its bonds, interest rates fell. Seeing that it could finance operations more cheaply by issuing new bonds with lower yields, the company might "call" its outstanding bonds, paying them off before they reach maturity. If you happen to own one of those bonds, you are suddenly faced with the problem of investing a wad of money that you didn't expect to have. You thought it was comfortably invested at 8%, and now the best available rate is 5% for a bond of similar duration and risk. At worst, a call can upset a carefully devised plan to reach a specific financial target by a specific date, requiring an adjustment in either the target or the date.

Reinvestment risk also applies to the periodic interest payments from bonds. When you hold a bond, you receive interest payments on a regular schedule, usually every six months. What you do with those payments can go a long way toward determining the final results of your bond investment. If you spend the payment, as do many retirees relying on bonds to supplement other retirement income, it's gone forever. But if you reinvest the payment, it will continue earning more money. How much depends on where you invest it and what the prevailing economic conditions are. Just remember that purchasing a bond isn't the end of the process. Reinvesting the proceeds will continue to be a challenge until the bond matures.

The risks we have discussed so far involve those found in the economy and in the overall bond market. Many individual bonds have more specific risks as well. Foremost is *ratings risk,* the chance that while you're holding the bond, the financial condition of the company or municipality that issued it will deteriorate. Smart investors who pay attention to their bond holdings will realize that things are getting worse since they are watching the company's balance sheet or have intimate knowledge of a town's finances. If you don't see it coming, you will realize that conditions have worsened only when the bond rating agencies announce a downgrade in their rating of the specific bond. Zap. The price drops. If you have to sell the bond, you will take a beating. Of course, you can continue to hold the bond in the hopes that the company can save itself. Usually, it can. But if your company is terminally ill, you'll face the bond holder's biggest risk and worst nightmare: *default.* When a company or city defaults on its bonds, regularly scheduled interest payments are delayed or, in the worst cases, are never made at all. If the company ultimately goes bankrupt, you may get some portion of your original investment back, or you may wind up losing it all. Not a pleasant thought, is it? Total default is rare but not impossible. You need to be aware that the danger exists.

Just as some stocks are more liquid—that is, readily bought and sold at the prevailing price—than others, bonds, too, can suffer from *liquidity risk.* Indeed, the overall bond market isn't nearly as liquid as the stock market because more investors tend to buy and hold bonds rather than trade them. Bond dealers, through whom you buy and sell bonds, will usually take an unpopular or thinly traded bond off your hands, but only at a low price. In fact, transaction costs in the bond market can be considerably larger than in the stock market because spreads—the difference between what a dealer will pay for a bond and what he will sell it for—tend to be wider. You will seldom know what the real spread is unless the broker truly is your friend (and as we've said before, he almost certainly isn't). If you think you may want to trade in and out of bonds, select ones with a high degree of liquidity.

Finally, to get Uncle Sam into the act, there's *tax risk,* the possibility that while you are holding a bond and receiving income from it, the tax laws will change. Since most interest payments on bonds are regarded as taxable income, any change in the tax laws that increases ordinary income taxes will decrease the value of the interest received. That isn't particularly hard to see: A 10% nominal yield is worth 7.5% if an investor's tax rate is 25% and is worth only 6% if the investor's tax bracket is 40%. Write your congressman.

THE MENU, PLEASE

Now that we have examined some of the risks that afflict the bond market, let's run through the variety of instruments that are available to the investor. We will pay special attention to how appropriate they are to a long-term investment portfolio, both as sources of income and as vehicles for capital appreciation.

U.S. Treasury Bonds

We consider U.S. Treasury bonds the kings of the bond market. There is no safer investment, provided the bond is held to maturity. Treasury bonds are backed by "the full faith and credit" of the U.S. government. That means the government will, if necessary to redeem its bonds, use its taxing powers to obtain the money. Regretfully for most of us, that's exactly what has been necessary. But for the bond investor it means there isn't any need to do the kind of tedious financial analysis that often accompanies the purchase of corporate or municipal bonds.

Treasury bonds and their shorter-term relatives, Treasury notes and bills, have many attributes to recommend them, but yield isn't one of them. Because of the almost total lack of default risk, Treasury securities carry among the lowest yields of any debt instruments. It's the classic case of risk and reward. Because you aren't taking much of a risk when you buy these securities, there isn't much reward. However, Treasuries do have something that can be nearly as important: liquidity. Treasury securities are so desired by so many different investors, including banks both here and abroad, that the market for them is among the most liquid in the world. If you decide to buy or sell a Treasury bond, you'll get quick service from your broker. The liquidity of Treasury bonds helps reduce transaction costs, too. But perhaps even more important for the investor seeking long-term income from Treasury securities is that the transaction costs can be virtually nil. The Treasury makes it exceedingly easy to buy notes, bills, and bonds at its regular auctions. Purchased at auction and held to maturity, there simply isn't an easier or safer way than a Treasury bond to lock in income. There is even a tax advantage to owning Treasuries: While the income from Treasury securities is taxed by the federal government, it is exempt from all state and local taxes. In certain high-tax states such as California and New York, that tax status can be a real advantage.

Are you convinced that Treasuries are absolutely safe? Wrong.

As with any fixed-income security, Treasury bonds are subject to inflation, interest rate, and market risks. Let's say inflation is running today at about 2.5% annually. Historically, Treasury bonds have yielded a little more than three percentage points above the going rate of inflation, which means you might expect to buy a 30-year government bond today that yields 5.5%. What happens if inflation five years from now is running at 6%, not 2.5%? Your income from that bond is only slightly ahead of inflation *before* taxes. And if you have to sell the bond before its maturity, market forces will have reduced the price substantially below what you paid for it. After all, we can presume that if inflation is 6%, new 30-year bonds are being sold that yield 9% or 9.5%.

Of course, those risks can work in your favor as well as against you. Turn the tables on this example and assume that inflation is running at 6% annually, and you just bought a 30-year Treasury bond that yields 9.5%. What happens five years from now if inflation has declined to just 3% a year? Your 9.5% yield looks great. You probably would want to

BUYING TREASURIES AT THE SOURCE

Investors who hate to pay for something that they can get free (and what smart investor wouldn't want to do that?) can buy new Treasury notes, bills, and bonds directly from the Treasury through a program called Treasury Direct. The process is relatively simple, although it does take a little time. You have to fill out an application, which can be obtained from the nearest branch office of the Federal Reserve (your banker will have the address and telephone number). The application basically sets up your personal account with the Treasury. It must be postmarked by midnight the day before an auction or, if delivered by hand, received by noon of the day of the auction. For Treasury bills, which are sold in minimum face value amounts of $10,000, you must deliver along with the application a certified check or cashier's check in that amount; they also take cash. New notes due in two or three years come in minimums of $5,000, and new notes and bonds with maturities of four years or more can be purchased for as little as $1,000; you can pay for all these with a personal check. Additional amounts beyond the minimums can be purchased in increments of $1,000.

Most investors using Treasury Direct submit what are called *non-competitive bids*, which means that you agree to accept the average price and yield set by the competitive bidding among major institutional investors at each auction. You won't receive a certificate showing ownership. Instead, your electronic account at the Treasury records your holdings. All principal and interest payments are sent directly by the Treasury to your bank account.

Because your bonds are held electronically in your Treasury account, it isn't easy to get to them quickly if, for instance, you decide you want to sell them. To sell, you would have to file an application to have the security transferred into a commercial book-entry account at a financial institution, a process that could take a week if everything goes smoothly.

One nice feature of the Treasury Direct system is that you can request your maturing 3-, 6- and 12-month bills be automatically reinvested at maturity for up to 104 weeks without having to go through the rigmarole of tendering a new bid. Yes, you can change your mind and cancel the automatic reinvestment if you give the Treasury a 20-day notice.

According to the Treasury's latest schedule, auctions of 3-month and 6-month bills are held every Monday (or, usually, the following Tuesday if there is a Monday holiday). Auctions of 12-month bills generally are held every fourth week, usually on a Thursday. Both 3- and 6-month bills are issued on the Thursday following the auction, and 12-month bills are usually issued one week following the auction.

Two-year and 5-year notes are usually issued at the end of each month. Three-year and 10-year notes are issued on the 15th of February, May, August, and November. Thirty-year bonds are issued three times a year, in February, August, and November. The current rate of frequency may decline if the U.S. government actually makes good on promises to cease and desist running budget deficits.

For more information: Issues Division, Federal Reserve Bank of New York, 33 Liberty Street, New York, NY 10045; (212) 720-6619.

hang on to it; you certainly won't be able to find any other fixed-income investment with such lucrative yields and low risk. But suppose you had to sell the bond for some reason. With the yield on new bonds running about 6.5%, there will be plenty of yield-hungry investors willing to pay a premium to you to buy your bond. Cash it in, and you've made a nice capital gain (taxable, by the way, at the lower capital gains rate, not the higher regular income rate). This example is one reason we heartily recommend that if ever you have a chance to lock in a long-term return of 9% or more in U.S. Treasury securities, do it. Over the years you're almost certainly going to profit by the decision.

U.S. Government Savings Bonds

Savings bonds are sometimes laughed at as a simplistic, low-yielding investment for people who don't know better. But don't listen to the scoffers. There are some facets of savings bonds that make them very appropriate to the conservative investor. We'll start with the Series EE bonds because you have to own them before moving on to their relatives, Series HH bonds. Series EE bonds are issued and backed by the U.S. government and have absolutely no risk of default on principal. They have a maturity of 12 years and are purchased at exactly half their face value from banks and from the Federal Reserve with no commission or other fees. Instead of paying regular interest payments, savings bonds *accrete* interest that is only realized when the bond is sold or redeemed. And since there isn't any income from a savings bond, there also isn't any tax to pay until the bond is sold or redeemed.

While the return on a savings bond isn't impressive, it is better than it used to be. In May 1997 the Treasury Department beefed up the return on savings bonds to stanch the sharp decline in sales. The interest rate, which is announced twice a year, on May 1 and November 1, now is calculated based on the yields of five-year Treasury notes rather than the yields of six-month Treasury notes for the first five years and on the five-year note thereafter. That would have amounted to a nice bump in rates on its own, but there was more: The Treasury also is offering bondholders 90% of the five-year note yields, up from 85% under the old system, and savings bonds now accrue interest monthly instead of every six months. This latter change helps avoid the possibility of losing five months of interest if bonds are redeemed early. The Treasury added only one provision in its favor, which basically hurts people who use savings bonds as a substitute for a savings account: A three-month interest penalty will be extracted from people who redeem their bonds within five years.

Though savings bonds don't offer the best rates around, the interest paid by a savings bond can rise if other rates rise. Savings bonds can't be sold on any secondary markets, so the price of a bond is never affected by the ups and downs of overall interest rates. Thus, an investor gets a product that is absolutely safe, has no transaction costs, is tax deferred, and has a guaranteed minimum payout with some protection if interest rates rise. The only disadvantage, besides the relatively low interest rate and the penalty if sold in the first five years of ownership, is that without regular interest payments, they are basically useless to an investor who needs a steady stream of income.

Series HH bonds differ slightly from Series EE bonds and can be obtained *only* by exchanging EE bonds. When your EE bonds mature, you simply exchange them for HH bonds, thus delaying any taxes due on the maturing EE bonds. Unlike EE bonds, HH bonds pay interest every six months and have a maturity of 20 years. The interest payments, while taxable for federal income tax purposes, are exempt from state and local taxes. They can be sold back to a bank or to the Federal Reserve after six months of owner-ship. Like the EE bonds, the Series HH bonds are fully backed by the government and therefore are risk free.

Certainly they aren't for everyone, and no investor should construct a portfolio with nothing else in it but sav-ings bonds. But for the conservative investor, savings bonds provide long-term, reduced-rate parking for excess cash.

The Mae Sisters (and Brother Freddie): Government Agency Bonds

There are bonds that, while not strictly government bonds, are nevertheless imbued with some of the characteristics of government issues. They are called government agency bonds, and the most popular forms for most investors are issued by the Government National Mortgage Association (GNMA), the Federal National Mortgage Association (FNMA)—known by their nicknames, Ginnie Mae and Fannie Mae—and by the Federal Home Loan Mortgage Corp., which somehow became known as Freddie Mac. These agencies aren't a direct part of the U.S. government, but because the government generally wants to encourage the growth and strength of the residential housing sector in this country, their financial obligations are backed by the govern-ment. Thus, chances of default are negligible at worst and more likely nonexistent.

The agencies issue two kinds of debt. The smaller amount is in the form of ordinary bonds that are similar to corporate debt issues but have that extra measure of securi-ty. The larger amount is in the form of *pass-through, mort-gage-backed bonds,* which are the more popular type with investors. Just to give you an idea, in 1997 Fannie Mae issued

$149.4 billion of mortgage-backed bonds and $39.6 billion of straight debt securities of varying maturities, some of which can be called. At the end of 1997, Fannie Mae had outstanding $709.6 billion of mortgage-backed debt and $372 billion of straight debt.

Mortgage-backed bonds require a little extra study before you go charging in to your broker with a purchase order.

Ginnie Mae, Fannie Mae, and Freddie Mac in effect purchase high-quality residential mortgages from lenders, package them into mortgage *pools*, then sell partial interests in those pools to investors like us through GNMA, FNMA, or FHLMC bonds. Like any bonds, these pay interest, but they pay it monthly rather than semiannually, a feature worth considering if you need or want monthly income. And unlike most bonds, which don't return an investor's principal until maturity, investors in mortgage-backed bonds get not only a monthly interest payment but also a partial repayment of the principal. That's because the agencies are passing on to you exactly what they receive from the homeowners who are paying off their mortgages. If you own a house, you know that each of your monthly mortgage payments covers some interest and some principal on your loan. The longer you pay on the loan, the interest component of each monthly payment falls while the principal repayment rises. Those changing proportions are reflected in agency bonds, which consist mostly of interest payments early in their lives while more seasoned bonds reflect heavier principal repayments.

You might wonder what happens if a few of those homeowners default on their mortgages that you seem to be holding. The answer is nothing. GNMA, FNMA, and FHLMC have plenty of their own assets, and they don't make their bondholders bear any mortgage default risk. If for some reason the agencies ran low on money to make good your payments, the Treasury would step in, thus assuring that you will never know if any defaults occur in your particular mortgage pool. It is a considerable safety advantage compared to holding the mortgages directly.

Pass-through mortgage-backed bonds are easily marketable, nearly as easy as Treasury bonds. They can be purchased from brokerage firms, which can provide you with new issues or older issues that are nearer to maturity. For someone in a high tax bracket, older issues may be preferable because the principal repayment, which is non-taxable, is a much higher percentage of the monthly payout than for newer issues, which consist mostly of interest payments that are fully taxable at the federal, state, and local levels. And more good news: Generally, agency issues like this yield as much as one percentage point more than similar Treasury issues.

So what's the bad news? Plenty, unfortunately. First, unlike most bonds that mature on a specific date, mortgage-backed bonds don't have a certain maturity. Although they are comprised of 30-year mortgages, which would suggest a 30-year maturity, it doesn't work like that. Homeowners are constantly buying and selling houses, retiring their mortgages in the process. The average lifespan of a mortgage is about seven years. Each time a mortgage in your particular pool is retired, you receive your portion of the entire principal of that mortgage in your monthly check. (Obviously, the size of your monthly check will vary, so don't buy one of these bonds if you need a set amount of assured income each month.) Over time, virtually the entire pool gets paid off early, and you get your principal back.

Worse still, the prices of agency bonds do not rise proportionately with a decline in interest rates. When interest rates fall, homeowners refinance their mortgages to get the lower rates. The farther rates fall, and the higher other bond prices rise, the more likely you are to have your mortgage-backed bond repaid much earlier than you expected.

This *repayment risk* hit home with a vengeance in the early 1990s as homeowners flocked to take advantage of the lowest mortgage rates in decades. Hundreds of thousands of GNMA, FNMA, and FHLMC bondholders who had counted on relatively steady income for years to come found themselves holding their principal and looking for another place to invest it. Unfortunately, they either had to accept much lower returns on their reinvestments or take much greater risks to duplicate what they had presumed their mortgage-backed bonds would be paying them for a decade or more.

One final risk depends on your ability to discipline yourself. Remember that each month you get back both some interest and some principal from a mortgage-backed investment. If you use that total income for living expenses or otherwise spend it, you will be committing one of the cardinal sins of the long-term investor: spending your principal. The challenge is to be sure that you have a clear-cut plan for reinvesting at least the principal amount of your mortgage-backed bond payments each month.

If you want to buy seasoned GNMA, FNMA, or FHLMC issues, be sure your broker tells you the *remaining face value* of any seasoned issue you are considering. Your objective should be to buy issues trading at a discount to their remaining face value. For instance, you may be offered a bond with a 7% current yield selling for $6,000. If the remaining face value is $6,300, you are buying it at a discount. But if the remaining face value is $5,850, you are paying a premium. The bond selling at a premium may provide higher current income, but you'll get back less principal at maturity.

You also might consider a variation on the standard mortgage-backed bond that offers adjustable rate bonds backed by both agencies. In the case of adjustable rate bonds, the homeowners in your mortgage pool have taken out adjustable rate mortgages, the interest rate on which changes periodically, usually every six months. If rates rise, the homeowner's mortgage payments are adjusted to reflect that rise. If rates fall, the mortgage payments fall, too. As a bondholder your payments will be adjusted as well, providing more interest income if overall rates rise, and less if they fall. Be aware, though, that adjustable rate mortgages have caps, or limits, beyond which the interest rate paid by the homeowner, and the interest payment received by you, will not rise. If overall rates go higher than the cap, you'll just have to make do with the highest payments allowed by the cap.

Both fixed-rate and adjustable-rate pass-through securities have been big hits with conservative individual investors who want government-backed safety but are looking for that little extra interest rate gain above Treasury bonds. The widespread disappointment created in the early 1990s due to the heavy refinancing of mortgages leads us to wonder if they will be as popular in years to come if interest rates remain low.

Municipal Bonds: Everybody's Favorite Tax Shelter

Everyone hates to pay taxes, which is what makes municipal bonds—munis, for short—so tantalizing. They have always been a favorite of the wealthy, and as taxes rise, their popularity is stretching more broadly across the population. The tax-exempt status of municipal bonds has its roots in an 1819 Supreme Court case, *McCullock v. Maryland.* In the decision, Chief Justice John Marshall declared that "the power to tax involves the power to destroy" and that "there is a plain repugnance in conferring on one government a power to control the constitutional measures of another." Subsequent court rulings broadened and added detail to the tax-exempt status of municipal bonds.

But don't be fooled. Muni bonds are not *totally* tax exempt. While the income from them escapes federal income tax, it doesn't always avoid state and local income taxes if the bonds you own are issued by authorities in states other than where you reside. Moreover, even the feds will be after you if you try to get away without paying taxes on any capital gains realized by buying a bond at one price and selling it later at a higher price. Muni bonds aren't exempt from federal estate or gift taxes, either.

Still, not paying taxes is more fun than paying them. Lots of people love to add up their municipal bond interest payments at the end of the year (as they are required to do on their federal tax form) so they can calculate how much

Figure 4.4 Tax-Free and Taxable Yield Equivalents

Here is what you would have to earn on a taxable bond to equal tax-exempt yields. State and local taxes, if they apply, would increase the amount you must earn from a taxable investment to equal the income from a bond that is free of such state and local taxes.

Tax-Exempt Yield	Equivalent Taxable Yield If Your Marginal Income Tax Rate Is		
	15%	28%	31%
4%	4.71%	5.56%	5.80%
5	5.88	6.94	7.25
6	7.06	8.33	8.7
7	8.24	9.72	10.14
8	9.41	11.11	11.59
9	10.59	12.5	13.04
10	11.76	13.89	14.49
11	12.94	15.28	15.94
12	14.12	16.67	17.39

they *aren't* sending the IRS. Take someone in the 31% federal income tax bracket. To keep the same amount of money that an 8% tax-exempt municipal security would provide, a couple filing jointly would have to earn 11.59% from a taxable investment. The savings are even more impressive in certain high-tax states where the income from municipal bonds issued within the state are exempt from state taxes, too. Of course, if you are in a lower tax bracket, the savings won't be as large, which explains the appeal of munis mostly to those investors with the highest incomes. Nevertheless, there is seldom a cheap lunch, much less a free one. Typically, muni bonds yield considerably less than other taxable investments of equal quality and duration, so don't assume that buying munis is going to ensure a better return. We're back to Mom's dictum: "Do your homework." It is much more important when buying munis than when buying Treasury bonds.

First, compare your after-tax yields from munis with other taxable investments to determine if it's really worth buying the munis. If you are getting only marginally more after-tax income from a muni than you would from a Treasury bond, chances are it simply isn't worth taking the additional risk.

What additional risk? you might ask. For openers, there is ratings risk. Municipal bonds are often rated based on the creditworthiness of the issuer. The most widely watched ratings are issued by Moody's Investors Service, Inc., and Standard & Poor's Corp. Some bonds also are rated by Fitch Investors Service, Inc. Moody's ratings range from Aaa (why they can't just be A through whatever is beyond us) to C. S&P offers similar ratings from AAA (which looks better to us than Aaa but isn't) to D, indicating an issue that is in default. You can call any of the ratings services to obtain their rating on a specific issue, or you can ask your friendly broker. Our advice is not to buy anything rated less than A.

The additional yield isn't worth the extra risk. Never, ever, under any circumstances, invest in a non-rated issue. Such investments are risky and probably not very liquid. And if you find that Moody's rating of an issue doesn't match S&P's, be alert. Find out why they don't agree or stay away from that issue. You should also ask whether the current rating has recently changed. A bond now rated A by S&P may have been a BBB a few months ago, but because the issuer's creditworthiness improved, it has been elevated. Or it may have been an AA bond, and the issuer's creditworthiness is declining. Finally, you want to know if a bond issue is "under review" by Moody's or on the "Creditwatch" list at S&P. Either can be a prelude to a ratings change, either up or down, that will affect the bond's price.

Before you put too much faith in a bond's rating, let us refresh your memory about how one of the richest counties in the United States ended up in a colossal financial mess. Orange County, California, and its $20 billion investment pool filed for bankruptcy court protection in December 1994 after the fund incurred $1.7 billion in losses from a risky investment strategy. It was the largest municipal bankruptcy in U.S. history, grabbing national headlines and pumping shock waves through the municipal bond industry. Something this big didn't happen overnight, of course; but months after the fund's highly leveraged portfolio started to collapse, S&P and Moody's continued to maintain high credit ratings on debt issued by Orange County and other local government participants in the fund. To unwary municipal bond investors, those seals of approval might have indicated that all was sublime with those issuers' finances.

Like many of the municipalities that invested in the county's investment pool, S&P and Moody's were long aware of the county's aggressive investment scheme. But they didn't feel it was necessary to highlight the risks to the public when they rated notes and bonds issued by partici-

Figure 4.5 Bond Ratings

A brief summary of what the credit ratings mean.

Moody's Investors Service, Inc.

Aaa Highest quality; principal is well protected and interest payments are virtually assured.

Aa High quality; marginally higher long-term risk than Aaa.

A Good quality; many favorable investment aspects, but some suggestion that credit risk could increase over the long term.

Baa Medium grade, neither highly protected nor poorly secured; lack outstanding investment characteristics and may be regarded as somewhat speculative.

Ba Speculative, with only moderate protection of principal and interest payments.

B Lack charactertistics of a desirable investment; protection of principal and interest payments over the long term is small.

Caa Poor quality; may be in default and protection of principal is questionable.

Ca Highly speculative; issues may be in default or have other large shortcomings.

C Lowest rated; extremely poor chances of ever attaining investment standing.

Standard & Poor's Corp.

AAA Highest quality; principal and interest payments well protected.

AA High quality; marginally higher long-term risk than AAA.

A Good quality; somewhat more susceptible to adverse conditions over the long term.

BBB Adequate; adverse conditions could threaten principal or interest payments.

BB Questionable; faces major uncertainties or exposure to adverse conditions that could jeopardize principal or interest payments.

B Speculative; adverse conditions would likely impair ability to pay interest or repay principal.

CCC Risky; has been identified as being vulnerable to default.

D In default.

pants in the fund—even in cases where the proceeds were used to speculate in the fund. As the county fund's losses began mounting earlier in 1994, both rating agencies likewise were aware that the fund's managers were being pressed by lenders to put up extra collateral against their investment positions. Yet in September of that year, S&P and Moody's both assigned their highest short-term ratings to an Orange County note issue. Bond investors who weren't in a position to do their own research into the fund's condition wouldn't have known what troubles were brewing.

The Orange County debacle occurred because the county treasurer was playing the "yield curve" game, or borrowing at low short-term rates and investing at higher long-term rates. He wasn't well supervised, and in particular he wasn't required to update the value of his portfolio to current market prices on a regular basis. As long as interest rates remained unchanged or continued to drop, as they did for much of 1993, his strategy was a winner. But it quickly came undone when interest rates started to rise in 1994.

Let's see, where were we? Oh, yes, telling you about the risks in municipal bonds. Don't forget *call risk*. Most municipal bonds have provisions allowing them to be called, or redeemed, before maturity. Typically, call provisions can't be invoked for 10 years after a muni bond is issued. But thousands of bondholders who purchased high-yielding munis in the early to mid 1980s have been shocked in recent years to have their bonds called. Many were counting on another 10 to 20 years of 12.5% yields to fund their retirements, only to face the prospect of reinvesting all that money when interest rates were at a 20-year low. It will be difficult, if not impossible, to escape call provisions, so make plans accordingly. Keep in mind, though, that if you are buying munis with interest rates close to their historical average, chances are less that they will fall far enough to trigger a call 10 years from now than if you were buying the bonds when yields were near their historic highs.

Finally, you incur relatively high transaction costs when you are buying and selling municipal bonds. Many individual investors fail to take those costs into account when comparing muni yields with after-tax yields on Treasuries and other taxable investments. Shopping around is essential to get the best prices. Even on large and liquid issues the difference in prices offered by brokers can be as much as $365 for a $10,000 bond. On smaller, less well-known issues the price discrepancy hit can be even harder. One broker may offer the best deal on a particular issue with which he's familiar but be way out of line on an issue that he doesn't know much about.

We aren't finished yet. You also need to know something about the different kinds of municipal bonds on the market to get an appreciation of what it is you are buying. The most basic distinction in muni bonds is between a *general obligation* bond and a *revenue* bond. A general obligation bond is supported by the taxing authority of the issuer. That is, a community issuing such a bond backs it with the promise that it will tax its citizens more if necessary to pay the interest and redeem the bond. Revenue bonds, on the other hand, depend on user fees for the payment of interest and redemption of the bond. By and large, it's easier to research revenue bonds because there is usually a specific project being financed by them, whether a hospital, water and sewer system, or toll bridge. But beware the industrial revenue bond, a kind of muni used by communities to attract new businesses. Usually the bond is backed solely by the creditworthiness of the corporation benefiting from the issue. General obligation bonds require some study of the underlying tax base of a community, a task requiring more judgment and skills by the ratings agency.

What all this comes down to is that investing in municipal bonds isn't the no-brainer that your broker or the late-night television advertisements make it out to be. The urge to avoid taxes is deep-seated in the American psyche. But don't let that urge push you into something that isn't suitable for your own financial circumstances.

Corporate Bonds

So you were surprised to discover how complicated investing in municipal bonds can be. Welcome to the next step of complexity: corporate bonds. Not only are corporate bonds subject to all the same risks as munis, but the earnings from them are fully taxable. Moreover, the company can't tax its customers to meet the interest payments on its bonds, as a municipality can. Corporations must rely on their ability to make a profit in a competitive and constantly changing environment. Therefore, as you might expect, bond ratings are even more important for corporate bonds than for munis. It's critical that investors pay attention to factors that would cause ratings to change. A recession, for instance, could jeopardize the ability of many companies to continue posting profits, not to mention increasing their profits. Liquidity is also a more important consideration when investing in corporate bonds. Generally, bonds that are listed—that is, trade on an exchange—are far more liquid than unlisted issues, something to keep in mind if you ever intend (or are forced) to trade your bonds.

For all their disadvantages, though, there is one benefit of corporate bonds that attracts investors: They pay higher yields. Here we are back at the risk-reward equation. Because corporate bonds by their very nature are more risky than Treasury or municipal bonds, they pay a higher interest rate. The question facing the investor is whether corporate bonds pay a big enough premium over competing investments to make their purchase worthwhile. While the answer depends to a great extent on your willingness to take risks, it also helps to know how big the premium is. Over the years the difference in yields between highly rated corporate bonds (probably the only ones you should consider) and equivalent Treasury bonds has varied widely. Usually, this spread between the two is widest when the economy is booming, demand for credit is high, and interest rates are soaring. In times of recession, when business activity is at an ebb, the spread narrows considerably.

All things considered, we don't feel that the spreads between corporate and Treasury bonds are usually sufficient to warrant the extra risk and work involved in buying and monitoring a portfolio of corporate bonds. Leave it to the pros who have the time and expertise to do the necessary credit research.

Zero-Coupon Bonds

When they first were created in the early 1980s, zero-coupon bonds were a little hard for the average investor to understand. An investment banker would take a perfectly normal Treasury bond and remove the coupons that entitled the owner of the bond to periodic interest payments. Then he would sell the pieces—each individual coupon and the principle amount— at what looked like an incredibly low price considering how much the investor would get back when the zero matured. The bonds paid no interest along the way (hence the name zeroes), and investors made their money from buying at the super-low discount price and receiving the face amount at maturity. They came with all sorts of ani-

malistic names derived from acronyms: TIGRS (Treasury Investment Growth Receipts), CATS (Certificates of Accrual on Treasury Securities), and LIONS (Lehman Investment Opportunity Notes). Yet zeroes have achieved a phenomenal acceptance among issuers and individual investors. You can buy government-backed zeroes, corporate zeroes, even zero-coupon certificates of deposit.

Zeroes are popular in part because they give investors a valuable planning tool. You know precisely how much you will receive when the bond matures. Plus, you don't have to worry about reinvesting periodic interest payments to achieve the maximum return on your investment because there aren't any periodic payments. What's more, zeroes tend to provide a somewhat higher yield than equivalently rated bonds of the same maturity (except for 30-year zeroes, where tremendous investor demand tends to push yields slightly lower).

Alas, we believe that zeroes have become *too* popular, at least in their use outside of such tax-advantaged plans as Individual Retirement Accounts and Keoghs. The problem is that since zero-coupon bonds offer no regular income payments, they are far more volatile than similar securities that provide regular income. When overall interest rates rise, the prices of zeroes plunge much farther than the prices of similar coupon bonds. If you are forced to sell for any reason, your losses can be astounding. Of course, when interest rates fall, the prices of zero-coupon bonds soar much higher than those of equivalent bonds, and your gains can be equally astounding. If you think you can predict interest rates, then you want to be trading zeroes. They give you the biggest bang for your buck. (U.S. Savings Bonds, discussed previously in this chapter, are zeroes, too, but there isn't any secondary market for them, which means no price volatility.)

A second problem with zero-coupon bonds is that while they don't pay interest periodically like a conventional bond, they are taxed as if they did. That's right: The government expects you to pay annual income tax on the amount of interest (the accreted interest) you would have earned had your zero been a conventional bond instead. If you think income taxes are a pain in the neck, try paying taxes on income you haven't received. This disadvantage disappears, of course, if the zero-coupon bond is held in your IRA, in which current earnings are protected from income tax. You will have to pay taxes eventually, though, when the money comes out of the IRA.

In any event, all the cautions that apply to buying conventional bonds apply equally if not more so to zeroes. Corporate and municipal zeroes are subject to call provisions just like regular corporate and municipal bonds. Ratings matter. And liquidity varies from one issue to another.

Collateralized Bonds

On the surface, these derivative bonds (created from other types of bonds) look like a good idea. In their basic form they are variations of mortgage-backed bonds. The backing can range from home mortgages to car and boat loans or even credit card receivables. Perhaps the most popular form they take, at least as far as individual investors are concerned, is that of the collateralized mortgage obligation, or CMO. CMOs are derivatives created from the government-backed mortgage bonds issued by one of the agencies mentioned previously. Indeed, slick brokers offer these securities by advertising them as "triple-A, government guaranteed" investments with what sound like amazingly good yields. And indeed the Ginnie Mae or Fannie Mae bonds from which CMOs are derived do enjoy the backing of the federal government. But CMOs are a different breed. Investment bankers created them to try to smooth out the rough spots encountered in agency bonds when prepayments occur. For all practical purposes they take a bunch of agency bonds and split them up into their component parts, principal and interest, before recombining them to form separate CMO offspring, or "tranches." Each tranche has its own maturity, interest rate, and seniority within the overall CMO structure. The idea is to transform standard mortgage-backed securities into an array of products with something to suit everyone from the most conservative investor, who wants to minimize prepayment risks, to the boldest, who is willing to take on extra prepayment risk to get substantially higher yields. The trouble is that individual investors are often ill-equipped to evaluate the relative risks of the various tranches. What usually happens is the clever broker seduces his victim with his pitch of high yields and government backing. Of course, the higher the yield, the more vulnerable a tranche is to the prepayment problem. Lower-yielding tranches have more protection from prepayment.

Both traditional mortgage-backed securities and CMOs had their reputations sullied in recent years as interest rates plunged and homeowners went on a refinancing binge. The lower home mortgage rates fall, the less likely these prepayment problems will recur. But it can happen. If you never buy an investment you don't understand, you won't be trapped. And because it is hard to understand CMOs, much less properly evaluate them, we recommend steering clear. If your broker calls with a deal that sounds too good to be true, it probably is.

Junk by Any Other Name

Unless you were in a coma during the 1980s, you have heard plenty about junk bonds. "High-yield bonds," your broker will call them. These are a subset of the corporate bond menu that the ratings agencies have either branded "speculative" or refuse to brand at all. They carry wonderfully high yields, along with amazingly big risks.

Your broker is probably going to get upset when you tell him what you have read in this book about junk bonds. He will tell you the media has never understood high-yield bonds and that Michael Milken went to jail not because he sold a lot of junk bonds but because he illegally manipulated the market for them; and, besides, all that's been cleaned up now, and where else are you going to get double-digit yields these days? If you don't particularly like the guy, just hang up. If he is otherwise an okay person to deal with, bear up and hear his spiel. Then tell him you are just not interested but does he maybe have a good Treasury floating around the office?

Junk bonds become junk in one of two ways. Sometimes they are just born that way. During the fevered merger and buyout business in the 1980s, Milken and his ilk created new junk bonds purposely to help pull off the deals they were making. The market was supported by criminal and/or stupid savings-and-loan officers who needed the high income to keep their institutions afloat. When it became evident that a lot of the deals just weren't working, Milken went to jail, the S&L industry collapsed, many junk bond issuers went bankrupt or into default, and junk prices plunged, eventually reaching a low enough level that they became worthwhile investments for risk-taking players capable of making a detailed study of the underlying creditworthiness of the issuers that had survived.

Other junk bonds start out as investment grade but become junk when the issuer gets into big trouble and the credit ratings agencies downgrade the bonds time and time again. Sometimes the company that issued the bonds manages to pull out of its tailspin and the holder of the bonds has a nice high-yielding security in his portfolio. But frequently the issuer continues to nose-dive until it crashes and burns, carrying the bond with it. *If* you have enough money to invest that you can buy a huge portfolio of different junk bonds to minimize the risk of default (with that much, you don't need this book) and *if* you are very good at analyzing financial statements and businesses, then *maybe* you have a shot at making and keeping some money from junk bond investments. Otherwise, accept with grace that junk bonds aren't for you and forget they exist.

Preferred Stocks and Convertible Bonds

Don't look so surprised. We figure preferred stocks belong in this chapter, not the previous one, because a preferred stock, despite the name, is really more of a bond without a maturity than it is a stock. Like the other hybrid discussed here, convertible bonds, you are buying preferred stock because you are scared to buy common stock. You are going for safety and income more than capital appreciation. Basically, a preferred stock pays a set dividend. It won't rise, but it won't fall, either, unless the company that issued it goes belly up. Even then, as a preferred shareholder, you have claim on the dead company's remains before mere common shareholders. With most healthy companies, however, the dividend yields on preferred stock aren't significantly better than those on Treasury or municipal bonds. The worse the company's health, the better the yield and, as always, the greater the risk. Don't forget that a company can decide to eliminate its preferred dividends at any time without triggering a default, as would a decision to halt timely interest payments on their outstanding bonds. Also, bondholders line up ahead of preferred stockholders to pick over a dead company's carcass. But because of the high dividend yield relative to other stocks, preferred stock doesn't appreciate nearly as fast as common stock of the same company. It doesn't lose value as fast, either.

There is a variation on the preferred stock theme that might be attractive to the conservative investor, however. Called *convertible preferred stock,* it gives you the right to receive your regular dividend *and* the right to convert your preferred stock into a specific amount of common stock. If the convertible preferred is trading close to the common stock's price, the convertible preferred stock will rise as the common stock rises. But be wary of convertible preferreds that are selling at a substantial premium to the company's common stock. There isn't any point in converting a preferred stock selling at $60 a share for five shares of common stock selling at $5 a share.

Convertible bonds, like convertible preferred stocks, give you the right to convert the bond into the common stock of the issuing company. But since the bond usually trades at a premium to the common stock—it usually yields more and has preference over common stock in the event of bankruptcy—you would seldom find it attractive to make the conversion.

Briefly, these are interesting variations on a theme. But they are neither fish nor fowl, and we don't find the case for owning either preferred stock or convertible bonds particularly compelling. If you want stock, buy stock. If you want bonds, buy bonds. Keep life simple.

STRATEGIES

So, after all this you have decided to make bonds a part of your portfolio. The only questions are which ones and how best to use them. If it wasn't clear in our discussion of the various kinds of bonds, we'll tell you right now that we love Treasuries. Safe, liquid, available in a wide range of maturities with very low transaction costs, they make the bond market about as simple and safe as it can get. Government agencies are okay, too, if you have a touch of greed in you that demands eking out that extra little bit of return. If your tax bracket is high or you think it will become higher during the time that you own bonds (much as we hate paying taxes, we wouldn't mind being pushed into a higher category), then certainly consider municipals. But get into munis only if you are willing and able to do the necessary shopping and home-work to get the most liquid and highly rated bonds in what-ever maturity you want. Zeroes are great for retirement accounts or other specialized needs, but their volatility and tax treatment make them less than desirable for most port-folios. We don't think corporates are worth the trouble they require, and certainly junk is out of the question for those of us barely able to read a balance sheet. The yield on collater-alized bonds is mighty tempting, but the prepayment factor makes them hard to value and raises the reinvestment risk to an unacceptable level in our minds. And preferred stock and convertible bonds just don't accomplish much, under most circumstances, that can't be done with ordinary stocks and bonds.

SHORT IS BETTER THAN LONG

Now let's consider some strategies for setting up the bond side of your portfolio. At its simplest, your bond portfolio will consist of one issue at a certain yield and a certain matu-rity. Obviously, if you have some relatively short-term goal in mind, say two years from now, a Treasury bond bought on the secondary market that matures just before you need the money is perfect. But if you are considering a goal much fur-ther away, say 15 to 25 years, your best bet might not be a bond that matures then. Under most circumstances you are not getting sufficient yield to justify the risk of price fluctua-tions. We recommend an intermediate-term Treasury. Historically—meaning on average since World War II but not always—5-year Treasuries have yielded about 97% of the yield on 30-year Treasuries. Yet should interest rates rise one percentage point, a 5-year Treasury would lose 4.1% of its value while the 30-year bond would give up 10.8% of its value. Clearly this strategy wouldn't apply if overall interest rates were near their all-time highs, as they were in the 1980s. Under those circumstances, if you lock in yields of 9% or more for as long as you can, you can still meet your goals. But since rates nowadays are much closer to their historic norms, it is best to protect yourself. If you are buying a municipal bond, remember that most call provisions kick in after 10 years, so it may not pay to buy a muni with a maturity of more than 10 years. A 20-year bond with a 10-year call provision offers no protection against price decline (rising interest rates), but the call provision eliminates any prospect of significant price appreciation and continued high interest income.

BUILDING A BOND LADDER

As your bond portfolio grows, and especially in a world of falling or low interest rates, it's easy to become a yield junkie, thirsting for the highest return possible on your investment money. But even if you stick to Treasuries, high yield can mean danger. Although the temptation will be strong to "go long" by buying long-term bonds, resist it. A much better approach is to build a bond ladder, each rung of which consists of a different maturity bond. At its simplest, a laddered portfolio would consist of bonds with maturities of 1 year, 2 years, 3 years, right on through 10 years. Bond laddering won't produce the highest possible yields, such as those you would get by buying nothing but 10-year bonds, but it provides an element of safety through diversification that you won't have if your portfolio is invested entirely in a single maturity.

Look at it this way: If interest rates rise sometime in the next few years, a single bet on the 10-year bond will be a loser. Either you'll be stuck with a subpar yield compared to what else is available, or you will have to take a loss on your 10-year bonds to get into something more lucrative. With a bond ladder, you will always be getting new money to invest as the rungs of the ladder mature. You also get some protection against falling rates because you have locked up higher yields on the longer-term rungs of your ladder. Another nice thing about the ladder is that it is simple and requires minimal maintenance.

Corporate and municipal bonds can complicate a ladder because they have to be watched for changing credit conditions. Callable bonds aren't a good idea for ladders because you could wind up losing a rung if that particular issue is called. While transaction costs can be relatively high for the investor with small amounts to invest, successful ladders can be constructed for $50,000 or less if you pick carefully and spread the rungs two years apart instead of just one year. Sure, it's a conservative approach. But if you are dealing with bonds, it's pretty certain that you are a conservative investor.

BOND TRADING: WHERE INVESTORS FEAR TO TREAD

There will be times when you are sorely tempted to do a little bond trading. After all, the pros do it all the time. But the pros can do things you can't do. Typically they employ such arcane strategies as riding the yield curve, substitution plays, and intermarket spread swaps. They can be complex and risky, and often require a knowledge and sense of the bond market that you probably don't have (and probably don't want). The gains the pros make often are small and would be wiped out by your transaction costs.

Still, you'll be tempted. The biggest temptation will come when interest rates have fallen significantly and your bond portfolio has appreciated very nicely. Why not lock in those hefty profits? Okay, so you lock them in, which means you sell them and turn your paper profits into real ones that you have to pay taxes on. Now what? Where are you going to put all those profits back to work? If it's just back into bonds, don't congratulate yourself. Not only did you incur a capital gains tax on your profits, but you also spent good money on a broker's commission and put what is left into instruments earning lower interest.

Selling appreciated bonds can be justified if you are rebalancing your portfolio and the proceeds from the sale will be moved into stocks or some other part of your portfolio that has underperformed and shrunk below your targeted weighting. Also, if for some reason your investment goals have changed, it might be wise to adjust the duration of your bond portfolio to fit the new needs, since the ultimate return on bonds held to maturity is far more predictable than the return on stocks.

The case for selling depreciated bonds is easier to make. If interest rates begin to rise, your bond holdings will begin to lose value. You are going to be stuck with the unpleasant choice of accepting lower yields than you might otherwise get (and that might be lower than the rate of inflation, resulting in a net loss each year on your bond portfolio); or you must take a loss on the sale of some bonds so that you can invest in securities with higher yields. The hard part is knowing how far interest rates are going to rise and how long they will stay there. If you panic and move too quickly, you will wind up with only marginally higher yields that don't justify the transaction costs involved, and you may still face the same problem if rates keep rising. If you wait too long, your loss when you sell your current bonds may be fairly substantial, and you will have forgone the higher yields that were available on more recently issued bonds.

So you expect us to tell you how to time your moves perfectly? Dream on. We wouldn't be writing this book if we could do that. Instead, our advice is for you to make a judgment about what you think interest rates are going to do based on the best possible information you have. If you expect rates to keep rising, shorten the average maturity of your fixed-income portfolio. Take your losses while they are small, put the money in the short-term high-quality instruments like Treasury bills or notes, and keep watching rates. If they do indeed reach high levels, start parceling your short-term money out into longer maturities. If, on the other hand, you do all this switching and then interest rates stabilize or even drop, you made a slight mistake. The consequences of this error, however, aren't much more than wasted transaction costs.

Going short to protect yourself against rising rates is a defensive measure for bond investors. If you are really bold and feel some degree of certainty about your ability to predict the direction of interest rates, you can go on the offensive and try to make really big money by going long when you think rates are about to fall. If you are playing this game, you may as well play with the big boys. Forget the safe stuff like Treasuries. Play with zeroes, which are far more volatile and sensitive to changes in interest rates. If it works, you can retire early. If it doesn't, you will be grinding away in the salt mines long after the rest of us have propped up our feet in that Arizona retirement community.

SUGGESTED READING

Investing in bonds isn't as interesting as investing in stocks, and it shows in the variety and style of books available on the subject. A good basic text put out by the New York Institute of Finance is called *Fixed Income Investments, A Personal Seminar*. It walks you through the panoply of fixed-income securities, asking questions to be sure you understand such concepts as discount pricing, current yield, and nominal yield.

You might also find useful *The Dow Jones–Irwin Guide to Bond and Money Market Investments* by Frank J. Fabozzi and Marcia Stigum, especially as a postgraduate course after the New York Institute of Finance's more simplified seminar.

5 Mutual Funds

"How would you like to hear how the mutual funds that control the affordability of your higher education are doing?"

When we wrote the first edition of this book, there were somewhat more than 3,200 mutual funds from which investors could choose. Part of the problem of using funds, we pointed out, was the daunting task of picking the right ones from among all the offerings. Well, in the past few years the problem has gotten much, much worse if you consider that at the beginning of 1998 there were an astounding 6,778 mutual funds out there vying for your business. There is, however, some good news in this bad news. Sure, sorting through thousands of funds to find the ones that are right for you is a challenge (although the guidelines we laid out in the first edition still hold true and will make the process much easier). But the good thing, we think, is that the whole world of mutual funds has gotten more attention from just about everyone: the regulators, the news media, the securities industry, and, yes, the little guy. The result of all this attention is that there is now more information about funds than ever before. Moreover, regulatory scrutiny is, in many cases, tighter than it has ever been. Best of all, the choices open to individual investors have never been greater.

For most investors, mutual funds should be the primary vehicles for putting their money to work. That might sound strange in a book about investing that is associated with the foremost publication for the individual investor, but let's look at the hard facts. Maintaining a diverse portfolio of stocks, bonds, and other types of assets isn't easy. You must know what you're doing, and you must devote large amounts of time to finding new stocks and deciding when to sell stocks you already own. The record keeping alone for a portfolio of 20 or more stocks and a handful of bonds can be overwhelming for the less-than-disciplined investor. Then there are the investment opportunities that the individual investor just can't take advantage of, including hot initial public offerings, many foreign stocks, and the commercial paper market, all of which are easily accessible through mutual funds. Of course, if you're an unusually devoted investor with particularly sharp analytical skills and the time to run a diverse investment portfolio, that's fine. You probably ought to *manage* a mutual fund. But if you're not all those things, you, like millions of others, are a candidate to invest in mutual funds.

That doesn't mean you can't or shouldn't buy individual stocks or bonds, or make other kinds of investments outside the mutual fund realm. Quite the contrary. By using mutual funds wisely, you'll still be able to pick that little rocket ship of a stock that the overpaid Wall Street analysts have ignored. You just won't have to pick as many of them (some of them inevitably sputter and fall back to earth with a crash anyhow). While you pore over *Barron's* looking for the perfect target, you can keep some of your investment pot simmering in a money market fund with a good rate of return while you diversify your portfolio with professionally chosen foreign stocks, or simply let a chunk of your money match the market through a low-cost index fund. Used that way, mutual funds actually free you to do a better job of investing in individual stocks and bonds without the dogged devotion that a full-blown portfolio would require. Of course, if you have other requirements on your time and energy, mutual funds can do it all for you. As few as four or five funds will give you a well-diversified portfolio that you can add to on a regular basis without the hassle—or fees—of dealing with brokers.

EVERYMAN'S MONEY MANAGER

The past several years have been a remarkable period for investors in the United States. The broad market has posted gains of more than 20% three years in a row, a record performance. The economy has been humming along in a state of remarkable balance, growing rapidly enough to keep unemployment low and profits high, but not so fast as to excite the inflation monster. The market's gains and the euphoria that has swept over investors have analysts pondering a classic chicken-or-egg proposition: Did the market rise because more investors decided that was the place for their money, or did more investors decide the market was the place for their money because it kept rising? Let them debate arcane questions like that. The point is, there is a vast army of individual investors out there who have poured huge amounts of money into the stock market through mutual funds and who have enjoyed spectacular results—results, we are confident to predict, that won't continue. The oft-repeated fear among the pros on Wall Street is that this vast herd of investors that has never experienced a true bear market will bolt and head for the hills when the going gets rough, as it inevitably will. Never mind that those same pros have been the ones to bolt and run at the first signs of trouble, giving all the individuals a chance to buy stocks cheaper than they could have if the pros had held firm. Certainly there are many individuals who don't currently realize how sick they'll feel when their portfolio drops 20% in value in a matter of weeks and then stays there for months. A portion of them won't be able to stand the pressure, and they will bolt, adding perhaps another 5% to the market's retreat. Their redemptions will likely force fund managers to sell stocks when they should be buying, and that ultimately will hurt everyone's performance.

But don't despair. The fact that you're reading this book suggests you're not among the fair weather investors. And we think the majority of converts to mutual funds in the past several years has a better understanding of the markets and of their own goals. The post-World War II baby boom produced a bulge in the U.S. population that through the 1980s was focused mostly on accumulating goods, including houses, furniture, and cars. But the older members of the baby boom bulge have had that behind them now for a few years. They're at the stage of life in which they're actively saving and investing for longer-term goals, especially retirement. They are more sophisticated investors and are apt to keep their wits in tough times. Indeed, it has usually been their buying which has turned around the momentary panics that have seized the Wall Street professionals. These investors have turned to mutual funds for the convenient, low-cost access they provide to professional money management. Many mutual fund investors have decided that they are better doctors, lawyers, executives, and journalists than they are money managers. They are devoting time to their careers while turning over some portion of their financial management chores to professionals.

Still, the question remains: How do you pick the 4 or 5 or even 20 funds that are right for you from among the vast array of funds that exist today? Many of the same procedures that an investor uses to pick individual stocks or bonds can be used to pick funds. When you are through with this sec-

tion, we think you'll be surprised at how easy it is to eliminate the vast majority of mutual funds before settling on the
few that truly suit your needs. But before we hand you the
menu, you should understand how a mutual fund works.

MUTUAL FUND MECHANICS

A mutual fund begins life as the creation of a sponsor, usually a financial services concern such as a mutual fund company, brokerage firm, insurance company, or bank. In ideal circumstances, the sponsor, presumably recognizing a desire
among investors to put money to work in a particular kind of
investment vehicle, hires a manager with some expertise in
that kind of investment, draws up the necessary legal papers,
and, after approval by the Securities and Exchange
Commission, begins advertising the availability of the fund.
As the money flows in, the manager invests it according to
the fund's objective. Different managers use different techniques, but we'll consider for a moment an aggressive growth
fund specializing in the stocks of small companies. Although
our fund manager is mostly intent on selecting stocks that
have the potential to appreciate quickly—in that sense, he
faces the same problems as any other small stock investor—
he probably also has some leeway to invest in a few larger
stocks or to leave a portion of the funds in cash, awaiting a
better investment climate. If the fund is large enough, he gets
calls from investment bankers about potentially hot new initial public offerings of small companies that are selling stock
for the first time. Those are the kinds of calls that few individual investors are likely to receive. Because our manager's
job depends on his ability to outperform rivals running similar funds, he probably has a very quick trigger finger. If a
stock isn't performing up to expectations, it is quickly sold

and replaced by another that is more promising. Even stocks that are still doing well but whose trajectories are starting to level off aren't immune to being sacrificed on the altar of explosive growth. If you visited the manager's office (it's highly unlikely you'll be invited), you would probably find him buried beneath a pile of paper, mostly proxies, prospectuses, and annual and quarterly reports. At the end of each hectic day the manager totes up his winners and losers, and compares them to the performance of his competitors and to whatever other benchmarks he is measured against by his bosses. It isn't an easy life. The hours are long and the pressures are intense. Public scrutiny of fund managers is greater than it has ever been, and star money managers are becoming celebrities in their own right. Of course, the fall from such dizzying heights can be painful if a manager slips. But running mutual fund money can be very lucrative. The best fund managers need never worry about how they will fund their own retirements.

But what we've just described is the ideal world. The real world is a little different. For example, the decision that leads to the creation of a fund often isn't the perceived desire of investors to put their money to work in a certain way. Rather, it's the desire of the sponsor to glom onto a well-established trend. The world simply doesn't need another growth fund or bond fund or any other kind of fund unless that fund can spectacularly outperform the existing ones. But that doesn't stop companies from creating them, knowing full well that they can't or won't pay the absolute best manager in the business to run their fund. The result? The creation of more mediocre funds who prey on the unwary or ignorant. Consider that the vast majority of mutual fund managers can't even manage to simply equal the returns produced by an unmanaged portfolio of stocks that resemble the Standard & Poor's 500-stock index. If they can't do that, why is anyone paying them a salary?

Regardless of whether a fund manager runs an aggressive growth fund or a much more conservative growth and income fund, her job is to provide investors with gains of some sort. Although the ways in which they seek to invest vary widely, all mutual funds have as their goal capital gains, income, or some blend of the two. How they intend to achieve that is laid out in the fund's prospectus, the single most important document in your quest to find the fund or funds most suited to your needs. The prospectus includes not only the statement of the fund's investment objective but also performance history going back as much as 10 years if it has been in existence that long. That history will include lots of details about expenses, dividends, and, most important of all, the *net asset value (NAV)*, or share price, at the end of each year, along with the increase or decrease in NAV. But that isn't all. You'll also get a sense of how fast the portfolio of stocks or bonds the fund owns turns over each year and whether the manager of the fund is new or is a veteran. All the information in the prospectus can have a bearing on your decision to invest or to look elsewhere.

Obviously, the performance of a fund should interest you most. The return on a mutual fund is affected not only by how skillfully the fund's managers invest your money but also by how much they charge you to do it. Basically, you need to be aware that funds can charge you to get into the fund (a load), to stay in it (management fees), and to get back out (redemption fees). You won't be able to escape the management fees; after all, nobody is going to help you invest your money without charging you to do it. But those fees vary widely from one fund to another. The investment management fee you pay can be as high as 3% of your invested assets each year, and other expenses, such as legal and accounting fees, can add another 1%. The annual rate at which the portfolio turns over naturally affects total brokerage commissions, which is another cost that fund shareholders must bear.

You can, and probably should, avoid charges to get into and out of funds. There isn't any evidence that load funds perform any better, on average, than no-load funds, so why put a hurdle (which can be as high as 8.5% of the money you invest) in the way of your potential gains? That's why you should beware of your broker's advice on mutual funds. His best interests (making money off you) aren't your best interests (making money *for* you) when it comes to mutual funds. He will almost certainly recommend a fund with a sales charge because he gets a cut of it. You must look elsewhere for advice about which fund or funds to buy.

As for funds with redemption charges, distinguish between those that are always levied and those that disappear six months to a year after you make your initial investment. These latter types are intended to discourage fund "traders," who move in and out of funds on a short-term basis and drive the investment managers nuts by making asset levels unpredictable. For long-term investors they shouldn't be a consideration. Just remember that if you need some quick cash, take it from a fund without a redemption charge or from one whose "back-end load" has expired.

It's exceedingly easy to deal with most mutual funds. Most of them have a toll-free number, and you need only ask to receive sales literature, including prospectuses. To buy a fund requires little more than filling out an application and mailing it, along with a check for your initial investment, back to the company. You will receive periodic reports on how the fund is doing, including confirmations each time you add to or withdraw funds or switch between funds. Most funds provide detailed annual statements that make your record-keeping and income tax chores much easier than if you maintained your own portfolio. When, for whatever reason, you want to get out of a fund, merely advise the fund that you wish to sell, and a check will be heading your way within a few days.

When you invest in a fund, you are basically buying shares of the fund. The price of those shares, stated as net asset value, is calculated at the end of each business day. You can monitor the performance of a fund by following the rise and fall of its net asset value on a daily, monthly, or quarterly basis. Daily is too often; it creates emotions that, if acted upon, will turn you into a mutual fund trader and make you poorer to boot. Monthly is about right. You can see trends developing, but you don't get jerked around by the ups and downs of daily moves. We think annual monitoring of your portfolio is a bit blasé if you have anything but insignificant sums in the fund.

The rate at which money comes into and leaves a given mutual fund depends on many variables. It's fair to say that in an overall bull market funds will be inundated with new money, and in a bear market they will be besieged by investors wanting to cash out. Thus, fund managers face problems that individual investors don't have to worry about. In a bull market, for instance, cash can come tumbling into a fund so fast that the harried manager finds it difficult to invest it wisely. He may let cash balances in the fund build, or he may take some risks in investing the money that he wouldn't ordinarily take. Another option for managers has been to invest in asset classes outside the purported scope of the fund's objectives. A small-cap fund can wind up owning some pretty big stocks, which may or may not help the fund's performance but certainly doesn't serve the needs of the investors who thought they were buying one thing only to find they own something different. If the manager decides to take extra risks to put all the money being thrown at him to work, he may get caught in the bull market's final euphoric frenzy before the fall. And in a bear market, when he should be concentrating on which stocks are real bargains, he may instead be trying to determine which good stocks already in the fund should be sold to meet redemption requests of investors bailing out of the fund. Thus, in both a bull and a bear market, the manager may be forced to take measures that he knows aren't the soundest investment strategies.

What's in a Name?

At the end of this chapter we provide you with the menu of fund categories that *Barron's* uses to make it easier to select funds that suit your needs. The next few sections explain some special kinds of funds: money market funds, bond funds, and index funds. But as you review various funds with an eye to selecting one, you're going to run into a problem: The way funds are categorized doesn't necessarily reflect their *real* investment strategies. The folks at Lipper Analytical Services, who supply much of the mutual fund performance data in *Barron's,* try to analyze funds for their real, as opposed to their stated, objectives. But fund holdings can change rapidly, and, besides, there is room for argument about what are, for instance, "growth stocks" or "value stocks." Indeed, the word "growth" is probably the most overused word in the fund industry. It can mean so many things to so many people that in the end it really means nothing. We like to think of growth stocks as the shares of companies whose earnings are growing faster than average. Yet when you review mutual fund literature, you'll find that many "growth" funds, and even some "aggressive growth" funds, are chock-full of companies that aren't producing very vigorous earnings growth. The same holds true for "value" funds. Our conception of value involves such standard measures as low price-earnings ratios and high dividend yields. Yet looking over some value fund holdings, you'll see some uncomfortably pricey stocks by any measure. And beware of funds that bill themselves as "equity income" or "balanced"

Figure 5.1 More Wealth of Information

Barron's mutual fund tables not only provide a detailed weekly summary of trading activity, but also show the latest income and capital gains distributions, plus the total distributions for the past 12 months.

						MUTUAL FUNDS						

52 Week High	Low	Fund Name	Week's High	Low	Close NAV	Wk's Chg.	---% Return--- 1-Wk	YTD	3-Yr	LATEST DIVIDEND Income+ Cap. gains	Record Date	12 MTH Inco. Divs.	Cap. Gain
18.60	14.98	OverseasB n	18.40	17.77	18.40	+ .11	+ .6	+ 17.5	...	.13+.96	12-05-97	.13	.96
14.84	9.72	MidCpB np	14.55	14.00	14.55	+ .16	+ 1.1	+ 12.9	...	...+1.38	12-19-97	...	1.38
11.72	10.93	StrInB n	11.32	11.25	11.32	− .02	− .1	+ 3.8	+ 40.9	.0526	4-01-98◊	.7102	.31
28.04	18.80	StrOppB n	27.18	26.42	27.17	+ .23	+ .9	+ 10.0	+ 73.4	...+.15	1-02-98	...	2.20
		Fidelity Advisor I:											
9.84	9.21	GovInl n	9.67	9.61	9.67	...	+ .1	+ 1.9	...	.0469	4-01-98◊	.5837	...
20.10	19.37	Balancedl	19.94	19.37	19.94	+ .24	+ 1.2	+ 10.1	...	.16	3-13-98	.64	1.26
53.99	37.27	EqGrl n	53.64	51.65	53.64	+ .82	+ 1.6	+ 15.4	+112.3	...+.42	1-02-98	.22	6.07
29.42	21.05	Eqlnl n	29.11	28.12	29.11	+ .37	+ 1.3	+ 13.3	+ 97.2	.08	3-13-98	.37	1.54
14.54	12.02	GroIncl	14.42	13.86	14.42	+ .27	+ 1.9	+ 15.0	...	.02	3-13-98	.07	.18
46.98	33.53	GrOppl n	46.88	45.24	46.88	+ .67	+ 1.4	+ 11.2	...	...+.21	1-02-98	.68	2.60
13.09	11.76	HiYldl n	12.86	12.80	12.86	− .04	− .2	+ 6.4	...	.0718	4-01-98◊	1.0909	.30
9.50	9.28	IShlGv	9.41	9.38	9.41	...	+ .1	+ 2.0	+ 22.6	.0507	4-01-98◊	.6191	...
10.73	10.31	IntBdl n	10.62	10.57	10.62	...	+ .1	+ 2.1	+ 23.0	.0521	4-01-98◊	.6302	...
14.99	12.79	MidCapl	14.71	14.15	14.71	+ .17	NA	NA	NA	...+.01	1-02-98	...	1.49
18.81	15.11	Ovrseal	18.62	17.98	18.62	+ .11	+ .6	+ 17.9	...	.26+.96	12-05-97	.26	.96
		Fidelity Advisor T:											
20.04	15.57	BalancT	19.87	19.31	19.87	+ .23	+ 1.2	+ 9.9	+ 59.5	.13	3-13-98	.54	1.26
12.24	10.30	EmMkInT	11.44	11.22	11.44	...	+ .1	+ 5.9	+114.9	.0779	4-01-98◊	1.043	...
53.15	36.88	EqGrT p	52.80	50.85	52.80	+ .80	+ 1.5	+ 15.2	+108.7	...+.42	1-02-98	...	6.04
29.19	20.92	EqInT	28.87	27.90	28.87	+ .36	+ 1.3	+ 13.1	+ 93.7	.05	3-13-98	.23	1.72
9.86	9.23	GovInT	9.69	9.62	9.69	...	+ .1	+ 1.8	+ 25.5	.0049	4-01-98◊	.5594	...
14.52	10.81	GroIncT	14.39	13.83	14.39	+ .27	+ 1.9	+ 14.7	...	.01	3-13-98	.03	.18
47.00	33.71	GrOppT	46.89	45.25	46.89	+ .67	+ 1.4	+ 11.0	+103.4	...+.21	1-02-98	.47	2.60
13.32	11.95	HiYldT	13.10	13.03	13.10	− .04	− .2	+ 6.2	+ 52.0	.0688	4-01-98◊	1.0577	.30
10.73	10.31	IntBdT	10.61	10.57	10.61	...	+ .1	+ 1.9	+ 21.9	.0496	4-01-98◊	.5992	...
10.76	10.19	ItMuniT	10.57	10.52	10.57	...	+ .1	+ .6	+ 21.1	.0372	4-01-98◊	.4381	.03
15.54	10.65	LgeCapT	15.34	14.81	15.34	+ .20	+ 1.3	+ 14.7	...	...+.80	12-19-97	...	.80
14.97	9.76	MidCapT p	14.69	14.13	14.69	+ .16	+ 1.1	+ 13.2	...	...+1.43	12-19-97	...	1.43
12.47	11.63	MuniIncT p	12.25	12.18	12.25	− .01	0.0	+ .9	+ 24.7	.05	4-01-98◊	.5848	...
19.01	14.72	OvrseaT	18.82	18.16	18.82	+ .12	+ .6	+ 17.8	+ 56.9	.16+.96	12-05-97	.16	.96
10.27	10.05	SIMuniT	10.16	10.14	10.16	...	+ .1	+ .7	+ 15.3	.0344	4-01-98◊	.4049	...
9.41	9.25	STFIT	9.33	9.31	9.33	...	+ .1	+ .9	+ 20.0	.0475	4-01-98◊	.5642	...

funds, both of which most investors assume are relatively low-risk investments. In their urge to rank high on performance lists, some of these fund managers adopt higher-risk strategies than the names of their funds imply. Investors who gravitate naturally toward the best performers in any category may end up buying funds that aren't nearly as low risk as they want.

Managers who have strayed from their investment mandates have created some real horror stories in recent years. Anybody who has been a longtime investor in Fidelity's Magellan Fund remembers the name Jeffrey Vinik—and not happily. Mr. Vinik in 1994 thought he saw the remarkable bull market in stocks hitting a peak, so he moved a huge proportion of Magellan's assets into bonds. Well, it wasn't the stock market that was peaking, it was the bond market. As a result, Magellan shareholders, who thought they had bought a growth stock fund, got creamed as bond prices plunged. Mr. Vinik no longer runs Magellan; in fact, Fidelity, along with other fund companies, has tightened restrictions on how far managers can stretch their mandates.

Nevertheless, in the end it's going to be up to you to determine if a fund suits your portfolio needs. There are an increasing number of publications, software, and Internet sites that will help you sort out the confusion, but they aren't necessarily cheap. How much you spend on research data may be determined by how sure you want to be that you are getting what you think you are getting. Just remember to include research expenses in your calculation of total return. It doesn't do you any good to think that such expenses don't count.

MONEY MARKET FUNDS

These funds are the parking lots of the mutual fund shopping center. They're a great place to leave some money while you shop among other, better, long-term investment choices. But like the parking lots where you leave your car while shopping, they aren't necessarily safe, so beware. Money market funds invest in a variety of short-term instruments, mostly short-term loans that are referred to in the finance industry as "commercial paper" or "government paper" depending on who is doing the borrowing. Some of this paper—that is, the loans—is considered very safe, and some is considered less than safe, perhaps even downright risky. As with much else in the investment business, risk carries reward. The riskiest borrowers have to pay you the highest rates. Thus, one money market fund may offer a yield of 5.75% while another has a yield of just 4.9%. All other things being equal, you can assume that, one way or another, the fund with the higher yield is a riskier fund than the one with the lower yield.

Money market funds try to maintain their funds in such a way that a share is always worth $1. You get extra shares or a check when the company or government agency makes an interest payment to the fund. Although you wouldn't know it by reviewing their records, some money market funds have been stuck with short-term investments that went into default. If the fund had accurately depicted its situation, the value of its shares would have fallen below $1 a share, an event called "breaking the buck." But since the money market industry has to cultivate the image of safety to compete against government-insured bank accounts, any fund that acknowledged the risks it had taken by breaking the buck would become anathema. So instead of lowering the share price, the fund companies that have run into trouble in the past have merely ponied up some of their own money to cover up the bad loans they made. But keep in mind that the money market funds are not *obligated* to do that; one day they might choose to let investors bear the brunt of such losses.

Most important, the returns on money funds tend to be poor over the long haul (although almost always better than whatever rates banks pay on certificates of deposit). Use them as a parking place—at least the money-market-fund meter dispenses small change rather than demanding to be fed—not as a long-term investment vehicle.

BOND FUNDS

Bond funds can sound awfully attractive to the conservative investor. After all, you're buying bonds, which are very safe, and you're getting diversification at the same time, aren't you? Well, yes and no. You do get a certain element of diversification in a bond fund; that is, the fund at any given moment owns many bonds instead of just one issue. But you're not really *buying* bonds in the sense that you will purchase a bond and then hold it to maturity, collecting periodic interest payments all the while. Instead, a bond fund *trades* bonds, striving all the time to maximize both its interest income and, by selling appreciated bonds, its capital gains. If that's what you want, fine. But if what you want is a money manager who tries to produce the maximum capital gains for you, why not go with a stock fund? If you want the safety that is implied by the term "bond," don't buy a bond fund, buy a bond.

Investors in one of Piper Jaffray's bond funds learned the hard way about what can happen even when you think you are invested in a conservative bond fund. The fund had been posting very impressive returns, and since it was a "government bond fund," it looked especially attractive. Imagine getting the safety of government bonds along with a spectacular return. It seemed almost too good to be true—and it was. The manager of the fund had been using derivatives to make speculative bets in government bonds on the direction of interest rates. He had been right for three years, and the fund reflected the returns of those correct speculative bets. But then, in the same 1994 downturn that caught the manager of Fidelity's Magellan Fund by surprise, bond prices plunged. At that point the speculative bond bets that the Piper Jaffray manager had made went against him—and his shareholders—with a vengeance. Instead of nice, level income from the fund, shareholders were looking at spectacular losses.

Most bond funds won't shock you that badly. But it's still going to be disconcerting from time to time to see in the financial columns that intermediate-term government bonds are yielding 5.2% while your year-end statement shows your intermediate government bond fund yielding just 4.7%.

Another thing to remember about bond funds is that costs matter more than they do in stock funds. A stock fund's performance stems in large part from the investment manager's ability to pick the right stocks from among many within an investment category. A high-expense stock fund with the right stocks can easily outperform a low-cost fund that holds the wrong stocks. But two bond funds with the same investment objectives are more likely to produce about the same results because bonds of similar maturity and quality tend to perform about the same. Thus, costs are a primary determinant whether the Tweedledee or Tweedledum bond fund produces the best results for investors. And costs can vary widely. One recent survey of government bond funds showed a range from 0.36% for the least expensive to 2.4% for the most expensive; the average was 1.14%.

INDEX FUNDS

Since Vanguard introduced the first indexed mutual fund for individual investors in 1976, the whole field of indexed investing has developed a significant and very happy following. In the interests of full disclosure, we should point out that *Barron's* is dedicated to the proposition that you can beat the market, and *Barron's* will help you do it. Indexed investing is the antithesis, namely the pursuit of average market returns rather than exceptional returns. Why, you ask, would anyone shoot for just average returns when you could have exceptional returns? The answer, we say, is that neither you nor anyone else can predict which "active" managers are going to supply those exceptional returns. Consider that in 1996 nearly 60% of active stock mutual fund managers failed to match the performance of Vanguard's Wilshire 5000 Equity Index, a fund aimed at matching the performance of the broad stock market. In 1995, some 77% of active managers failed to beat it. The question therefore seems to us to be: Why are investors paying 77% of all stock fund managers fat salaries when those investors could get better performance at a lower price?

At the heart of the argument for mutual funds is the issue of costs. Historically, stocks have produced an average annual return of 10.7% before costs. The after-costs return, however, varies depending on what you paid to achieve those returns. The costs of investing can add up to a pretty hefty chunk, exceeding 2% of the assets invested in some cases. Those costs come from a variety of sources, including management fees, brokerage and trading costs, and sales charges (loads). In any event, if costs add up to 2% of the assets under management and those assets return a little over 10% per year, then costs are eating up a total of nearly 20% of your returns. Wow! That's a big number. Now consider the advantage of an index fund, which, if it is properly run, should pay low management expenses, keep transaction costs to a minimum, and never, ever assess a sales charge. All those savings contribute to an overall expense ratio of about 0.3%, nearly seven times lower than the typical actively managed fund. So not only do you keep more of your money invested, but your money also compounds faster over the years.

There are other advantages to index funds, including a tax advantage. Since index funds, by their very nature, do not trade stocks nearly as frequently as most actively managed funds (where turnover can exceed 100% in a year), an investor is likely to incur much lower capital gains taxes, whether short-term or long-term. And money not paid to Uncle Sam is money that keeps on working for you.

Active money managers, trying to justify their salaries and bonuses, often pooh-pooh index funds, arguing that a monkey could run an index fund. But it isn't that simple (and think what that says about the many, many money managers who can't beat an index). To match as closely as possible the performance of a specific index (a fund's return will always fall slightly short of the actual index's performance because even small management fees detract from overall performance), an index fund manager cannot have any excess cash lying around. He must therefore know the most efficient way to put to work the hundreds of thousands of dollars he may receive in any given day. That is often done using computer programs to calculate how much of which stocks must be bought at the end of every trading day. (Funds hardly ever own the exact stocks in the exact proportions that are in the target index.) Conversely, since he has no cash pool from which to pay shareholders who are redeeming, he must know exactly which and how much of each stock to sell to meet redemptions. So while it is cheaper to run an index fund, only the smartest monkeys need apply.

The fact that there is no spare cash lying around is one reason that index funds tend to outperform active managers. After all, if you have $100,000 at work in the broad market and the market rises 10%, you'll have $110,000. But if, as many active money managers do, you have just $90,000 of that $100,000 in the market and $10,000 in cash reserves, a 10% market gain gives you $109,000. Of course, it works the other way, too. In a falling market, the fact that there is no cash cushion will hurt an index fund more than it hurts an actively managed fund holding some portion of its assets in cash.

By far the most popular index fund is Vanguard's 500 Index Portfolio, which seeks to match as closely as possible the performance of the Standard & Poor's 500-stock index. At the end of 1997 it was the second largest stock fund in the United States, behind only Fidelity's Magellan. But Vanguard, the pioneer in indexing, offers many other types of index funds, as do other fund companies. Some of the other index funds are offshoots of the basic 500 Portfolio and include a "value" fund that concentrates on the stocks in the S&P 500 that pay the highest dividends, and a "growth" portfolio that duplicates the performance of the fastest-growing stocks in the S&P 500. Other index funds cover a broader range of stocks, such as the Total Stock Market Portfolio that duplicates the performance of the Wilshire 5000 Equity Index, a barometer that includes all regularly traded U.S. stocks and several international and small-cap indexes. For bond fund aficionados (don't forget we warned you about bond funds), there are even four indexed bond portfolios.

We can make a strong argument that your entire stock portfolio should consist of index funds. But we know that most of you just can't stand the idea of simply matching the market; you want to beat it. Acknowledging that, we recommend that you make index funds a goodly part of your portfolio, say 50%, and then devote the remaining 50% of your money to buying whatever kinds of funds you think will be able to outstrip the average market over the long haul.

EXCHANGE-LISTED INDEX FUNDS

A new wrinkle on the investment scene is exchange-listed index funds. As we write, all of them are at the American Stock Exchange, but we doubt that exclusivity will last.

Exchange-listed funds are really unit investment trusts, which we describe later on, but the distinction isn't important for you. What does make a difference is that you can get into and out of them at any point during the trading day. With mutual funds, you buy in or cash out only at the end of the day, when the net asset value is established. If you place your fund order in the morning, you can only guess what the NAV will be at day's end. Not so with the exchange-listed funds, which you buy and sell just like a stock—knowing from the moment your order is confirmed what you paid or what you received. As with funds, holders of these trust units collect their proportionate share of dividends.

The original exchange-listed funds were based on Standard & Poor's indexes, starting with the 500. They were named Standard & Poor's Depositary Receipts and immediately became known as "Spiders." Next came "Webs," which are unit trusts based on Morgan Stanley Capital International's indexes for nearly two dozen foreign stock markets. The arachnid nomenclature disappeared with the third entry in early 1998: "Diamonds," based on the Dow Jones Industrial Average.

Spiders have become so popular that most days they lead the most-active listings on the Amex. Some Webs are heavily traded, too. Diamonds set a new-product volume record when trading began. This kind of success on Wall Street is sure to inspire more variations on the listed-fund theme. Their popularity seems to stem from the ability of investors to trade these market-exposure vehicles through their regular stock broker rather than dial a whole new number to reach a futures commission merchant (to trade index-based futures) or a mutual fund. And investors can hold these index-related trust shares for as long as they like; they don't have finite life spans as options do.

In short, exchange-listed funds are a worthy consideration if you are looking for indexed investments. The brokerage commission will be an extra cost (compared to a no-load mutual fund), but the management fees are among the lowest in the financial services industry. Meanwhile, keep an eye on this kind of investment; your choices are almost certain to grow in the years ahead.

CHOOSING THE RIGHT FUND

The question remains: How do you choose among the many thousands of mutual funds out there that are all vying for your dollars? Selecting the right fund or funds requires that you know what shape you want your portfolio to take. If, for instance, you are young and are just starting a long-term investment program with a small grubstake and a few hundred dollars each month to invest, your best bet probably would be a fund specializing in small-company growth stocks. Over the long haul the best of those funds provide some of the healthiest returns. But if you are pretty far along in your investment program and think you need to diversify into international investments, then an international stock fund would be among your targets. In any event, by determining the kind or kinds of funds you want to buy, you will have automatically eliminated the vast majority of the nearly 7,000 funds that so mystify other investors.

Once you have narrowed the search to a specific type or types of funds, go through the list and eliminate any fund that charges a sales fee (called a load). What's the point of throwing money away on a sales commission when the same or a better performance will be available from a no-load fund?

Now you can employ screening techniques similar to those used to pick individual stocks. When you examine advertisements for mutual funds, you'll see the warning: "Past performance is not necessarily indicative of future results." Right. But since there isn't much else on which to base your decision, we think the first screen you should use is past performance. We don't mean short-term past performance or even intermediate-term performance. Last quarter's

Figure 5.2 Mutual Fund Performance, 1988-1997

Benchmark performance, in percent, of various types of mutual funds, as tracked by indexes from Lipper Analytical Services.

	1988	1989	1990	1991	1992	1993	1994	1995	1996	1997	Average
A-Rated Bonds	9.19	12.51	6.65	17.47	7.53	11.90	-4.92	19.81	2.60	9.43	9.00
BBB-Rated Bonds	9.22	10.52	6.51	17.24	8.11	12.79	-4.54	20.17	4.12	9.88	9.20
Balanced Stocks & Bonds	11.18	19.70	0.66	25.83	7.46	11.95	-2.05	24.89	13.01	20.05	12.90
Capital Appreciation	12.85	28.30	-7.78	37.56	7.56	15.75	-2.46	31.59	14.95	19.86	15.00
Convertible Securities	12.34	14.36	-4.36	24.07	14.41	14.84	-3.65	21.07	14.64	16.91	12.09
Equity Income	17.06	22.64	-5.11	26.68	9.74	14.84	-0.92	29.83	17.89	27.51	15.45
General US Govt. Bonds	6.66	12.41	8.02	14.63	6.10	8.32	-4.74	16.94	2.01	8.81	7.75
Global	14.59	22.12	-9.23	20.30	0.07	32.76	-2.20	14.60	16.25	14.01	11.67
Gold	-18.77	33.48	-24.27	-0.61	-19.10	87.02	-5.97	-3.91	4.74	-43.92	-4.14
Growth & Income	18.35	23.73	-5.99	27.75	9.63	14.62	-0.41	31.14	20.69	26.96	16.03
Growth	14.13	27.47	-5.41	36.33	7.63	11.98	-1.57	32.65	17.48	28.08	16.08
High-Yield Bonds	13.57	-2.77	-11.12	40.22	18.36	19.84	-3.68	17.38	12.66	12.91	10.88
International	15.90	22.32	-12.37	13.17	-4.28	39.18	-0.74	10.02	14.43	7.27	9.64
Money Market	7.21	8.95	7.93	5.83	3.45	2.72	3.74	5.53	4.95	4.71	5.48
Science & Technology	8.12	27.84	-7.23	45.00	9.78	21.85	9.35	38.55	16.91	7.75	16.85
Small-Cap Stocks	20.34	21.06	-13.78	48.53	11.18	16.93	-0.48	31.62	14.37	15.05	15.38

number one fund in whatever category you're examining could be a serious long-term loser. Even the best performing funds have a bad quarter or a bad year over the long run. Five-year performance data are more reassuring, but they, too, can be misleading, especially if the fund manager responsible for it has since departed. Ten-year performance data are the best measure of a fund's ability to weather the ups and downs of market cycles and the ins and outs of investment styles. But ten-year data won't always be available, especially considering that nearly half of all mutual funds in existence today have been created in the past four years. Should you rule out all the new funds without a ten-year history? Not necessarily. If a fund has a strong performance over a period of two or more years, you might consider it. Just keep in mind that through the end of 1997 there hadn't been a prolonged downturn in the market for more than a decade. If you choose one of the upstart new funds, you might find yourself regretting the decision in the midst of the next bear market. You can review *Barron's* quarterly mutual fund report to identify the funds with the overall best and worst performance for the past quarter, year, 5 years, 10 years, and 15 years. But you'll still have to do your own research to pinpoint the best performers in the category of your choice.

Once you have compiled a list of a half dozen or so individual funds that could potentially meet your specific investment needs, the next step is to figure out which ones do best in bad times. Because there haven't been many bad times in the market for five or six years, picking a period to measure isn't easy. The worst performance year recently was in 1994 when the market basically moved sideways for a year. If the funds you've picked were around then, it's worth noting how they fared. Were they significantly worse than whatever benchmark is appropriate? When comparing funds, you want the one that held up best in bad times. That won't necessarily mean that the fund didn't post negative returns for a quarter or even a year, only that its returns weren't as bad as other funds with comparable investment objectives. For most big growth funds the Dow Jones Industrial Average or Standard & Poor's 500-stock index are useful benchmarks for overall comparison. The Wilshire 5000 is a good broad market index, and the Russell 2000 is considered a benchmark for small-capitalization funds. Take the best-performing funds from this list and move on to the next step: checking out the managers.

In many cases the performance of smaller funds is dependent almost solely on the manager of the fund. In that sense the manager *is* the fund rather than the administrative apparatus that processes your paperwork. You are therefore buying his or her skill at managing a portfolio of investments. If your manager has been running the fund you're interested in for the past 10 years, you're in luck. Presumably he has been able to manage the portfolio to achieve superior results in good times and bad. Don't make the mistake of comparing one manager's 10-year record with that of a fund manager who has been in business during the spectacular bull market of the last few years. The manager of the older fund will have the benefit of tempering and experience that the young hotshot lacks, which can be an important factor in long-term performance. If a fund you're considering has changed managers in the past year or so, we advise that you stay clear. He or she may be great, but without a track record you'll be taking a gamble. Keep an eye on the fund as a potential future investment but let somebody else learn just how good the manager is before you commit your money.

After Fidelity's unfortunate experience with Jeffrey Vinik, there has been an effort among some of the larger fund companies to de-emphasize single managers. One reason is that a sort of cult has grown around some fund managers, making the individuals the financial equivalent of rock stars. If a fund company lost such a manager, fans could be expected to follow him or her to a new fund. Instead, the big fund companies now try to sell the *team* that runs a fund, including the research staff that provides the analyses that guide the fund manager's decisions. But don't let them fool you. A good stock picker is a good stock picker, and the best will be good with or without big staff support. There aren't many, which is why we argue strongly in favor of index funds, but if you find one that influences you to buy a certain fund, stick with that person. If the person leaves to go to another fund, go with him or her (to the extent that you don't incur huge capital gains making transfers).

While you are looking at funds, you inevitably will find a few that look pretty attractive but that may not yet be well established enough to have a reassuring track record. If you're really serious about using mutual funds as the core of your investment portfolio, it isn't a bad idea to establish a "shadow" fund portfolio consisting of the runners-up to the ones you actually put money into. Monitor the shadow portfolio along with your real one. You will be able to keep closer tabs on your real managers' performances against what probably is their toughest competitor. If one of your chosen managers leaves or falls down on the job, your shadow funds comprise a ready-made list of alternative homes for your money. If a shadow portfolio isn't your style, you should at least keep the fund managers you choose under review to make sure that they maintain their batting averages and, more important, that they don't leave your funds for greener pastures.

Mutual funds are well suited to the dollar cost averaging approach to investing. You can even arrange for many mutual funds to deduct your periodic investment directly from your checking or savings account. As we discussed earlier, dollar cost averaging is a good way for individuals who don't have substantial lump sums to invest to get into the market. It's also good for those conservative investors with large sums ready to invest but who want to get wet slowly. Studies have shown, though, that parceling out a lump sum from a conservative investment, like a money fund, into a more risky investment, such as a foreign stock fund, produces lower overall returns than if you just invest the whole amount on the spot. We think the best approach is the one that is most comfortable for you. But if you do elect to invest a lump sum, be careful of the timing. Mutual funds distribute capital gains and other income to their shareholders at more or less regular intervals and at least each December before the tax year ends. Investors, even those who invested for the first time only a few days earlier, must report these payouts on their tax returns. These tax bills can be unexpectedly hefty, and they sharply reduce your return on the fund; by coming so soon after you get in, such taxes in effect amount to a fast loss on your capital. If you are thinking of investing in the fourth quarter of the year, you should call the fund to get an idea of the "record" date of the payout and how much it will be. If it's substantial, just hold off until after the record date.

MULTIFUND INVESTING— A MUTUAL FUND PORTFOLIO

You need not use mutual funds only as a vehicle to start an investment program or to handle just a portion of your port-folio. Your entire investment program can be built on mutu-al funds, ranging from short-term money market funds where you park investable funds to a full range of stock, bond, and global funds that provide the maximum possible diversity. How many funds are enough? It depends on how complex and thoroughly diversified you want your portfolio to be. But we think you could profit handsomely from a portfolio of just four funds while keeping risks within tolerable limits for most investors. More recently, as the investing public has become enamored of funds, a better question might be: How many funds are too many? Having more than 20 funds strikes us as overkill, but the real answer to the question is whether you have time to adequately monitor and adjust whatever number of funds you own. If the answer is no, then you have too many.

At the core of a minimal mutual fund portfolio would be one or more domestic stock funds: an index fund based on the S&P 500 or the Dow Jones Industrial Average is a good, cheap anchor for everything else, perhaps supplemented by an aggressive, small-cap growth fund for the adventurous investor or a more conservative growth and income or equity income fund for those who would rather reduce the volatility of their portfolio. With the domestic side taken care of, at least one international fund would be useful. A money market fund to serve as the parking place for funds before they are invested rounds out the basic no-hassle, low-cost approach to fund investing.

You doubtlessly noticed that there aren't any bond funds in our basic brew. We'll say it again: Bond funds are much riskier than bonds. If you don't mind the risk, buy stock funds. If you don't want the risk, buy bonds, not bond funds.

The basic portfolio that we just described will provide ample diversification for just about any investor. What's more, a portfolio of five or six mutual funds will be considerably easier to monitor than one consisting of a dozen or more individual stocks and bonds. At worst, if you really don't like the investing process, such a portfolio could almost run itself for a few years. But we prefer to check our portfolios, no matter how simple, at least once a month. That way we are alert to any problems that might be developing. If you think one of your funds is getting into trouble—maybe it's lagging the appropriate index or falling behind competitor funds—you can take steps to fix the situation before you've fallen too far behind. Just be sure the fund really is in trouble and not just undergoing a slow period. Switching funds frequently to chase the best quarterly performance is a waste of money, time, and effort.

Be wary of second-guessing yourself into a too-big fund portfolio. If you have the courage of your convictions, you will decide early on that you don't mind taking risks and will put your money into volatile funds. Or you will decide that you really don't like risk and will go with conservative funds. Whatever your decision, stick with it. Don't try to hedge your bets by buying some risky funds and some safe funds, then adding to that the best performers of the last few quarters until you have some huge hodgepodge portfolio. The end result of that will be average or below-average performance. You would be better off just putting your money in a single broad-based index fund and forgetting about it.

VARIABLE ANNUITIES

There is one last way you can own mutual funds, and it allows you to enjoy a tax benefit to boot. Variable annuities are products sold by insurance companies, brokerage firms, and banks that basically take the place of the old Individual Retirement Accounts for those of us who no longer qualify for IRAs. You put up a lump sum of money that is invested in your choices of funds run by the offering institution. Like the old IRAs, your dividends and capital gains aren't taxed until you withdraw those funds, perhaps years later. As an additional bonus, the contracts for variable annuities provide that if you die, your heirs will receive at least the amount you invested in the annuity, regardless of the performance of the investments you selected.

But, of course, there are some not-so-favorable characteristics of variable annuities. First, the funds offered by the firms that sell annuities typically aren't the ones you would buy if you were doing your own picking. Suffice it to say, they aren't the stellar performers in the mutual fund universe. Indeed, a considerable number do poorly enough that you'd be better off investing in a taxable fund with a better record. Next are the high fees. The companies selling these things

216 BARRON'S GUIDE TO MAKING INVESTMENT DECISIONS

don't do it as a kindness; they do it to make money. The fees they charge go a long way toward negating the tax advantages offered by variable annuities. That's especially true if you are among the many conservative investors who hate paying taxes but hate taking risks, too. You would be amazed at the number of people who buy a variable annuity to avoid taxes, invest their funds in a money market account, and basically wind up paying more in fees than they make in income.

Our advice is to steer clear of variable annuities. If you insist on buying one, study the performance of the funds offered by the firms selling annuities, just as you study any mutual fund purchase. Look for funds that have at least a three-year performance record. Assume you are buying the fund to make money, not just avoid taxes. Once you assemble a list of annuities with decently performing funds, select the one with the lowest fee.

WHEN FUNDS AREN'T APPROPRIATE

There are some types of funds that you probably will want to avoid. One is the sector fund, which invests in a single industry. Presumably, you are paying the managers of your funds to do a measure of asset allocation for you. When you buy a sector fund, you have taken on a big part of the asset allocation decision and left that handsomely rewarded manager only the problem of picking some stocks. If you know enough about economic conditions in a specific industry, you can probably do your own stock picking. If you don't, then you have no business buying the sector fund in the first place.

Many investors are attracted to tax-free municipal bond funds. If you hate paying taxes that badly, then own municipal bonds, not a muni-bond fund. Even though capital gains taxes are lower than ordinary income taxes, you will still be sending Uncle Sam a larger-than-you-think share of investment gains if you invest in a muni-bond fund. As we pointed out earlier, bond fund managers treat bonds as tradable instruments, not buy-and-hold investments. Your bond fund manager is going to be doing some buying and selling that will produce capital gains within the portfolio—those are gains on which you are going to be taxed. It's better just to own the bonds outright. You, not the fund manager, can decide whether you want to take capital gains at all and, if so, when the best time is from your personal tax standpoint.

THE MENU, PLEASE

Broadly speaking, the people who monitor mutual fund results divide them into approximately the same categories. For obvious reasons we'll use the categories that appear quarterly in *Barron's* mutual fund review. The categories are those used by Lipper Analytical Services, which assigns individual funds to the categories based on both the language in the fund's prospectus and the actual investment practices of the fund. The categories are presented in broader groups that identify the overall investment approach. It's a long list, but it provides you with an overview of the best array of funds from which you can choose.

Debt and Equity Funds

BALANCED: Goal is preserving principal; fund maintains a 60/40 or so ratio of stocks to bonds.

Balanced Target: Invests to provide a guaranteed return of principal at maturity. Some assets are in zero-coupon Treasury bonds, the remainder in long-term growth stocks.

Canadian: Invests primarily in securities traded in Canadian markets.

Capital Appreciation: Seeks maximum capital appreciation through strategies such as 100% or more portfolio turnover, leveraging, and purchasing unregistered securities or options. The fund may also take large cash positions.

China: Concentrates on companies whose primary trading markets or operations are concentrated in the China region.

Convertibles: Invests primarily in convertible bonds and preferred stock.

Dual-Purpose Capital: Closed-end fund that seeks capital appreciation, capital preservation, and income. These shares incur no fees, receive no income, and bear all capital gains and losses.

Dual-Purpose Income: See Dual-Purpose Capital. Unlike capital shares, these have a priority on redemption at NAV, bear all expenses, and receive all net investment income.

Emerging Markets: Puts at least 65% of assets in equities of emerging markets.

Emerging-Markets Debt: Has at least 65% of assets in emerging-markets debt.

ENVIRONMENT: Invests at least 65% of assets in companies contributing to cleaner and healthier environment, such as waste-management outfits.

EQUITY INCOME: Normally has over 60% of assets in equities; seeks high income.

EUROPEAN: Focuses on one or more European stock markets.

FINANCIAL SERVICES: Invests 65% of assets in stocks of financial service companies, including banks, insurers, and securities firms.

FIXED INCOME: Typically has more than 75% of assets in fixed-income securities, such as bonds, preferred stocks, and money-market instruments.

FLEXIBLE: Aims for high total return by allocating its portfolio among a wide range of asset classes.

GLOBAL: At least 25% of its portfolio is in non-U.S. securities.

GLOBAL FLEXIBLE: Similar to flexible; invests at least 25% of assets in securities traded outside the United States.

GLOBAL SMALL CAP: Has at least 25% of its assets outside the United States; limits 65% of its holdings on the basis of market cap.

GOLD: Has at least 65% of its assets in gold mining or gold-oriented shares, gold coins, or bullion.

GROWTH: Invests in companies whose long-term earnings it expects to grow faster than those of the stocks in the major market indexes.

GROWTH AND INCOME: Seeks earnings growth as well as dividend income.

HEALTH/BIOTECH: Has 65% of its portfolio in health care, medical, and biotech companies.

INCOME: Seeks high current income through stocks, bonds, and money-market instruments; has a maximum equity exposure of 60% and maximum fixed-income exposure of 75%.

INTERNATIONAL: Invests in securities traded primarily outside the United States.

INTERNATIONAL INCOME: Invests in non-U.S. debt.

INTERNATIONAL SMALL CAP: Invests in non-U.S. companies with market caps below $1 billion.

JAPANESE: Focuses on securities traded in Tokyo.

LATIN AMERICA: Invests primarily in securities in Mexico, Brazil, Chile, and other Latin American countries.

MICRO CAP: Invests in companies with market caps of less than $300 million at time of purchase.

MID CAP: Owns companies with market caps below $5 billion.

MULTISECTOR INCOME: Allocates assets among several fixed-income sectors, including U.S. government, foreign, and below-investment-grade paper; no more than 65% in one sector.

NATURAL RESOURCE: Usually has over 65% of its equity holdings in natural-resource stocks.

PACIFIC REGION: Concentrates on stocks trading in one or more of the Pacific Basin markets.

PACIFIC EX-JAPAN: Concentrates on stocks trading in the Pacific Region but does not invest in Japan.

REAL ESTATE: Puts 65% of its assets into real estate securities.

S&P 500-STOCK INDEX: Designed to replicate the performance of the Standard & Poor's 500-stock index on a reinvested basis; passively managed, with adviser fee no higher than 0.5%.

SCIENCE AND TECHNOLOGY: Has 65% of assets in science and technology stocks.

SMALL CAP GROWTH: Limits investment to companies on basis of size.

SPECIALTY: Limits its investments to a specific industry, such as retailing, transportation, or paper, or falls outside other classifications.

TELECOMMUNICATIONS: Has at least 65% of assets in companies developing, making, or selling telecommunications services or equipment.

UTILITY: Utilities comprise 65% of its equities.

World Income: May own common and preferred, but invests primarily in U.S. and foreign debt.

Municipal Bond Funds

General Muni: Puts at least 65% of its assets in municipal bonds carrying the top four credit ratings.

Insured Muni: At least 65% of its holdings have been insured for timely payment of interest.

Intermediate Muni: Its tax-exempt debt holdings have an average maturity of 5 to 10 years.

High-Yield Muni: Can put 50%-plus of assets in low-rated credits.

Short-Intermediate Muni: Invests in tax-exempt debt maturing, on average, in five years.

Short Muni: Invests in munis with average maturities of less than three years.

Single-State Muni: Limits investments to securities exempt from taxation in a particular state.

SUGGESTED READING

With so many new funds coming on the market in recent years, it is difficult to keep up with the ever-expanding array of possibilities. But don't feel overwhelmed to the point you feel obligated to shell out money for advisory services and the like. There are lots of purported experts trying to capital-ize on the popularity of mutual funds by offering (for a price, of course) to guide you through the maze. Sample as much as you can in your local library before spending money that you could be investing.

For the dedicated mutual fund enthusiast who wants to go beyond the mutual fund coverage and tables provided in *Barron's* and other periodicals, we recommend investigat-ing the services offered by Morningstar. It has several publi-cations (including material available on the web and as soft-ware) and has devised an excellent format for presenting fund information. Beware, though: Subscriptions for all this neat stuff are costly and may be overkill. If you want more information, contact Morningstar at 225 West Wacker Drive, Suite 400, Chicago, Illinois 60606. The toll-free line is 800-735-0700.

If you're looking for more information about how mutual funds work (or should work, at least), there is a clas-sic by John Bogle, the founder of Vanguard: *Bogle on Mutual Funds* (Irwin, 1993). More straightforward dope on funds can be found in *Mutual Funds for Dummies* by Eric Tyson (IDG Books, 1995) and in *Mutual Fund Mastery* by Kurt Brouwer and Stephen Janachowski (Random House, 1997).

There are jillions of newsletters entirely or partly devoted to mutual funds. None of them is essential, and some may even be detrimental if you fool yourself into thinking that subscribing to one or more of them fulfills your obliga-tion to do your homework. Some fund families are big enough that newsletters specialize in them. For example, *Fidelity Insights* is an independent newsletter that analyzes the ins and outs and ups and downs of the various funds sponsored by Fidelity Investments.

6 Warm, Fuzzy Investing

(with Your Very Own Money Manager)

"We've had lunch and we've finished our martinis.
Time to go pick some more stocks."

Mutual funds are a good way to cut down on the time and effort involved in running an investment portfolio. But money managers are the best way. They are expensive, but the cost is well worth it if the alternative is a cobbled-together portfolio done haphazardly and never adjusted because you don't have the time or interest.

A growing number of fee-based advisers are changing the way many Americans, particularly those outside big cities, manage their money. As small investors become more reliant on the stock market—and bewildered by the huge array of options—the advisers are ready to offer a large menu of mutual funds, securities, and other financial products. With the help of technology, they open offices in remote areas and grow to manage hundreds of accounts.

Many of these advisers are former stockbrokers, accountants, bank officers, and insurance agents. They do much of the same work as traditional financial planners, but they also invest their clients' money, typically in no-load mutual funds. They usually charge an annual fee based on the amount of money under their management. Planners, by contrast, generally come up with financial game plans for clients, typically for a onetime fee; their clients must handle the actual investing.

Largely unregulated, the fee-based advisers are tapping into a huge market of consumers who are eager to invest in equities—often after receiving large sums through inheritances or retirement plans. The clients frequently don't have the time to do their own research, and they distrust the hard sell of brokers dependent on commissions. What they want are reliable returns layered with personal service.

Between 1992 and 1996, the number of fee-based advisers jumped 13%, to 10,650, according to Cerulli Associates, a Cambridge, Massachusetts, research firm. Due in part to the surging market, their assets under control were $370 billion in 1996, up 48% from 1995, and triple the assets of 1992. Most firms manage less than $50 million, but some have more than $250 million.

If you decide you need or want professional management, be sure you get the best you can find—and afford. There are thousands of purported "money managers" and "financial advisers" out there. Many of them either don't know what they are doing or use their position to steer unwary clients into costly but not particularly lucrative investments that put more money into the adviser's pocket than into the investor's.

If someone soliciting your business tells you he is a "registered investment adviser," don't be impressed. Anyone who receives a fee for providing investment advice to 15 or more individual clients must be registered with the Securities and Exchange Commission, but the registration is amazingly simple to obtain and requires no educational background or any demonstration of proficiency in evaluating investment vehicles. The SEC oversees about 22,500 advisers—from huge mutual fund companies to mom-and-pop outfits—and the agency says it typically concentrates enforcement efforts on the largest 100 firms. Most states require investment

Do You Enjoy Science Fiction?
Then Join Us At
Philcon® 2008

November 21-23, 2008 • Fri 5:00 pm–Sun 4:00 pm
Crowne Plaza Hotel, Cherry Hill NJ
2349 W. Marlton Pike (Rte. 70)• Free parking • Accessible by public transit

Principal Speaker: **Tim Powers**
Multiple-award-winning novelist
Guest Artist: **John Picacio**
Multiple-award-winning artist, 2008 Hugo & Locus Awards nominee
Special Guest: **Scott Christian Sava**
Webcomic creator of *The Dreamland Chronicles*, etc.

Philcon is the annual Philadelphia Conference on Science Fiction & Fantasy (SF&F), first held in 1936.

At Philcon, you can:
Meet about 1,000 other people who enjoy SF&F • Learn & have fun • Meet hundreds of SF&F professionals • Participate in activities for the entire family

And enjoy:
Panels on science fiction, fantasy, science & more with authors, artists, editors, scientists & other experts • Large art show • Movie & anime screenings • Vendors • Costuming & masquerade performances • Gaming • Singing SF&F songs • Writers' contest • Autographs (at no extra charge) • Music • *Surprises* • and more…

Early registration rates available. For latest info & details, see:
www.philcon.org

advisers to register with them but don't mandate any experience or skill level. And investment advisers don't have to disclose their returns. They do have to report to the SEC whether they receive commissions. That information is public record, but the advisers don't have to tell their clients. While it is illegal for advisers to misrepresent how they receive their income, the SEC says it has never taken disciplinary action against a fee-based adviser who lies about collecting commissions.

In short, being a registered investment adviser means nothing. At least brokers have to pass a test. Even so, we don't consider them money managers, either; they are salespeople.

In any event, you begin a search for a money manager the same way you search for a mutual fund: by knowing what kind of investor you are and what kind of portfolio you want to have. The trouble is, money managers aren't nearly so easy to evaluate as mutual funds are, so the shopping will be considerably more difficult.

To begin with, most money managers also have minimum account sizes, ranging from $50,000 up to $5 million. If you have less than $100,000 to invest with a manager, you might want to work with mutual funds for a while to build your kitty to the size at which you can engage a money management firm.

If you have your heart set on a money manager despite your portfolio being a few dollars short, you could do worse than inquire at your bank. The booming demand for financial advice—particularly from people who charge flat fees instead of commissions—is prompting some banks and fee-based financial advisers to join forces. The advisory firms are teaching small banks how to create and run asset-management divisions. In return, banks are outsourcing money management duties to the advisers. What this arrangement means for investors is that through some banks they can now get the services of professional money managers even though their portfolios don't meet the managers' minimums. For example, one advisory firm that normally accepts no accounts smaller than $1 million takes them at half that amount through the bank with which it has this kind of relationship.

The fees in these arrangements aren't out of line, thanks to the increasing competition among money managers to gather assets, but they aren't *de minimus,* either. In one bank-manager relationship, in which the manager parcels assets among mutual funds rather than individual securities, a typical client is charged a fee of 1.5% annually.

Not to be outdone, brokerage firms also have geared up to work directly with advisers. Previously, advisers dealt with mutual fund companies separately, and customers received a barrage of statements. But in 1987, Charles Schwab & Co. developed software that enabled advisers to keep their assets at Schwab, then use the discount broker to trade stocks or many no-load mutual funds and produce consolidated statements. Schwab charges the fund companies to hold their funds, and it charges advisers' customers transaction fees for trading securities and some funds. Fidelity Investments and other discount brokers now offer similar services, as do the Vanguard Group and Dreyfus Corp.

Finally, Lockwood Financial Group of Malvern, Pennsylvania, has introduced a program that provides access to more than 50 institutional money managers with a range of investment styles and niches, including growth, value, and international. Lockwood's "money-manager supermarket" is geared to independent advisers, a group that includes financial planners, accountants, attorneys, brokers, and insurance agents. Currently, independent advisers don't have any simple way to line up clients with money managers who can then put together a separate portfolio of securities.

One appeal to investors is that the fees are comparable to adviser programs at Schwab and Fidelity—and they decline as accounts grow larger. The minimum investment is $100,000 for each separately managed account. Separate accounts have tax advantages over mutual funds, in which all investors' money is mingled. With a separately managed account, you own the securities, so you pay only for the gains you realize. When you buy into a mutual fund, you might get stuck paying capital gains taxes on "profits" that occurred before you joined the party. Also, investors with individual-stock ownership can sell portions of their portfolio to offset other gains and losses they incur during the year. That isn't as easy to do with mutual funds.

As with mutual funds, past performance doesn't guarantee future results but nonetheless is the best place to begin evaluating money managers. There is a complication, however. Money managers' results are seldom made public, as are mutual fund results, so there is little outside documentation about their performance. Basically, you are going to have to rely on the money management firm to tell you the truth about how it has done over the past several years. Clearly, they are going to put their performance in the best possible light. But they do have to tell you how they calculated their performance data, so you aren't completely at their mercy. You'll want to see annual and quarterly results going back ten years if possible, and they should be results *after* fees and brokerage commissions. The results should also reflect accounts of approximately the same size as yours invested in the manner in which you wish to invest. Don't trust results based on "model" accounts that don't really exist anywhere but in a computer spreadsheet.

Once you have obtained a money manager's results that you feel you can trust, compare his or her performance to an appropriate benchmark, such as the S&P 500, or to the performance of mutual funds with similar investment goals. Be particularly wary of managers who outperform the averages by large amounts, especially in short periods. They may be taking a lot more risk to get those returns than you would like. It would be better to stick with the manager who gives investors a small but consistent edge over the indexes year in and year out. You also want to know if a manager attempts to time the market or uses essentially a buy-and-hold approach in which your money is nearly always fully invested in the assets you want to own. Timing is by far the riskier approach, although it can produce impressive short-term gains.

Certainly you will want to determine at the outset how diversified your portfolio will be. If you are looking for a money manager who invests exclusively in stocks, be sure they are the kind you would want to own if you were managing your own portfolio. If you are looking for a manager who will spread the risks around more broadly, try to find one with some international expertise because some of the best returns are made abroad. Many small money-management firms don't have the qualifications or ability to engage in foreign investing.

Finally, you pay a premium for personalized money management, so be sure you get your money's worth. Can you pick up the phone and talk to the person directing your account, or will you be foisted off to a marketing person? If a firm tries to discourage you from talking to the investment professionals running your account, find another firm.

Once you have narrowed your search to a few firms, it's time to weigh fees. Most money managers charge a management fee that is based on the assets under management. That is appropriate because if the manager is successful, the asset base will grow and so will his compensation. Management fees range from 0.5% to 3% of assets annually, but you should be able to find a good manager for 2% or less. The costs don't stop with management fees, however. You also will have to bear transaction costs, which of course depend on how often your manager trades, but they will seldom exceed 1% annually. And there might be an incentive fee in which you pay more if your manager does especially well. The more of the total fees you can get into the incentive category, the better off you'll be.

THE WRAP ACCOUNT

The wrap account is simply another variation of matching individual investors with the professionals, whether in mutual funds or separate portfolios, but they have become so popular that they deserve their own section in this chapter. At the end of 1996, wrap-fee programs held $139.4 billion in assets, up 34% from 1995, according to Cerulli Associates. Although more than 60 firms sponsor wrap programs, just three—Smith Barney Inc., a unit of Travelers Group Inc.; Merrill Lynch & Co.; and Morgan Stanley Dean Witter Co.—control more than two-thirds of the market. Fidelity Investments, the Boston mutual fund giant, is also a big player.

Wrap accounts seem like a dream come true, largely because they are marketed that way. In a wrap account a broker matches you with one or more professional money managers who will more or less tailor a portfolio for you, overseen by your broker. The attraction is that not only do you get professional management without having to ante up the hefty minimums that most money managers require, but also your brokerage commissions and money management charges are "wrapped" into one all-inclusive annual fee. Simplicity sells!

But notice that fee! Typically, a wrap account will cost 3% of assets, more than what you would have to pay to get a good money manager. In addition, hidden fees called "execution costs" can really hammer you. Execution costs include the spreads that managers must deal with when they buy or sell securities. Ordinarily, a money manager shops around to get the best spreads and execution of orders. But when he agrees to participate in a wrap account, the manager often surrenders that privilege, agreeing to funnel all the trades through the sponsoring brokerage firm. Although it doesn't necessarily happen, this lack of transaction choice could sharply increase the manager's costs of trading. Not that he cares; he gets all that new money funneled to him by the brokerage firm and usually is happy to do whatever he's told. Some experts estimate that in a "worst case" situation the execution costs could eat up as much as 10% of a poorly managed portfolio, although 5% would be more likely in a merely bad situation.

When you stop to think about it, wrap accounts seem like glorified mutual funds. Indeed, the Securities and Exchange Commission for years has worried about the fuzzy line between legitimate wrap programs and those that pool investment capital, which is basically what a mutual fund does. A legitimate wrap program offers individually tailored investment advice rather than a "one-size-fits-all" formula. To ensure that wrap programs are customized, the SEC believes clients must be free to put "reasonable restrictions" on their accounts, as long as they don't make too many requests, or make them too often. Excluding individual stocks, stocks of an industry group, or stocks from a specific country generally are considered reasonable restrictions, the SEC says. Wrap-fee clients would be free to veto tobacco company stocks, for instance, but requests that conflict with a sponsor's basic investment philosophy or strategy would be deemed "unreasonable."

If you are considering a wrap account, inquire deeply into the money manager's track record. Brokerage firms' wrap programs aren't tracked by independent analysts the way money managers and mutual funds are. And brokerage firms are shy about publishing performance figures. While potential clients are shown a money manager's profile, the performance numbers included may blend the manager's record of handling money for big institutional clients with the performance of much smaller accounts for individuals. Ask to see performance figures for the money manager that cover wrap accounts *only,* not blends of institutional and individual accounts. Also, be sure the performance numbers factor in the wrap fee, which can make a considerable difference over time.

Here are some other shopping tips:

■ Watch out for wrap accounts that would charge you the same hefty 3% fee on the cash in your portfolio—which usually is parked in a money market fund with its own management fees and expenses. Ask to have that part of your account exempted from the wrap fee.

■ Check the rate of securities turnover in the prospective manager's wrap accounts, because every sale your manager makes affects your annual capital gains taxes. On the other hand, if your manager has low turnover (50% a year or less), ask for a wrap-fee discount so that you don't pay a premium for service you aren't using.

■ Come to think of it, ask for a discount anyway, on general principles.

■ Finally, avoid programs where brokers receive incentives to choose in-house managers or where—worst of all—the broker *is* the manager.

Mutual fund wrap accounts are very similar to money management wraps, but with an extra kicker that could work against you: When you pay a brokerage firm a wrap account fee for setting you up in mutual funds, every fund the broker puts you into automatically becomes a "load" fund, even those that normally are no-load funds. If your broker bows to temptation, he will wind up putting you in funds that pay him a fee for directing new clients to them. The broker cashes in while you are saddled with fees that could range as high as 3%, and that's before the mutual fund's fees are added on.

Before you get involved in a mutual fund wrap account, find out who the adviser is and what his or her qualifications are. Some mutual fund wrap accounts are run by brokers with no particular skill in managing money. Instead, they subscribe to services that periodically provide them with recommended asset allocation schemes. At best, you would be paying a handsome fee for very little service; at worst, such brokers could put you in bad funds or move you from one fund to another more frequently than is warranted.

No doubt about it, wrap accounts are popular with the investing public. But to avoid being stung, you must—all together, now—do your homework. If you are just looking for some advice on how to spread your investments among different funds, most of the big mutual fund firms will provide that service free or at a small charge. Our last word on wrap accounts is "Danger: Use with Caution."

UNIT INVESTMENT TRUSTS

If you are particularly interested in bonds as an investment vehicle, there is yet one more way to have your portfolio professionally managed, or at least professionally assembled: a unit investment trust. UITs are nothing more than a pool of bonds in which investors buy shares. The trust is formed, sells its shares, and then continues to throw off periodic income to its shareholders until the bonds mature. You pay an up-front fee to get into a unit trust, but that fee tends to be lower than it would be for a mutual fund. Unit trusts have some of the hallmarks of a mutual fund in that you and other investors pool your money to be able to obtain diversification. But unlike an actively managed mutual fund, a unit trust tends to have minimal management requirements. Managers will, if necessary, sell bonds of a company that is getting into trouble, and they will handle the paperwork if a bond is called by its issuer. Otherwise, there isn't any turnover. The advantage of a unit trust is that you know before you decide to buy it exactly which bonds are in it, what their ratings and maturities are, and approximately how much income you will realize. In addition, you can decide when you will receive your income; unit trusts can provide monthly, quarterly, or semi-annual payments. Unit trusts tend to be fairly liquid, so you can get out if you must, but the value of the fund when you sell will be affected by the relative level of interest rates. Unit trusts are often used as vehicles for investing in foreign and high-yield, or junk, bonds. Taken together, unit trusts are an appealing alternative to buying and holding individual bonds for an investor who wants steady income but doesn't want to be bothered with constantly monitoring a portfolio of bonds.

Unit trusts can also hold stocks. Among the more popular are those that hold the five or ten highest-yielding stocks in the Dow Jones Industrial Average, which are nicknamed "the dogs of the Dow." These trusts last for one year, at which point it is time to clean out the kennel and bring in a fresh bunch of "dogs."

The trouble with stock-oriented unit investment trusts is that the lineup of stocks hardly ever changes. With rare exceptions, such as the dogs of the Dow, investors don't like fixed stock portfolios for prolonged periods. They either want portfolios that can change holdings in response to market moves, or they want fixed portfolios they can get into and out of easily. That's why the exchange-listed unit trusts are gaining popularity. They are index-based and can be traded like stocks. We mentioned the main ones in the previous chapter.

7 Investing Globally

"Do you have any tours to the various stock exchanges of the world?"

For years American investors have been quite content to sit comfortably at home. The immense diversity of the U.S. stock and bond markets seemed to offer something for everybody, and there appeared to be little need to deal with markets and investments abroad. If anything, this attitude was reinforced in the mid-1990s when the U.S. market surged by more than 20% annually for three successive years.

While American investors enjoyed insularity, foreign investors were busily exploring one another's markets in an attempt to find a wider mix of investment vehicles than they had at home, as well as to capture the best possible returns in any given circumstance.

Notwithstanding the string of tremendous performance by the U.S. market in the mid-1990s, the returns for the past 20 years have proven the wisdom of the foreign investors. In that period, U.S. stocks, the best performing of all U.S. asset classes, gained an average of 11.6% per year. Foreign stocks in the same period rose an average of 13.9%. American investors are becoming increasingly aware of the appeal of overseas markets and are investing more and more abroad. But the total amount of U.S. capital invested in foreign markets remains minuscule. We urge you to do your part to make that proportion larger.

OVER THERE, OVER THERE

Why should foreign stocks or bonds be any more appealing than U.S. investments? After all, the United States is easily the world's strongest economy. But as we know, economies move in cycles, sometimes growing and sometimes shrinking, or at least slowing. And we learned earlier that a properly diversified portfolio should have investments in assets that do not usually move up and down together. A close look at the growth rates of foreign economies compared to that of the United States reveals that their economies follow their own cycles, pretty much independently of what is happening in the United States. While the U.S. economy is growing, some foreign economies are slumping. And while the U.S. economy is slipping into recession, other foreign economies are recovering from downturns and enjoying robust growth. Because foreign stock and bond markets tend to reflect the changing economic conditions in their home countries, they, too, move in different directions from the U.S. stock and bond markets. Thus, putting a portion of a portfolio abroad increases the total diversification of the portfolio.

Economies also tend to be at different stages of development and thus tend to grow at different average rates. The United States, Great Britain, Germany, France, and Japan are all mature economies growing at comparatively slow rates. But in smaller economies, where demand for capital is still greatest for such basics as highways and telecommunications, growth rates are considerably higher. Investors willing to help finance that growth can be richly rewarded. Of course, financial markets in those countries aren't nearly as developed as our own, but even that can create opportunity for an investor who is willing to search carefully for bargains. The chances of finding such uncommon values are much greater in less sophisticated markets than in the United States where information is disseminated and digested very fast.

RISKS APLENTY

But what about the risks? Make no mistake about it, there are many. That's one reason the relative rewards of investing abroad are so high. We have counseled you repeatedly not to invest in something you don't understand, so it's only fair for us to help you understand the risks of investing abroad. Let's

Figure 7.1 Foreign Investments Become More Alluring

Amounts, both gross and net, that U.S. investors have invested abroad annually, 1980-1997, in billions of dollars.

	Foreign Stocks			Foreign Bonds	
Year	Gross	Net	Year	Gross	Net
1980	$17.9	$2.1	1980	$35.2	$1.0
1981	18.8	0.2	1981	40.6	5.5
1982	15.7	1.3	1982	66.4	6.6
1983	30.3	3.8	1983	76.0	3.1
1984	30.4	1.2	1984	118.8	4.1
1985	45.6	3.9	1985	166.4	3.9
1986	100.2	1.9	1986	337.7	3.7
1987	189.4	-1.1	1987	405.9	7.8
1988	152.7	2.0	1988	444.5	7.4
1989	232.7	13.1	1989	474.5	6.0
1990	254.5	9.2	1990	651.6	22.5
1991	273.2	32.0	1991	675.5	14.8
1992	332.4	32.3	1992	992.1	19.6
1993	554.0	63.3	1993	1729.2	69.5
1994	815.1	47.1	1994	1829.4	20.3
1995	741.4	50.3	1995	1827.5	48.4
1996	976.5	57.9	1996	2281.5	45.2
1997	1477.0	38.6	1997	2989.5	45.8

Source: Securities Industry Association

start with some relatively small risks before dealing with the Mother of All Risks, currency fluctuations.

As we said, many foreign financial markets aren't as sophisticated as our own. One of the things the new international investor first notices on going abroad is the lack of information about both markets and companies. Even Germany, which has developed a reputation for financial responsibility, doesn't have anywhere near the statistical background on its stock market that we have in the United States. Technical analysts accustomed to manipulating all sorts of market data to discern patterns that can guide their investment decisions are appalled by the lack of such information abroad. Further, the stringent financial reporting requirements imposed by our own Securities and Exchange Commission frequently are absent in other countries, as are the detailed accounting procedures that we impose on companies here. The result is that it is easy to underestimate or overestimate the relative value of foreign stocks when comparing them to similar U.S. stocks. Overcoming such risks obviously requires considerable research into the differences in accounting and reporting procedures. Still, using certain analytical techniques that are common in the United States is difficult, if not impossible, abroad.

We have already seen that it isn't always easy to determine what your transaction costs are in the U.S. markets. It can be doubly difficult abroad, and the costs can amount to a substantial portion of a portfolio. For example, in some countries the commission charged by a broker is fully negotiable. What you pay for a transaction depends on your ability to bargain with the broker. Beyond that, other countries impose various taxes and fees that won't be familiar to the U.S. investor. And while we generally assume that a transaction will be settled in a matter of minutes, hours, or, at worst, a few days, settlement times abroad can run into months. Some foreign markets are also relatively inactive. Buying and selling shares isn't easy, and the spreads between bid and ask prices can be painfully large.

If you aren't discouraged enough at this point, let's get into the biggest risk of all facing U.S. investors abroad: *currency risk*. Stocks or bonds bought in other countries are usually purchased in the local currency. That means an American investor has to convert his dollars into the appropriate currency before making an investment. When he wants to get out of that investment he must translate the local currency received in the sale transaction back into dollars. The trouble is that the rates of exchanging the value of one currency for another fluctuate constantly and somewhat unpredictably. When you convert your dollars into a foreign currency prior to making an investment abroad, you will receive a specific amount of that currency for each dollar converted. A few weeks, months, or years later when you close out that investment and exchange the proceeds for dollars, you won't necessarily receive dollars in the same ratio that you originally exchanged them. If the values of the dollar and the foreign currency have moved sufficiently against you, the currency translation process could effectively wipe out what would otherwise have been a handsome return. Of course, currency fluctuations can work in your favor, too, turning an otherwise mediocre profit or even a loss into a tidy gain in dollars. Here are some examples of how the process works:

Suppose you want to invest $50,000 in a German stock selling for 20 marks a share. Further assume that on the day you want to make that investment the dollar is valued at 1.800 marks. First, you must convert dollars to marks. That exchange gives you 90,000 marks ($50,000 times 1.80 marks). That means you can buy 4,500 shares of the German company. You hold the stock for three years, and over that period it rises to 30 marks a share, an impressive 50% gain. When you sell it, you will receive 135,000 marks. Now you must convert the marks back to dollars. Let's say that during the three-year period you held your investment, the mark weakened, or fell, against the dollar, and today the dollar is worth 2.8 marks instead of 1.8. (Wait a minute, you say. That looks like the mark went up. Ah, but the more marks a dollar can purchase means a weaker mark and a stronger dollar. Look at it the other way: It now takes 2.8 marks to buy one U.S. dollar instead of 1.8. This counterintuitive combination of language and numbers confuses everybody except professional currency traders, but they aren't allowed to cross the street by themselves. Now, back to our example.) When your 135,000 marks is turned into dollars, you'll get $48,214—a modest loss in dollars for what was a 50% gain in marks. Turn the situation around and assume that the mark strengthened against the dollar, to 1.4 marks per dollar. Your 135,000 marks now convert to $96,429, a 93% dollar gain on an investment that increased 50% in marks.

As you can see, currency fluctuations can play havoc with international investors. Some professionals try to use it to their advantage, attempting to pull off a "triple whammy" by buying a cheap stock or bond in a currency that they hope will strengthen against the dollar. If they are successful, they reap not only the capital appreciation as the stock or bond price rises, along with the income from the stock's dividend or bond's income, but also an extra "kicker" from the appreciating currency. Other international money managers, fearful that the currency moves will go against them, try to negate the effect of currency changes by hedging. That is, they use the futures and options markets (or an arcane process controlled by big banks called the interbank forward market) to lock in a certain exchange rate. They argue that if you want to speculate in currency movements, there are more "pure" ways to do that than by taking the extra risk of buying stocks and bonds. They prefer to eliminate currency risk and concentrate on what they know best: the identification of good stocks and bonds to own. But hedging costs money, which lowers the ultimate return from foreign investing. Some really long-range investors simply ignore currency fluctuations, figuring that in the long run the ups and downs cancel each other out.

As we write, the European Monetary Union appears assured to begin on January 1, 1999. Eleven countries—including France, Germany, and Italy, but not Great Britain—will adopt the Euro as their common currency. For investors, it amounts to a big reduction in currency risk. Among auto stocks alone, for example, Renault in France, Volkswagen in Germany, and Fiat in Italy, all will have the same currency risk. If EMU succeeds, more countries will join in the future, easing the currency-risk factor even further.

APPROACHES TO GLOBAL INVESTING

So what's an investor to do about investing abroad? Let's start with how much of your portfolio ought to be in non-U.S. investments. The United States stock and bond markets represent roughly 50% of the total value of all the world's stocks and bonds. Some of the leading lights in investment theory thus conclude that to be truly diversified an investor should be holding about half of his or her portfolio in U.S. assets. The remaining 50%, according to these wizards, should be distributed around the world in various markets in relation to their weighting within the global economy. While we know people who follow this logic, we believe your comfort level should dictate how much you invest overseas. Start with 10%, and if you find it doesn't give you anxiety attacks, gradually boost the proportion to 20% or 25%. At that level you'll have enough exposure to foreign markets to benefit from the diversification effects—provided you stick with it for at least five years—but not so much that you'll miss opportunities in the country with the world's biggest stock market, which happens to be where you live.

As for the investments themselves, the choices, frankly, are few. It isn't practical for most individual investors to attempt to buy stocks in foreign markets. Lack of knowledge is usually the biggest barrier. It's difficult enough for a professional investor to get the necessary details even when his firm has an office in the country he is investing in. The individual doesn't have those resources and must therefore place an undue amount of trust in guidance from a broker, most of whom aren't well informed about foreign investing. Even then, the costs of investing abroad are enormous. The fees for simply getting into and out of foreign currencies could easily cost an individual 5% of his portfolio before a dime is invested. And that's before he incurs the costs of hedging if he wants to neutralize the effects of currency fluctuations. Because even professional currency traders frequently get slammed by volatile moves in currencies, it would be unwise at best for an individual to buy foreign investments directly without hedging.

U.S. Multinational Companies

Some investment professionals, especially those not large enough or sophisticated enough to actually engage in overseas investing, will tell clients that they can get exposure to international markets while avoiding currency risks by buying shares of U.S. multinational companies with extensive operations abroad. It's true that in the past the profits from prosperous European operations of a company such as Ford Motor have effectively reversed sizable losses the company suffered in the U.S. auto market. But when you are trying to diversify by buying foreign stocks, you aren't buying just a foreign economy, you're buying a foreign stock market. Until the world becomes much smaller than it is now, stock markets will respond overwhelmingly to the actions of local investors. The U.S. stock market rises and falls largely on the perceptions of U.S. investors. Likewise, the German stock market will rise or fall depending on what German investors think will happen to stock prices, and those are the stock market moves that you want to capture by investing globally. Don't let some clever broker or money manager convince you that you can gain the benefits of international diversification by buying stocks of companies based in the United States, no matter how big their overseas operations.

American Depositary Receipts

While buying shares of U.S. multinationals doesn't achieve international diversification, there are foreign stocks that, in a sense, trade on U.S. exchanges. Instruments called American Depositary Receipts, or ADRs, are not foreign stocks even though they are traded on the New York Stock Exchange, NASDAQ, and the American Stock Exchange. Rather, they are certificates representing the ownership of foreign shares that are actually held abroad, usually by a big U.S. bank with foreign operations. The ADR entitles the investor to receive all the dividends and capital appreciation that the actual stock abroad enjoys and thus, for all practical purposes, is just like owning the stock. Indeed, for an additional fee an ADR holder can actually lay his hands on the underlying stock certificates, although there usually is little point in doing so. The nice thing about ADRs is that they can be purchased in dollars and their dividends are paid in dollars (adjusted, of course, for currency fluctuations and minus a small charge for the institution handling the ADR). But if an investor is interested in anything more than a nominal foreign investment, ADRs aren't the solution. For the most part,

ADRs are available only from the biggest and best-known companies in any given country. Limiting your foreign investments to them effectively precludes you from the shares of small, rapidly growing companies that often produce the most spectacular gains in foreign stock markets.

In addition, some foreign companies are braving the full-disclosure requirements of the Securities and Exchange Commission and exploring the possibility of listing their shares on U.S. exchanges. A few are here already. Like ADRs, they offer the convenience of dollar-denominated transactions and the disadvantage of almost always being shares of big blue chip companies.

INTERNATIONAL AND GLOBAL MUTUAL FUNDS

The mutual fund concept—a large number of investors pooling their funds to hire a professional manager skilled in a specific kind of investment—lends itself especially well to foreign investing. A mutual fund manager with millions to invest can negotiate much smaller fees for currency exchange and for hedging services, and he or she probably can tap a big reservoir of research on specific countries and companies that would be beyond the reach of the average individual investor. But choosing the right mutual fund to handle your overseas investing can be tricky.

The first question is whether you want a "global" or an "international" fund. Don't laugh, there's a difference. A global fund is allowed to invest anywhere in the world, including the United States. An international fund, on the other hand, is restricted to investing only outside the United States. In some cases an international fund has even more specific goals, such as investing mostly in Europe, in Asia, or in so-called emerging markets. Which one you choose depends largely on how the rest of your portfolio is structured. If, for instance, you already own an extensive array of U.S. stocks, both large and small, or you own one or more specialized mutual funds that concentrate on U.S. stocks, then a broad-based international fund might be appropriate. But if you have only a small smattering of U.S. stocks in your portfolio or own a single U.S.-oriented mutual fund, then the global approach may be more satisfactory.

In either case, you must do much of the same homework and make many of the same decisions that you would in selecting any mutual fund. We covered that process in Chapter Five. *Additionally,* you will have to decide if you want to shoulder currency risks by buying a fund that hedges currency exposure only minimally or not at all, or avoid currency risks altogether by seeking out funds that employ extensive hedging techniques. The additional costs of widespread hedging can pale into insignificance if the dollar strengthens and wipes out most of your overseas gains.

If you decide on a global fund, use all the techniques available (again, see Chapter Five) for narrowing your choices to ensure you pick one of the best. If you conclude that an international fund would be more useful for your particular portfolio, you must decide if you want to emphasize any particular part of the globe or characteristics of markets. A strong case could be made, for instance, that in the late 1990s it made more sense to invest in countries around the Pacific Basin than in Europe because the Asian economies were battered severely by a financial crisis that came to a head in 1997-98; their theory was that these Asian markets couldn't fall much further, but the sky is the limit in how strongly they might snap back. Of course, if you had heeded the advice to invest overseas and climbed aboard the Japanese stock market when it was still soaring on the edge of the stratosphere,

Figure 7.2 The World Market's Performance

The Dow Jones Global Indexes track 3,000 stocks worldwide, both by
country and by industry groups. Here are four overviews of how world
markets have performed since the end of 1991.

The Americas

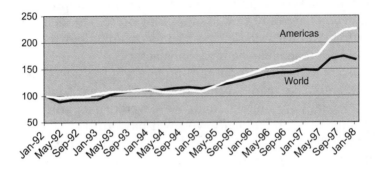

Asia/Pacific

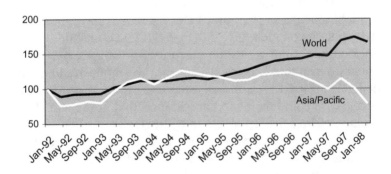

Figure 7.2 *continued*

Europe

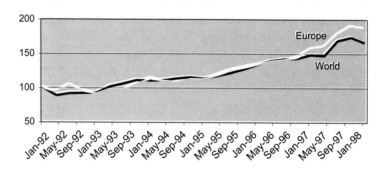

World (except United States)

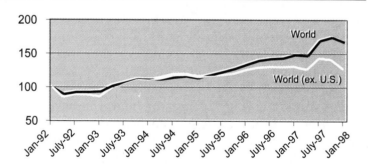

250 BARRON'S GUIDE TO MAKING INVESTMENT DECISIONS

you would sorely regret it today. That market peaked in early 1990, and as we write this, it hovers at a level some 70% lower. Of course, to the true investor, such a condition spells opportunity. One of the tricks is to get into these markets when they are out of favor. The Latin American debt crisis of the 1980s left many people wary of investing in South America or Central America, for example, but it appears now that some of those countries are in a position to enjoy strong growth well into the twenty-first century.

In fact, funds specializing in emerging markets may present the best single foreign investment opportunity of them all. Funds that invest in countries such as Malaysia, India, Taiwan, Brazil, and Peru will almost certainly be highly volatile—witness their dismal performance in 1997 and early 1998—but those countries are poised on the brink of what could become an enormous economic expansion, producing possibly the biggest stock market gains seen in years. Mutual fund managers will certainly have to be nimble to make the most of such an opportunity, but we think that it's worth at least a small part of your portfolio to tap into the potential boom.

We generally steer investors clear of sector funds that invest in one industry or one country on the grounds that if you are hiring a mutual fund manager to invest your money, you must think he or she knows more about where to invest it than you do. If you buy a sector fund, you have already made a big part of the decision about where the value is in international markets. Of course, you may by virtue of your occupation have some intimate knowledge about a particular country or company that would increase your confidence in buying a single-country fund. If that's the case, by all means put that knowledge to use. But most investors make the mistake of buying whichever single-country fund happens to have performed most spectacularly over the past six months. The tremendous volatility in many smaller foreign stock

markets makes it unlikely that any fantastic boom six months old will last another six months. Chasing those kinds of profits will cost you valuable time and money that would be better spent on broader goals.

CLOSED-END FUNDS

While many investors think of closed-end funds as being a kind of a mutual fund (a.k.a. open-end fund), closed-end funds are different in several important ways. A mutual fund allows investors to enter and leave anytime they wish by redeeming their investment at the current net asset value (NAV). If a new investor wishes to invest in a mutual fund, the fund simply creates more shares. The number of shares it can create is virtually unlimited. A closed-end fund, on the other hand, creates a specific number of shares that are sold to investors. The proceeds of those share sales are used to invest in specific securities, typically stocks or bonds. Shares of a closed-end fund are traded on an exchange just like stocks. Although the price of closed-end fund shares are often close to the net asset value per share (the value of all the stocks and bonds that the fund owns), the price can vary considerably from the NAV. Some trade at premiums to the NAV, and others—including many that invest in stocks— tend to trade at a modest discount to the NAV. The price of a closed-end fund is determined more by supply and demand factors—how many investors want to own or unload the limited number of shares—than by the value of the assets the fund owns. (The exchange-traded funds, mentioned in Chapter Five, are like closed-end funds but don't have the premium-discount characteristic. That's because they are a hybrid; they trade on an exchange but can easily create new shares if investor demand warrants.)

Closed-end funds have become relatively popular as vehicles for investing abroad. For one thing, they don't have the administrative and marketing costs that burden mutual funds, and costs are an important consideration because they tend to be higher for any fund that invests overseas. More important, closed-end funds don't experience the sometimes overwhelming influx of new investment money—or the opposite, a sickening outflow—that plague open-end mutual funds periodically. That means the fund manager can keep focused on his or her strategy without worrying about peripatetic shareholders.

Finally, closed-end funds that trade at a discount to their NAV seem to offer investors something of a "bargain."

There are a number of reasons that a fund would sell at a discount, not the least of which is the uncertainty about the prices the fund could obtain if it sold some stocks it held. Some of these funds hold large stakes in some companies, and if they unloaded one of those stocks, the price could fall far and fast. If, for whatever reason, demand for the fund declines, its share price will decline regardless of what happens to the underlying value of its portfolio. But for the investor looking abroad, the discount is often the result of uncertainties about the particular market. As we have seen, it is very difficult to predict *any* market's behavior, but investors are much more comfortable dealing with the U.S. market than they are dealing with the stock markets of Greece, Peru, or Turkey. The investor hopes, of course, that rising values in those markets will persuade other investors that they, too, should invest there. As additional money bids for a closed-end fund's shares, the price will rise. Some closed-end funds represent the *only* way foreign investors can get into some markets, such as India.

But closed-end funds aren't without their investment warts. Single-country closed-end funds suffer from the same volatility that afflicts single-country mutual funds. When a country's stock market is doing well, prices of closed-end funds investing in that market climb, as do the NAVs of mutual funds specializing in that country. When the market plunges, so do the share prices and NAVs of the closed-end and mutual funds.

A RECOMMENDED APPROACH

Given the limited options available to investors who seek to put a part of their portfolio abroad, we recommend the broad-based global or international funds as our first choice, followed probably by one or more regional mutual funds, especially those with some emphasis on emerging markets. Single-country funds are simply too volatile for most investors. Multi-country closed-end funds can be attractive alternatives to mutual funds as long as they trade at a discount to their NAV. If you want to get into a country and the only way to do it is through a closed-end fund trading at a premium, keep in mind that you are raising the risk level of your portfolio in the process. If you want to keep your overall risk level about the same, consider making some risk-reducing adjustments in other parts of your portfolio.

If you take the broad-brush approach, you won't have to worry specifically about what's going on in the main regions of the world, at least in investment terms. But with regional or country funds, you should be following the news rather closely. As we write this, Asia is in the tank, Latin America is wobbling, Europe has been looking good but faces uncertainties from monetary union, and North America has been doing so well that many analysts are skeptical that the good times will roll much longer. By the time you read this, all these conditions will be different.

So our message here boils down to this: International investing is an opportunity too good for you to pass up. It is strictly a long-term enterprise, which means that you shouldn't worry overly much about market timing, but don't foolishly jump into foreign markets just as they are peaking. If you turn your international portfolio over to an international fund manager, you must keep your eye only on him or her. If you assume some of the decision-making yourself in the form of ADRs, or regional and country-specific funds, you should be willing to spend significant additional time on your homework.

SUGGESTED READING

Investors who want to think about getting their feet wet internationally can dip into a really terrific book that takes the same simple, straightforward approach to the subject as you are finding in this volume. We know it's terrific because we wrote it. *The Wall Street Journal Book of International Investing* (Hyperion) was first published in hardcover in 1997, and an updated paperback version came out in 1998. In addition to far more detail on the why and wherefore of international investing, the book helps you put together an international portfolio and add it to your existing investments.

Other possibilities are John Dessauer's *Passport to Profit,* and for the more dedicated reader, *The Handbook of International Investing* edited by Carl Beidleman. This latter tome presents a sophisticated approach to international investing, but the extra detail will be well worthwhile to those who seriously intend to diversify their portfolio globally.

For those interested in emerging markets, try a new volume from Burton Malkiel—a Princeton University professor who advocated indexing as an investment style long before it became popular—and J. P. Mei, a New York University professor. It's entitled *Global Bargain Hunting* (Simon & Schuster, 1998).

Finally, if you want to play with the pros, delve into *Global Investing: A Handbook for Sophisticated Investors* by Sumner N. Levine. Full of theories and formulas, this one is for only the most dedicated individual investors.

8 Futures and Options

"You seem a thousand miles away. Is it me, Lisa, or coffee futures?"

Hah! Caught you looking at this chapter anyway, despite our pointed warnings in Chapter One. All right, as long as you're here, you might as well get acquainted with this X-rated corner of the investment world. As the sign in the greasy spoon says, "Management Is Not Responsible for Any Lost Articles"—in this case, your shirt.

Now it's true that you can also lose your shirt in the stock market or the bond market, or in mutual funds. And while it is possible that such losses could occur in the blink of an eye, they don't very often. But this isn't the case with futures and options. When they move, they move fast. Thousands of people have doubled or tripled their money in a matter of days. You also can lose everything just as speedily, as hundreds of thousands have. This speed is one of the great attractions for investors who get bored buying stocks and waiting for them to go up or watching bonds dribble interest into their accounts once every six months. Futures and options appeal to the same sort of instincts that compel some people to visit Las Vegas, buy overpowered sports cars, or take up skydiving as a hobby. An investment portfolio can have many purposes, but in our view emotional release shouldn't be one of them.

At this point you may well ask: If futures and options are so terrible, why include them in this book at all? Our answer is, they aren't terrible, but chances are you will be terrible at playing them. Investment vehicles are just tools, like hammers, wrenches or—and this is our point here—chain saws. Any of these tools can be used constructively, as in building a house, or destructively, as in murdering your mother-in-law. We think you can devise a perfectly good investment portfolio without touching futures or options. We have. For those of you who insist on a full tool kit, we will show you how we would use futures and options if we were so inclined.

WELCOME TO WONDERLAND

The *nom du jour* for futures and options is "derivatives" (although this term really is broader and includes certain warrants and other exotica). As that term implies, they are at least once removed from something real, such as gold or corn or Treasury bonds, and sometimes two or three times removed. While they have strong ties to the prices of whatever they are based on, they can and do move independently. That's because they are oriented toward future, not current, performance of their "underlying" markets. Yes, we know, buying a stock is in effect an anticipation of a company's future success. But a stock is a real share of corporate ownership. You receive dividends, vote at annual meetings, and if you like, you can get a fancy certificate to show. There is nothing tangible about futures or options even though their second names are contracts. To the extent they exist at all, they are bits and bytes in computers somewhere. If you asked for a contract, you would get (following the blank stare) a recitation of what is in the contract but not a contract itself.

Befitting the electronic impulses that they are, futures and options can be created or liquidated at will. In fact, they are born to be terminated. You can hold a stock forever and a Treasury bond for up to 30 years. But most futures and options expire within months, a few more go out a year or 18 months, and a very few, introduced relatively recently, last three years. They are both zero-sum markets, if you disregard commissions. That is, for every dollar made there is a dollar lost. This isn't the same thing as saying for every winner there's a loser (because all traders aren't in the markets for the exact same periods and number of contracts), but you get the idea: Profits are made in these markets at somebody else's expense.

At this point, futures and options separate onto their own, though roughly parallel, tracks. While both have to do with establishing prices now regardless of what the future brings, they go about it in different ways. Someone who buys a futures contract is obligated to accept delivery of the specified quantity of gold, corn, or Treasury bonds at the future time that is part of the name: March corn, June T-bonds, and so forth. Further, that person is obligated to pay the price established when the contract was bought, be it $3.57 for a bushel of corn or $98^{27}\!/_{32}\%$ of the $1,000 face value of a T-bond. For someone who sells a futures contract, all this works in reverse. He or she is obligated to make delivery of the item at a future time and to receive the price established when the contract was sold.

Most people who buy futures (who are said to be "long" in whatever the futures are based on) don't want 5,000 bushels of corn and couldn't afford $100,000 of T-bonds, which are the amounts called for in those particular contracts. What they really want—if their expectations that prompted them to buy the futures are borne out—is the price increase that has occurred since they got into the game. This increase happened in the market for real corn or actual T-bonds (known in the investment world as the "cash market" because you have to pay full price, in cash, to buy something) and has been reflected in futures prices. Instead of hanging around until the contract comes due, they sell it in the futures market and pocket the difference between what they paid and what they receive from the sale, less commissions. Similarly, most people who sell futures (who are said to be "short") probably don't have 5,000 bushels of corn to deliver on the due date and wouldn't know where to get it if they had to. They really want the price decrease that they anticipated in selling the futures. So, to neutralize their initial sale, they buy a futures contract, again profiting from the difference between what they received in the sale and what they paid to buy.

Thus, the futures market might be described as people selling what they don't have to people who don't want it anyhow. If this is too weird for you, skip ahead to the next chapter. Meanwhile, we should tell you that 98% of all futures contracts are canceled through offsetting trades prior to their due dates; only in the remaining 2% is the ownership of real corn, T-bonds, or whatever transferred from one party to another.

Options work in much the same way. Their chief difference is that they aren't obligations to buy or sell something at a specified time and price; they are, well, options to buy or sell, which means they may be exercised or not as the holders so choose. Naturally, holders bother to exercise options only if there is profit to be made. Also, holders may forgo exercising a profitable option and simply trade it away in the options market; in this case, as in futures, the profit is the difference between the price paid to buy and the price received in selling. This choice must be made before the option's life span runs out, however. Left unexercised, an option expires worthless, and the holder walks away poorer by the amount paid for it.

Following along so far? Good—then have another helping of options complexities. Unlike futures, there are different kinds of options. An option to buy whatever it is in the underlying market is a call, and an option to sell whatever is a put. Call options rise in value as prices in the underlying market go up; put options gain value as underlying market prices decline. Both calls and puts can be bought and sold—indeed, they have to be, for even options aren't exempt from the basic law of markets that for every buyer there must be a seller and vice versa. (Actually, there is an independent institution called a clearinghouse sitting in the middle of each trade to guarantee financial integrity of the transaction; a similar setup exists in futures. Buyers buy from the clearinghouse, and sellers sell to it. None of this is important to the investment aspect, but at least you personally don't have to worry whether the joker who bought your Exxon call options has the wherewithal to pay for them.)

If you initiate your market position by selling an option, you are said to be "writing" an option; buyers are just plain buyers. If you write an option on something you already own, it is a "covered" option. That is, if you own 100 shares of Exxon and you write a call option on them, you are writing an Exxon covered call. You collect the premium—that's what option prices are called, premiums—but if the price of Exxon stock moves against you, your stock could be "called away" at the agreed-upon price (known as the "striking price"), unless you get out of this situation (by buying back the option you previously sold) before that happens. If you write an option on something you don't own, it is a "naked" option. These are the riskiest of options positions, capable of inflicting unlimited losses on individual investors. In options, as in life, it is best to go naked circumspectly.

One last piece of introductory business. Futures for the most part are just one step away from something real. Options can be as close as one step—the 100 shares of Exxon, for example—or two or three steps removed. Most futures contracts have options on them, for instance, which places the options two steps away from the underlying market. (If you exercise a hog futures call option, you are in the hog futures market, not in the hog pen.) And then there are index futures and options. These are based on, for example, a stock index such as the Dow Jones Industrial Average or Standard & Poor's 500, which are themselves one step away from real stocks by being a mathematical construct intended to reflect or measure an important segment of the stock market. So you can buy or sell options on futures on the Dow Jones industrials and not be any closer to owning a part of corporate America than a kid with his face pressed against the toy store window is to his own electric train.

We dwell on this because it is important to understand that in futures and options markets you are trading shadows. Like your own elongated or shortened shadow, futures and options are sometimes distorted versions of the real underlying markets. The further away from reality, the greater the possible distortion. Indeed, there are Wall Street traders with heavy-duty computers who specialize in making money from the distortions—the degree to which prices in the derivative markets are out of synch with those in the underlying markets. These traders are called arbitragers (or arbitrageurs for those of you who go to movies with subtitles). When they move in a pack, as their computers often cause them to do, they can produce otherwise inexplicable jumps and dips in all the affected markets. There is nothing you can do about it, but we thought you ought to know. The main lesson for you is that while futures and options usually track the markets they are based on, sometimes they don't. That difference can cost you money and on other occasions give you a little extra. Just one more loose end for you to think about.

THE TWO-EDGED SWORD OF LEVERAGE

There is more bang per buck, or drubbing per dollar, in futures and options than in any other investment vehicle. That's because they are leveraged—which almost everywhere else in the financial world is euphemism for being in debt, but not here. This kind of leverage is more akin to what Archimedes had in mind when he said, "Give me where to stand, and I will move the earth." In this case, the outlay of relatively little capital can produce either comparatively huge profits or mammoth losses.

You can get into the futures game with either a buy or a sell order by putting up only 10% or so of a contract's full value. The exchanges set the minimum amounts, the clearinghouses add a little extra for safety, and the brokerage firm you deal with probably tacks on a bit more as well (especially if you are a neophyte). Still, you could enter an order to buy a futures contract for 5,000 bushels of corn worth $16,250 (if corn is going for $3.25 a bushel) by having maybe $2,000 of uncommitted capital in your brokerage account. Then corn jumps 10%, to $3.575 a bushel, and you sell your contract for $17,875. You get to keep all your profit of $1,625, and you still have the $2,000 that paved your way into the futures market. Your account has swelled 81%, to $3,625, thanks to the 10% price increase in corn. That's leverage.

Let's go back through this example, moving the shells and the pea more slowly. You did *not* buy a corn futures contract for $2,000. You merely said you would buy corn some future day, and you let your broker hold your $2,000 to show there was moolah where your mouth was. This good faith money is officially known as margin, which is confusing because in the stock market, where you must pay in full for everything, margin is the term applied to the amount an investor borrows to buy stock; the Federal Reserve says no more than 50% of a stock purchase may be paid with borrowed money. Same word, different meaning. Anyway, after the price went up, you didn't sell corn; you merely passed along your previous promise to buy it to someone else. At that point, your broker releases your $2,000 and credits your account with the profit on the trade.

What happens if the price of corn falls between the times you say, "I'll buy 5,000 bushels" and "No, on second thought, I won't"? The leverage works in reverse and clobbers you. A 10% drop from $3.25 a bushel socks you with a $1,600 loss, or 80% of that original $2,000. But you can't slip away with your remaining $400 to quietly lick your wounds. A futures market that moves against an investor extracts its due in a torturous manner. As your paper losses mount, the brokerage firm phones and demands you put up more money—typically by the end of that very day—to maintain your position in the market. The trigger points vary, as do the "maintenance margin" levels, but there is nothing like a margin call for $500 to $1,000 per contract to sour the gastric juices. Even if you can afford the money, you must struggle with deciding whether to stick to your guns on this trade or throw in the towel. In a particularly fast-moving market, you could get a margin call in the morning and another after lunch. And if you shrug these calls off (or, worse, you don't hear about them in time because you're in a long meeting or out of town), the brokerage firm is empowered to close out your position plus cash out any other investments it can get its hands on until the loss is covered.

Are we having fun yet?

Options are more attractive to many people because their potential losses can be limited while leverage works on their behalf on profits. While true, it isn't that simple. The whole truth is that in options, too, you can be hammered straight into bankruptcy if you are greedy, careless, or both. Just ask the folks who, in the summer of 1987 as the stock market levitated to one record high after another, wrote put options on the S&P 500 with exercise levels that were 10% to 15% under the index itself. They fully expected to keep those premiums because even if the market started dropping, they thought, they would have time to buy offsetting put contracts. Imagine their surprise when, on October 19, the market dropped like an anvil by more than 20%, and they couldn't get out because their brokers' phones were busy or off the hook. After the close, however, their brokers were able to call them with the news that the put options they wrote had been "put back" to them and would they please send a cashier's check for the full amount. (S&P options settle in cash only, not in securities, seaside villas, or old master paintings.) Some people had to sell every security they owned to raise the money, which contributed to the extreme volatility of the financial markets for weeks afterward.

As a result, the Securities and Exchange Commission made it known that it wanted stricter policing of who was allowed to play options. That's why, if you should decide options trading has a place in your portfolio, your broker will invite you in for a little chat. No bright light is beamed into your face, but you will be grilled on your investment philosophy. Your net worth will be strip searched, and you will be required to sign a bunch of documents that, among other things, certify you know all about options, like to take risks, and will never sue your broker no matter how far down the primrose path you go.

But we digress from explaining how much safer options are than futures. Actually, option buyers do have "downside protection," as they say in the financial business. If you buy either a call or a put and don't exercise it, all you can lose when it expires is the premium you paid for it. That means you know going in how much you could lose, which doesn't prevent you from losing it but at least doesn't give you a heart attack when it happens. And "covered" call option writers, or sellers who already own the security or whatever they are writing options on, also are insulated from disaster: Either it isn't exercised and the writer keeps the premium received, or it is exercised and the writer satisfies the demand out of his or her portfolio. Only naked option writers are exposed to unlimited risk. The bottom line is that options are somewhat safer than futures, but they aren't foolproof.

Now to leverage, which is the ultimate topic here. The theory of options pricing involves formulas that take into account the price of the underlying whatever, how volatile the price of whatever has been over the preceding year, the current rate of interest on an annualized basis, and the time remaining until expiration. We aren't going into any further depth, inasmuch as our idea of high math is making sure after three glasses of wine that the waiter isn't stiffing us on the sales tax. Besides, an option really is worth only what somebody is willing to pay for it, which is another basic law of markets. (To be fair, investment professionals keep their pricing models chugging away in their computers to spot those options whose premiums deviate from where they should be, but arbitrage is not the way for you to play options.)

Here's the nut of options leverage: The further away an option's exercise price is from the actual price of the underlying whatever (a condition known as "out of the money"), the cheaper the premium. For a call expiring in six months, the premium is, as we write this, about 10% of the price of whatever it is an option on. As the underlying whatever's price moves closer and closer to the strike price, the option premium goes up—and at an accelerating pace. If and when the underlying whatever's price surpasses the strike price (the option then being "in the money"), the option's premium moves more and more in tandem with the underlying whatever until, when the option becomes "deep in the money," it moves point for point. So if you were so prescient as to buy cheap out-of-the-money options that became deeply in the money, you would make a bundle. Working against this leverage is the steadily approaching expiration date, the factor that causes an option to be known in investment circles as "a wasting asset." The closer an out-of-the-money option is to expiration, the more "time decay" will whittle its price. Similarly, an option whose strike price is about the same as the underlying whatever (you got it, "at the money") will experience increasing time decay the closer it moves to expiration.

How does this work in real life? In late November 1997, you could have bought an Oracle January 30 put option for 1¼; at the time, Oracle was a bellwether computer software stock, trading in the mid-30s. You figured the bubble might burst. It did, on December 8 when Oracle announced earnings that were 17% below Wall Street's expectations and expressed doubt that profits would recover quickly. The stock, at 32⅜ before the news hit the fan, plunged 29% on December 9, on a thunderous volume of 171 million shares— the biggest one-day turnover ever for any single stock, except for one case of a stock priced at less than $1 a share. In ensuing weeks Oracle spiraled 21% lower as the entire technology sector fell under intense investor scrutiny. The January 30 put option, meanwhile, had soared to 7 ¾. Flush with success and only a month to expiration, you close out your position. Now let's go to the calculator: While you were in the game, the stock dropped 44%, from 32 to 18. The put option rose from 1 ¼ to 7 ¾, a 5200% move. That's leverage.

TAKING THE PLUNGE (SORRY ABOUT THAT) IN FUTURES

All right, we're getting as bored with school as you are. The question here is, should you dabble in futures or not? You already know our bias, so we'll be gracious and begin with reasons you should:

1. You can make a lot of money in futures. Some of the great traders have years in which they earn returns of 50%, 75%, or better. That's after deducting losses sustained on the majority of their trades. Naturally, they don't do this well each and every year, but a few—such as Paul Tudor Jones and Richard Dennis, to name two—have built sizable fortunes mainly from futures trading.

2. Futures provide desirable diversification for your portfolio. Most of the markets in which futures are available—farm and industrial commodities, energy and currencies—march to drummers that are very different from the ones stocks and bonds do. Prices in every market are determined by supply and demand, but the supply of and demand for, say, soybeans develop from factors most dissimilar to those affecting the Dow Jones Industrial Average. This lack of correlation is the very essence of diversification, and it is why more stodgy pension funds and other fiduciary responsibility types have been sidling into the formerly off-limits futures markets in recent years. Your portfolio doesn't have to be as big as theirs to benefit from diversification.

3. Even the interest rate and stock index futures, which of course do correlate closely to the bond and stock markets, provide worthwhile protection services for investors primarily interested in securities: They can be used to keep a market from running over you by hedging portfolios against price declines during periods of uncertainty. And they can be used to constrain a rising market from running away from you by establishing an entry price level for initial or enlarged stock and bond positions without having to hurriedly research and select specific securities.

4. Futures are in many cases the "purest" play you can make on certain investment themes, meaning they will respond more fully than further removed vehicles and thus offer the greatest potential return. If we are coming out of a recession, then home building should take off soon, if it hasn't already. Lumber and copper futures beckon invitingly because demand for two-by-fours and insulated cable is likely to increase faster than supply. It's possible to play this same theme by buying stocks of home builders and copper mining companies, but these choices drag along all sorts of baggage that can affect your return: How good is the management? Will the home builder's geographic area of operation lead or lag the recovery? Does the copper company make wire, which has higher profit margins than just selling metal? And so forth.

Now our consciences demand we give you reasons that you shouldn't get into futures. We'll stick with four, just to keep things in balance (but we have more if you want 'em):

1. Somewhere between 75% and 90% of all futures traders lose money on an annual basis. Unless you are very smart, diligent, and lucky—all three are required—you are probably going to be in that vast majority. Another statistic comes from a Chicago discount commodities brokerage firm, which found its individual investor accounts were kept open an average of only 11 months. At that point, these humbled investors scraped up the last bits of their initial capital stakes, if any, and retreated to the familiar territory of stocks, bonds, and mutual funds.

2. The people you have to do business with can—and do—clip you coming and going. In every investment the individual is up against professionals, but in futures markets the professionals are manning the toll booths on the only road in and out. Orders are executed on the floor of futures exchanges in what is known as an "open outcry" method of "price discovery" but looks like a maddened crowd on the verge of running amok. When one of these hyper traders gets your order to execute, he or she receives a fee from your brokerage firm for doing the job. But more is better, right? As professionals with on-the-scene knowledge of where the market is, has been, and appears to be headed, the trader at the very least can profit from the bid-ask "spread" by acquiring a contract at the lowest price currently available and selling it to you at the highest price then prevailing. If a market is in a strong trend higher or lower, the trader can do even better by taking care of his or her own account first and then—after the price has already moved considerably beyond where you hoped to get in—executing your order. It is perfectly legal on most exchanges for floor traders to both service their own accounts and handle customers' orders; the arrangement has the pretentious name of "dual trading" but is actually a government-sanctioned conflict of interest whose alleged purpose is to keep these markets active enough to allow people to trade easily when they want to. Of course, there are rules about how traders should give customer orders precedence over their own accounts, but, well, it can get awfully confusing down there on the floor.

3. Fast-moving futures markets work against the individual investor in another way, too. Suppose you buy soybean futures because a prolonged drought and hot spell seem likely to push prices higher. Wise as you are, you put in a stop-loss order at a price 15% lower in case a rainstorm shows up. It does, and the market plunges. But the advisory slip from the broker says you were "stopped out" at a price far below the level specified in your order, say 20% or 25% under your buy-in price instead of 15%. More shenanigans at work? You may have been hit with some number two (see above), but not necessarily. Futures prices sometimes do move faster than brokers' and traders' abilities to execute all the transactions at the prices people want. This is called "slippage," and it, including whatever number two ends up costing you (you'd have a devil of a time trying to quantify it), trims your profit or enlarges your loss significantly. Put another way, slippage and commissions combined mean the price of whatever has to move 10% to 18% in your favor—*before* the futures contract matures within months or weeks—for you just to break even. Hurdles, anyone?

4. Ever have a nightmare in which you are trapped inside a plunging elevator or a rocket to Mars? Futures can be just as entertaining because these markets have limits on how much their prices can move in any single trading session. The idea is to give crazed traders time to cool off and think things over, sort of like a trading halt in a stock. But if your stock is halted on the New York Stock Exchange, you can still sell it on a regional exchange or, failing that, in the "third market," which is a loose collection of firms that accommodate investors who can't or won't trade through standard channels. No such alternative exists in futures, where each contract is proprietary to the exchange on which it is traded. If a contract's price rises or falls the allowable limit, trading ceases until prices back away from the limit or the session ends, whichever comes sooner. So there you are, holding Mexican peso futures because you think that country is on a roll, but then the Mexican government unexpectedly devalues its currency. Or there you are, holding short lumber futures because you think the U.S. economic recovery is weaker than generally believed, but then home building takes off like another baby boom happened, and meanwhile the government has placated environmentalists by limiting logging on public lands. Prices slam up/down against the limit, and trading screeches to a standstill. You can't get out. Today's crazed traders come back tomorrow just as crazed, and the market "locks up" or "locks down" the limit again. This can go on for days until the price gets to the level that traders deem fair or until the exchange changes the rules to get things unstuck. By that time you have lost 20 pounds in cold sweat alone. Both the Mexican peso and lumber situations happened within our working life memories; peso futures resumed trading after five days at a price nearly 40% lower than when the lock-down first occurred, and lumber futures were locked up 22 days to resume at a price about 58% higher. It doesn't happen often, but it happens. Always unpredictably.

GUIDELINES FOR THE UNDAUNTED

If after all this you still want to trade futures, at least heed some commonsense guidelines:

- Learn about futures trading by thoroughly studying an entry-level book or two. We give some suggestions in the usual place at the end of this chapter.

- Before jumping in, practice by making trades on paper. It isn't the same as playing for real money, we acknowledge, but if you pay attention to when you get in, and why, and when you get out, and why, you can at least raise your instincts to a near-conscious level. Keep notes. Refer to them when you actually do start trading.

- Avoid buying "trading systems," which are available on disk for computers and on paper for people at costs ranging from hundreds to thousands of dollars. Some of these systems have a reality-based rationale, and others are full of baloney. You won't be able to tell the difference until you become comfortable with your own approach, risk tolerance, and so forth. You may lose money in futures, but at least gain the benefit of learning the hard lessons of your own experience rather than only being able to blame some "system" you never really understood.

- Use only risk capital in trading futures. Risk capital is a fancy term for money you can afford to lose, which in turn means neither your standard of living nor your disposition will be affected by its loss. It also means that the rest of your portfolio can generate enough money to replace the loss within a year. In practical terms, start with no more than 10% of your portfolio's value; 5% is even better for beginners. More practicality: A brokerage account for trading futures shouldn't be any smaller than $10,000—$20,000 is better—or you will find your trading strategies limited to low-priced contracts, which is like tying one hand behind your back. The bottom line of this advice is don't even think about futures unless you have a portfolio worth a bare minimum of $100,000, with $400,000 being much more prudent.

■   Arrange to spend the time required to monitor your futures positions. You must have the ability to check the markets two or three times a day (which probably means you should have a way of getting price quotes without calling your broker all the time) and to drop everything else and focus on your futures if trouble seems to be brewing. This means you shouldn't go on vacation with futures trades still open. It also means that between researching trades you might want to make and monitoring positions you are already in, you will find yourself spending a grand total of 5 to 10 hours a week on 10% of your portfolio and only 1 or 2 hours on the other 90%. This is what it takes to make a killing someday, maybe. If you can't abide this disproportionate allocation of your attention, stay out of futures.

■   If you want the portfolio diversification that futures offer without the hassle of doing your own trading, consider commodity funds or pools. These are like mutual funds in that professionals manage your investment for you. They are unlike mutual funds in that they charge very high fees—in the neighborhood of 10% to 15% of your assets annually, compared to 1% to 1.5% for ordinary stocks-and-bonds mutual funds. Many of them have minimum investments of $50,000 and up. Some are structured as limited partnerships with lives of a specified number of years, which means you usually can't get out early without sustaining a big loss. Still interested? You find them through major brokerage concerns. Always ask to see the past performance statistics of the professionals who are—or will be, in the case of a new fund or pool—managing your money. Be wary of those with track records of less than five years and of those who previously have managed only much smaller funds than the one you're considering. (Some professionals who can go gangbusters with relatively small amounts of capital, say $1 million to $5 million, fall on their kiesters when handed a $20 million bundle to manage.) Don't be content with the average annual return figure, which almost always will make you salivate. Ask to see the actual returns of their best year and worst year, and prepare to be amazed by the win-big-lose-big swings. Another performance statistic to examine is the professionals' "drawdown," both average and maximum. This is the amount of capital they have lost from the funds they were managing, and it's an indication of how wild a ride you can expect. A professional with an average drawdown of 30% could turn your $50,000 stake into $35,000 and still be performing as advertised. Resolve before you get in to stick with the fund you have selected for at least five years—the same length of time you demanded in experience for the manager. Avoid funds "guaranteed" to pay a minimum annual return or to preserve your original investment. These funds, also charging high fees, make good on these guarantees by putting most of their capital into Treasury bills and bonds, which you can do yourself for free. That leaves these funds little or no money to play with in futures markets, which means you wouldn't be getting any portfolio diversification much less a chance for a big profit.

TAKING THE PLUNGE (OOPS, DID IT AGAIN) IN OPTIONS

Though exchange-listed options have been around for 25 years, the field is still evolving in terms of investment strategies and even vehicles. Options nowadays are at the exploding center of the new galaxy of derivative investments. Resist the temptation to invest in them just because they are *chi-chi*. Stand under a cold shower and repeat after us: I will make no investment before I understand it.

Options are sort of investment tofu, taking on whatever flavor and texture you want. You can raise your level of risk by speculating with them, or you can use them in ways that reduce risk. Guess which we prefer. Granted, we all wish we were the 30-year-old physician described in The Striking Price column of *Barron's* on March 15, 1993. Within six weeks the good doctor allegedly made over $700,000 buying—and, in a matter of days, selling—hundreds of puts and calls on such stocks as Philip Morris and General Motors and on the S&P 100-stock index. If we can't have the hot streak for ourselves, we at least would like to be that doctor's brokers—but not patients. Of course, anybody who makes seven profitable trades in a row—of anything, not just options—is going to do all right, especially if that's when they stop keeping score. Perhaps the doctor's next seven trades were clinkers. People in the business tell us that options traders lose money 60% of the time. And while it is true that you can't lose more in options than the typically small amount you pay for them, it is also true that if you keep losing a limited amount of money, you eventually will be wiped out.

GROUND RULES FOR USING OPTIONS

So let's establish some ground rules for using options in your portfolio, the first of which is suggested by the preceding phrasing:

■ You don't *invest* in options, you *use* them for some purpose. The purpose may be as foolish as low-stakes crapshooting or as conservative as an elegant portfolio hedge, but time-limited options cannot be the core of your investment program. We recommend allocating no more than 20% of

your portfolio assets to options trading, and then only if you enjoy the process and are willing to work at doing it well.

■ Don't trade options on futures unless you are already very experienced in the futures markets. Because they are twice removed from something real, options on futures can be tricky for a newcomer. This ground rule effectively prevents you from using options to play commodities. What are left are stocks and stock indexes, Treasury bills and bonds, and currencies.

■ Don't use options to speculate on a stock you don't already own or intend to own. The purpose of this ground rule is to keep you from trading options on stocks you don't know anything about. We presume you will do your homework before buying a company's shares. Do the same before you trade options on that company's stock. And for heaven's sake, don't buy a stock just because it has listed options available for trading; the presence or absence of options has nothing to do with a stock's investment merits.

■ In fact, don't use options to speculate, period. Use them to enhance your portfolio (examples will follow), not to play hunches about the economy or the markets. If you have a little gambling itch, scratch it by organizing a Friday night poker game or something.

■ When you do trade options, never deal in single contracts. The minimum transaction costs are too high for one-contract trades. Two or three are okay; four or five are better.

UP THE RISK STAIRCASE

The most fundamental level of options trading is writing (that means initiating a trade by selling, remember) covered calls. This is what someone with absolutely zero options experience would be allowed to do by a brokerage firm. You have 500 shares of Exxon in your portfolio. How many calls can you write? Wrong answer: 500. Right answer: 5. Each call (and put, for that matter) on an individual stock is for 100 shares. An all-too-common beginner's mistake is to equate one share with one option. It's so common, in fact, that the options departments in many brokerage firms will routinely look into any new account that just bought or sold 100 options to make sure the customer (and, not incidentally, the customer's broker) knows what he or she is doing. If you write 500 call options and you own only 500 shares, you're in trouble if those calls are exercised. You must buy 4,500 more shares in the stock market, and you would probably have to sell a big chunk of your own portfolio to raise the necessary cash. Ouch. And you must pay taxes on any investment you sell at a profit even if you sold it solely to satisfy an option obligation. Double ouch.

It's supposed to work this way: It's early May, and Exxon is trading at 66. You write five Exxon calls with a 70 strike price, expiring in October. You collect a premium of 1 ⁵⁄₁₆ per option, or about $600 after commissions. The stock rises to 68 ½, then levels off. The calls expire worthless, and you keep the $600. Exxon pays a per-share dividend of $2.88 annually, which would be a yield of 4.2% (dividing the dividend by the share price of 68½). But adding your net option profit raises the effective annual yield on your Exxon to 6%. If you pull off your covered call trick three times a year with about the same results, the yield on your Exxon zooms to 9%. Pretty neat, huh? Thousands of retired geezers in Florida and Arizona occupy some of their ample hours with this game, only for some of them it became a survival strategy as interest rates fell on their CDs and other fixed-income investments in the early 1990s.

Playing the covered-call game successfully requires writing the calls at strike prices far enough above the stock's market price so that the calls are unlikely to get "in the money"—at which point the writer would have to buy five calls to neutralize his position, losing everything he had collected in premiums and incurring more commissions to boot, or risk losing the stock. If he was thinking about getting out anyway, having the shares called away isn't so bad. But there is little point in writing calls so far out of the money that the premium is less than a dollar a share, or $100 per option, because commissions eat up too much of the proceeds. In short, picking the right strike price depends on becoming intimately familiar with the price-fluctuation behavior of the underlying stock.

Writing covered calls can be used for another purpose: reaching the price objective you established for a stock. Suppose you bought 1,000 shares of XYZ at 20 in the belief it would rise about 50%. XYZ goes up to 28 and holds for a while; should you forget your goal and take a nothing-to-sneeze-at 40% profit instead? It's a decision you don't have to make. You could sell 10 in-the-money XYZ 25 calls at 6 (a total of $6,000) or 10 slightly out-of-the-money XYZ 30 calls at 1 (a total of $1,000), using options expiring in about six months. In the first instance your shares probably would be called away at 25, but with the 6 from the call premium, your effective selling price is 31, a 55% profit on your XYZ stock. In the second instance, your shares will be called away only if the market price reaches 30, which is your objective anyhow. And if for some reason your shares aren't called or the stock doesn't quite make it to 30 before the options expire, you keep the $1,000.

The next step up the risk ladder is buying options. Brokerage firms look for at least a year's experience in writing calls or for some prior experience speculating in stocks or other securities. You buy a call if you expect the underlying stock, stock index, bond, or currency to go up; you buy a put if you expect the price to decline. Some full-service firms restrict you to buying options only on stocks their own analysts follow and on which they have issued current recommendations. Discount brokers don't analyze stocks, so you can do what you want through them.

The Prudent Speculator

Our ground rules permit you to speculate on a stock you have researched and wouldn't mind having in your portfolio. Here is how we would recommend going about it:

■ Preset your level of gain and level of pain. Begin by forming a clear conviction about the stock, which means more than "it's sure to go up" or "it simply has to come back to earth." Exactly how far do you expect the price to rise or fall from its present level? Set the goal and then shave off a little for safety. Write that number down, along with the reasons you think the stock will move the way you predict. This is a reminder to yourself why you are taking this position and at what point you would consider your trade a success. At the same time, write down the price level you would consider maximum tolerable failure if the stock moves against you. Your object here is to salvage some of the capital you put into this trade and not settle for a 100% loss. These price levels are your exit points. Never change them unless a significant adjustment occurs in the thesis that led you to do the trade. If you are keeping score with option premiums rather than stock prices, here are good rules of thumb: Sell if you double your money in the options trade; if the stock is still moving toward your target, at least sell enough of the options to recoup your initial investment and take the rest of the ride for free. Also, get out totally if your option trade has a paper loss of 50%, because if it has lost that much, it's going to lose more.

■ Determine when you think the stock will reach your price goal. Not "pretty soon" but a specific date. To make money in options, you have to be right about both the stock and the timing. If you can't honestly tell when a stock might climb, you are better off buying the stock than a call option because stocks don't expire. (Another possibility is a long-term option; see the section on LEAPS later in this chapter.) If you don't know when a stock might fall, either hold off buying the put until there is some movement or buy the put with a far-off expiration.

■ Pick an option with the striking price and expiration corresponding to your "how much" and "by when" targets. Don't assume you should always buy the most distantly expiring, out-of-the-money option—unless your strategy demands it—because with these usually inactive options you will pay a little more getting in and take a little less getting out. If you are expecting a modest move in the stock, you probably will do best buying an option that already is a little in the money. If you think a large move is in the cards, go for an option that is a little out of the money. Only in the rare case where you forecast a huge move should you buy a "deep-out-of-the-money" option (note the acronym DOOM). The main reason so many people lose in the options market is that they buy out-of-the-money calls and watch them expire worthless. As for the "when" aspect, four expirations are always available for trading: the two nearest months and two more on one of three possible quarterly cycles (March-June-September-December, January-April-July-October, and February-May-August-November). For many buying strategies, the option just after the soonest-to-expire one offers the best combination of price and time for the target to be reached.

■ Execute the strategy with strict discipline. If the stock price moves against you, get out (sell the option) when it reaches the level of maximum tolerable loss. (Many firms and some exchanges don't accept stop-loss orders on options, so you have to monitor your trade closely.) If the stock price moves in your favor, be ready as it approaches your target to do one of two things: First, reexamine your reasons—which you wrote down, remember—for doing the trade; if the thesis has improved, raise your target and seek more profit. But if the thesis really hasn't changed, sell your option without fail when the target is reached. The object is to make money on the trade, not scoop up every dime and quarter of possible profit. If the stock keeps moving well past your target, analyze where you fell short in translating your thesis into a price-move projection and attempt to do better next time. The next time could be another option gambit on the same stock, provided you have a clear conviction about where the stock is headed. (Return to the first bullet above and start over.)

SOME OPTIONS STRATEGIES

Even within these seemingly strait-laced procedures there is room to reflect your personal circumstances, including risk tolerance. You pick a strategy reflecting your attitude toward risk and accentuate that attitude by how you implement the strategy. In buying calls, for instance, you indicate a willingness to take a risk. But an aggressive risk-taking investor buys out-of-the-money calls, the moderate investor goes for at-the-money calls, and the conservative investor takes in-the-money calls as a substitute for buying the stock.

One option-buying strategy is actually risk-reducing rather than risky. It is called the "married put" strategy because it consists of simultaneously buying a stock and a put option on that stock. You think the stock will go up, but the put option constitutes a safety net if you are wrong. It serves the same purpose as a stop-loss order but is far more accurate. A fast-sinking stock is likely to roll right through your stop-loss price level before your order is executed, leaving you with a bigger loss than you were willing to accept. Or an even worse scenario: A stock dips down to your stop-loss price, your shares are sold as ordered, and then the stock takes off for the heavens without you. Both experiences can be psychologically devastating to some investors who take setbacks too personally. A married put gives you much more peace of mind because the put option increases in value as the stock sinks, offsetting much of your "paper" loss in the stock. As a result, you can afford to wait a little and see if your original thesis was truly wrong or just early. However, if you were right in the first place, your put options will expire worthless, and you'll be out the money you paid for them— which, if you are keeping score meticulously as we advise, reduces your true return on the stock. But so what? If the married put raised your comfort level on this particular stock purchase, it was worth the price. Think of it as buying term insurance. Watch out, though, that you don't become insurance-poor by continually buying puts on the same stock, which gets to be expensive. If your confidence in the stock is that shaky, sell out and find one you believe in more.

The next two rungs on the option-risk ladder are "spread" or "straddle" trading (simultaneously buying and writing options on the same stock or whatever, usually at different striking prices) and "naked" option writing. By the time you have enough experience to do these kinds of trades (or be allowed to do them by your brokerage firm), you will be far beyond the purview of this book. Meanwhile, turn a deaf ear to anyone who tries to talk you into such trading.

As usual with options, however, there is an exception that might appeal to investors in certain situations. It is called a "covered straddle," and it works like this: Suppose you have decided to buy 2,000 shares of XYZ stock. You don't. Instead, you buy half your intended stake, or 1,000 shares, and simultaneously write 10 calls and 10 puts. If XYZ goes up, you are basically playing the covered call gambit described earlier, except that you have collected both the call premiums and the put premiums—which together either greatly enhance the return on the 1,000 shares you have or reduce the effective cost of buying your second 1,000-share stake. What happens if XYZ goes down instead? You are forced to buy another 1,000 shares at the puts' striking price. That's what you wanted to do in the first place, only with this strategy you got the first half at 50, say, and the second half at 45, for an average total cost in this example of 5% less than if you had bought all 2,000 at 50. Moreover, the premiums you collected on the calls and puts further reduce the cost of the strategy.

If you liked the part about reducing average cost, here is a simpler way of doing only that: Buy half the number of shares you eventually want to own and sell put options for the rest at a striking price where you would be willing to buy more. If the stock dips down to that level, you are forced to buy the shares you wanted anyway at a lower price, with the total cost further reduced by the put premiums you collected. If the stock rises instead, the put premiums compensate for having to acquire the rest of your stake at a higher market price, assuming you don't let the stock run up too far before you act.

There is even a "naked" strategy that is permissible under our ground rules. Suppose you are interested in buying a stock whose price, in your opinion, has gotten a little ahead of itself. XYZ is trading at 65, and you would be willing to buy below 60. Write XYZ puts equivalent to the number of shares you want (one option for each 100 shares, remember), selecting an expiration at least six months off to allow plenty of time for your wishes to come true. You collect a premium of, say, 1, or $100 for each option you write. If the stock falls to 60 or less, the holder of the options "puts back" the shares to you at the price you wanted to pay, and your real cost is 1 less than that. Just be sure you still want to own the stock at that time. And have plenty of intestinal fortitude on hand, because you likely will be buying the stock in a falling market. Context changes the whole picture for some people, but it needn't if you are buying for the long term.

If you use options as we have described here—strictly as an adjunct to your stock investing—you could add 0.5 to 1.5 percentage point a month to the return on a stock portfolio—that is, if you are reasonably energetic about employing options strategies. It isn't much, considering that you must spend a fair amount of time learning and monitoring options strategies. But it can amount to a nice piece of change if your portfolio is big enough, which it should be to get involved with options in the first place. The key benefit, though, could be making yourself much more comfortable with stock investing by knowing you are doing what you can to enhance income, reduce risk, and lower your acquisition costs.

OPTIONS ON OTHER STUFF

Options on stock indexes should be used sparingly to hedge your stock portfolio against a broad-scale market decline. Suppose you think stock prices have run up too far too fast and the market is due for a "correction" or maybe even a prolonged decline, yet it's too expensive to sell all your stocks and wait to get back in later. You could buy put options on a stock index roughly matching the kinds of stocks you own (the Dow Jones Industrial Average, for instance, if you have big stocks, or the Standard & Poor's Mid-Cap index if your stocks tend to be medium-sized). How many options? That depends on the index. All of them are settled in cash, with the value typically calculated by multiplying the index level by $100. It would take 10 options on an index standing at 100 to hedge a $100,000 portfolio, but only three if the index were at 300. Wait a minute, you say, that second hedge would cover only a $90,000 portfolio. True, and that's the trouble with index hedging: It's very imprecise. Rarely, if ever, will you be able to create a hedge of the exact same size as your portfolio on an index that your stocks mimic to a T. Just come as close as you can on both counts. Don't overhedge, meaning don't buy more options than needed to cover your portfolio; the objective is to cushion an adverse market move, not protect every penny. To the extent your hedge falls short of your portfolio's value, consider it like buying insurance with a deductible. Also, don't be hedging all the time. It's expensive. If you have a diversified portfolio and are in the market for the long haul, time will erase most losses. And time is free.

Of course, some people like the idea of speculating on moves of the whole stock market with stock-index options. Gambling is more like it. If it is hard to get enough information on one company to determine whether you should buy its stock, how can you get enough information on the entire market? You can't. You're spending money on guesses. If you are super-disciplined in following the option-buying steps described earlier, you conceivably could make some money playing index options. But if you prudently restrict the capital you devote to options trading to 20% or less of your portfolio, the money you put into stock-index trades isn't available for the other strategies involving individual stocks, where the payoffs are steadier if less spectacular.

What about options on interest rates and currencies? We recommend you use them only to hedge your portfolios of bonds and of foreign securities, not to speculate on the direction of interest rates or the strength of the Japanese yen. Very experienced people are burned regularly when they try to do that. You may not need to hedge, either, or at least not your entire portfolio. If, for example, you tend to hold bonds until they mature, your hedging can be restricted to the portion of your holdings that will mature within the next six to nine months and expose you to reinvestment risk. As for foreign securities, the whole idea is to strive for diversification—the very nature of which suggests you won't have enough exposure in any one currency to justify the cost of hedging. At the risk of boring you with repetition, we must reiterate: Hedges cost money and should be used only when the perceived risk and the pertinent part of your portfolio are sizable enough to warrant the time and expense. Most people reading this book shouldn't bother. (Nor should you bother if the overseas portion of your portfolio is in mutual or closed-end funds; some of these do their own hedging to bolster their performances.)

TAKING LEAPS

As if the guideline-guru dodge weren't tough enough, along comes a new flavor of options that by changing one thing transform themselves into something quite different. They are Long-term Equity Anticipation Securities, from which has been teased the acronym LEAPS. As their name suggests, the thing that changed is time until expiration. LEAPS stretch out up to three years, instead of six or seven months, a period that exceeds the time investors hold some stocks. Except for their life span, they act like other options on stocks and stock indexes. But their extended existence qualifies them for removal from the high-risk ranks and into a special category of Stock Substitutes, Equity Lite, Lease-a-Stock, or whatever.

If you want to savor the security of putting a three-year floor under your stock, you can—by buying a LEAPS put. Thrill to the opportunity of locking in a purchase price now for a stock you might buy in three years; a LEAPS call will do it all. Expose your portfolio to broad market moves with LEAPS index options, while you put the capital that didn't go into individual stocks at work in other investments. Many, many a possibility LEAPS to mind.

But—and there always is a but, isn't there?—in the end, LEAPS just give you more time to make decisions; they don't make the decisions themselves any easier, and they sure don't eliminate them. (They do, however, eliminate your collection of dividends, which are paid only to shareholders, not LEAPS holders.) So stick to the game plan. Use the LEAPS to meet your objectives rather than allowing their longevity to lull you into relaxed self-discipline. You don't buy a LEAPS call before you get around to researching a stock; you buy it afterward if you buy it at all. Before you get in, figure out exactly where and when you will get out—and then do it, no matter how good everything is going, unless the original thesis for the trade has changed.

LEAPS look more expensive than regular options, but according to people in the business, they are actually cheaper if you figure in their entire life span. Be that as it may, they aren't free, so don't go overboard. The money you put into them counts toward the less-than-20% of your stock portfolio allowed in options, which means that loading up on LEAPS can leave you with limited capital to pursue strategies involving regular options. That is worth considering. There are more than 2,000 stocks with regular options on them, while at this writing roughly 300 stocks have LEAPS available, and most of those are big blue chips. The number is bound to grow, but who knows how quickly.

Breaking In a Broker

If you plan to become active in options, find a broker you can trust—not one you can make into a friend but one who knows what he or she is talking about, is able to discern strategies that fit your comfort level and investing style, and is willing to help you monitor your positions and spot opportunities. Go to a brokerage firm and ask to see a broker who has experience with options clients. Soon after you meet, ask to see his or her track record in options with those clients.

You are bound to be asked what sort of option trades you have been considering, and you can use that opportunity to spring a little test: Mention an option (Exxon April 45 call, for example) and see if the broker can find the option symbol to look up the premium on a quotation terminal. If he or she can't figure out the symbol, look for another broker.

Assuming the broker passes the test, ease into the relationship slowly. Be wary if the broker suddenly starts pressing you to try strategies you don't need or understand. For your part, don't be overly demanding, such as constantly calling for quotes, for example. But do expect the broker to spend time explaining things to your satisfaction. Start with a trade and see how it goes. Close out the first one before proceeding with the next. After you have three under your belt, and you and your broker have become comfortable working together, you can expand your horizons and have two or more trades going at once. If the going gets rough and some trades don't work, call a time-out and discuss the failed trades in detail with your broker. If it's your fault, live and learn. But if the broker's bad advice or incomplete advice or miscommunicated advice is the problem, get ready to move on. Having an options broker you don't trust is hazardous to your net worth.

SUGGESTED READING

We think you should read about and study futures and options trading extensively before trying it with real money. If you are bound and determined to trade commodities, you also will have to study the individual market(s) you are interested in. The mechanics of trading corn futures are about the same for trading cocoa futures. But the fundamentals of those markets couldn't be more dissimilar, and the information you gather about corn will do you absolutely no good in formulating a bullish or bearish opinion about cocoa.

Our duty is fulfilled by steering you to some basic books about the futures market. One that has been around for twenty years is *Getting Started in Commodity Futures Trading* by Mark J. Powers. It's probably out of print, so look in your library. A more recent book on the same theme is *Getting Started in Futures* by Todd Lofton. We especially like Mr. Lofton's dedication to his wife, who "bought one contract of silver coin futures 15 years ago, sold it 3 weeks later for a $750 profit, bought a color TV, and retired from the markets." Other possibilities are *Facts on Futures* by Jake Bernstein and *Futures: A Personal Seminar,* which is based on a classroom seminar conducted by the New York Institute of Finance.

For basic options books, try *Options as a Strategic Investment* by Lawrence McMillan. Be sure to get the most recent edition. If you don't mind having the fox show you around the henhouse, slog through *Options: Essential Concepts and Trading Strategies.* It's edited by The Options Institute, which is the educational arm of The Chicago Board Options Exchange. And the winner of the best-title award is *The Conservative Investor's Guide to Trading Options* by Leroy Gross. The author is dead, but the book was reissued.

A helpful book about long-term options is *LEAPS: What They Are and How to Use Them for Profit and Protection.* The author is Harrison Roth, who we are sad to say died while we were at work on the second edition of this book.

9 Real Estate and Other "Hard" Assets

"You have to look down, if you want something that goes up."

Inflation has been much in the news as we write this, and not because it's rising. Rather, economists, bond traders, and all sorts of other "experts," ranging up to and including the chairman of the Federal Reserve, are astounded and mystified that prices in the United States are so well behaved. The way they see it, conditions would seem ripe for an upward price explosion: Unemployment is at 20-year lows, well below the 5% level that many of these experts have long assumed would trigger a rising wage-price spiral. That spiral would start with businesses, desperate for help, jacking up pay offers to try to attract employees away from other businesses. Unions, wielding the threat of a strike at companies running full tilt to meet demand, would win big pay settlements. Once workers began rolling in all that money, they would compete with one another for a limited supply of goods and services. As demand for all sorts of things climbed, the reasoning went, producers would begin to jack up prices. Rising prices would convince workers to ask for higher pay, and another spin around the 'inflation block would ratchet the whole process up another notch until a frightened Federal Reserve slammed on the monetary brakes to bring the whole economy to a skidding halt.

Instead of that grim scenario, we see an economy humming along at a sustainable rate, albeit with spotty labor shortages. Wages are rising, but hardly at a frightening pace. There have been a few notable strikes, not the least of which was one that shut down United Parcel Service and showed many of us just how dependent we have become on catalog shopping instead of trekking to the local mall. While businesses would undoubtedly love to raise prices—they'd love to raise them no matter what was happening to the economy!—they can't seem to get away with it. Competition, from both here and abroad, is just too tough. Instead, they have to boost profits through streamlining their operations to be more efficient. Talk of any Fed rate hikes has faded as we wait to see how the financial crisis in East Asia works its way through our economy. Many U.S. businesses are bracing for a wave of low-priced imports as East Asian nations use their currency advantage to undercut other manufacturers in the burgeoning U.S. market. Of course, many U.S. manufacturers produce at least some of their own products in Asia and will benefit as well from the currency problems there. If anything, conditions seem ripe for prices to fall in this country, not rise, in the foreseeable future.

INFLATION? WHAT INFLATION?

For those of us with enough gray hair to remember the early 1980s, the scene today is nirvana. Back then, inflation was pushing relentlessly higher. Of course, rising inflation resulted in some stunning interest rates from bonds and short-term money market accounts. But most of us knew the truth: Inflation is a thief. What it gives with one hand, it takes back, plus a little more, with the other. As long-term investors we were deeply worried about the prospect of nonstop inflation ruining our retirement plans even as we gloried in money market returns of 18%.

For some investors the inflationary pressures of that era were more than welcome. These people held "hard assets" in the form of real estate or gold, and the value of those assets in most parts of the country were soaring along with inflation. Gold hit an amazing $800 an ounce at the height of the inflation panic of the early 1980s.

With no real prospect of that kind of inflationary binge ahead of us today, the question becomes this: Should you as a prudent investor own real estate or precious metals as a diversification tool within your portfolio to protect you from inflation? The answer is both yes and no. There are still powerful arguments for owning real estate as a diversification tool. Demand for housing in many sections of the country has driven home prices up sharply in the past few years, despite the near absence of inflation; those rising home values have put a nice shine on many an investor's net worth. But gold is another matter altogether. Not only is there an absence of inflation to drive demand for gold, there is also a growing inclination among some of the world's biggest gold hoarders—central banks—to get rid of at least some of their gold holdings. That potent combination of falling demand and growing supply has dealt gold a hard blow in the past few years. Indeed, late in 1997 the price of gold sank below $300 an ounce for the first time in 12 years. And short of an unexpected world economic crisis (triggered, perhaps, by East Asia's problems) there is little reason to expect a resurgence of demand for gold.

REAL ESTATE

Real estate is a real head scratcher for investors. It does provide a worthwhile diversification tool when added to a portfolio of cash, stocks, and bonds. The trouble is, it's difficult to invest in real estate in a manner that puts it on the proper scale when measured against your other investments. Owning your own house is certainly a real estate investment, and a big one for most of us. But owning a house as an investment isn't much different from putting all your stock investment money in a single stock. There is no diversification. There are real estate stocks, called real estate investment trusts, that do achieve a measure of diversification in that they hold properties in different parts of the country. Trouble is, REIT stocks behave as much like stocks as they do real estate. Again, you aren't getting a pure, diversified play on real estate. The real solution is to join a limited partnership or some other investment vehicle that allows you to take a long-term stake in a diversified portfolio of property. But that solution is available only to the fortunate few among us with a million bucks or so to invest in the partnership. (An investment of that size implies, if you really are diversifying your portfolio, that you have $5 million or so in stocks and bonds.) So let's take a closer look at the world of real estate. Our goal is to help you put it in perspective and find a way to make it an effective part of your portfolio.

Real estate—they're not making any more of it. That's right. But when a real estate broker presents this fixed supply argument as a reason to invest in it, he is glossing over the second half of that fundamental law of markets: supply *and demand*. Sure, the supply of land is finite, and we will even forget for the moment that the vast majority of the United States is *un*developed. But the demand for what land there is varies. And it varies a lot, you should pardon the pun. Demand for real estate fluctuates not only from year to year but also from decade to decade. That long-term variance is what you should be thinking about if you are interested in making real estate a part of your portfolio.

When World War II ended and the soldiers and sailors came home, they went to work—not just at jobs or at getting an education but also at producing families. Well, maybe it wasn't all work. In any event, their efforts produced in subsequent years a huge surge in the population of the United States that has come to be known as the baby boom.

By the mid-1960s those at the leading edge of the boomers were out of school and had started their own families. As might be expected, the boomers and their children needed shelter, and they embarked on a house-buying binge of unprecedented proportions. The quest for shelter continued well into the 1980s as boomers bought their second, third, or even fourth homes, some as a result of corporate transfers around the nation and others simply to upgrade their lifestyles. That massive demand for houses, coupled with a serious inflation problem in the late 1970s and early 1980s, pushed home prices right through the roof. Those rising prices, in turn, persuaded even more people to buy houses, until home ownership became the preeminent financial goal of most Americans. Most homeowners considered their houses not places to reside but investments that would appreciate steadily and spectacularly. Living in a house was just a side benefit of the investment.

But what of that generation, and the ones following it, today? Most boomers are well into that period of their lives when they would seek to buy their first home. More important, the members of the leading edge of what we might call Boomertown are hitting their fifties and are in the midst of or still recovering from financing their children's college educations. Certainly they are old enough to grasp their own mortality and to recognize that retirement is no longer some fuzzy concept but a stark reality that they are going to face in the very foreseeable future. By and large, they are much less interested in paying bigger mortgages than they are in amassing an investment portfolio to carry them comfortably through the years of retirement. As the boomer population ages, the portion of the population in the prime home-buying ages, between 25 and 35, is declining markedly. What all this demographics amounts to is that the residential real estate market is running out of steam.

This isn't to say that real estate is not enjoying high old times in some parts of the country. New York City lives and breathes by the stock market, and the unprecedented gains of the past few years has driven an enormous demand for prize properties in Manhattan and the ritzier suburbs. Young traders and investment bankers fight for the privilege of paying $2 million for a two-bedroom apartment in a prestigious building. Out in the Hamptons, the older, more seasoned (and better paid) Wall Street veterans compete to see who can put the most ostentatious adornments on their seaside estates. Elevators to whisk their guests to the second floor are the latest manifestation of that one-upsmanship. Yet while that crazed bidding occurs, people living only a few miles away in the surrounding boroughs are finding themselves far under water if they bought more mundane co-ops or condos at the height of the last real estate boom that swept New York in the 1980s. Wall Street wealth doesn't trickle down very far. Then there's San Francisco. Even jaded New Yorkers suffer sticker shock when they transfer out to the Silicon Valley area.

Still, new homes are being thrown up in most of the rest of the country at a pretty fast clip, more than meeting demand. And, not to be ghoulish about it, a sizable proportion of the nation's housing stock—about 25% by some estimates—is owned by people 65 years or older. These homes are likely to come on the market in the next 20 years or so, especially since the Tax Relief Act of 1997 granted most of those owners the right to keep every penny of profits when they sell those houses. So the supply and demand equation, it seems to us, works out this way: plenty of supply, not so much demand. Does that sound like a market in which you want to sink a goodly portion of your wealth?

Commercial real estate seems to be in somewhat better shape, but again it is very region-specific. Overbuilding in the late 1980s and early 1990s resulted in some spectacular collapses. But since then, a cutback in construction coupled with growing demand by expanding companies in many parts of the country has brought the supply of commercial space into fairly good balance on a national basis. Of course, when that happens, every builder and his brother-in-law get the urge to throw up a speculative office park on some piece of suburban farmland, so it's hard to predict how long that balance will last. Certainly, as we look around New York City, there are plenty of cranes and steelworkers putting up new edifices.

The bottom line: There are problems with real estate as an investment. Let's take a closer look now at each piece of the puzzle to see what might fit into your portfolio.

Figure 9.1 Real Estate's Ups and Downs

The U.S. real estate investment industry group of the Dow Jones Global Indexes includes some development companies as well as real estate investment trusts (REITs). The U.S. market index is a broad measure of about 725 stocks.

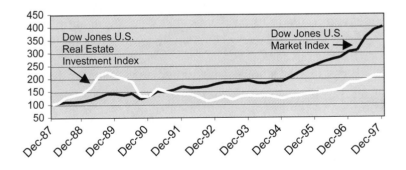

Costs, Risks, and Benefits of Owning a Home

To evaluate any investment, you must know the costs of getting into it. Let's consider the costs of "investing" in a $300,000 house. First, there is the down payment. Although you can find lenders that will accept less, 20% is the usual amount advanced on a house purchase. That's $60,000. Add a few thousand more, probably at least $5,000, for fees and closing costs. That brings us to $65,000, and we haven't even moved in yet. The $240,000 mortgage will cost you more than $2,200 a month if you take out a 15-year mortgage, somewhat less with a 30-year loan. Then there's maintenance, which will tack on a few more thousand each year and property taxes, which can range from a few thousand to as much as $10,000 in some areas. You do get a tax deduction for the mortgage interest and real estate taxes, which can save you nearly 40% on those two items in some high-tax states if you're in the upper brackets. The net result of all this is a monthly payment of about $1,820. Don't forget that when you sell your abode, you're likely to be paying a real estate agent 6% or 7% of the selling price as well as shelling out a few thousand more for various fees.

But buying a house isn't all bad news. That tax deduction for mortgage interest and real estate taxes is a powerful incentive. All things considered, a mortgage loan is apt to be the cheapest money you'll ever borrow. And courtesy of the Taxpayer Relief Act of 1997, the government gives you yet another powerful incentive to own a home: the absence of any capital gains tax on profits of up to $500,000 on the sale of your house. How much encouragement do you need to make this "investment" in a house?

Still, before you start scouring neighborhoods for that center-hall colonial, consider the alternative: renting. We figure that, on average, a house similar to the $300,000 structure mentioned above would rent for about $1,200 a month. No down payment required. No property tax bill. Minimal upkeep, if any. No closing costs at purchase or real estate commission on the sale. Just $1,200 a month. That means not only would you have $65,000 in a lump sum for some other kind of investment—stocks or bonds, say—but you would also have more than $600 a month, or $7,200 annually, to dollar-cost average into other investments as well.

That's just a snapshot of the costs of owning a home versus renting. We really haven't delved into appreciation or, heaven forbid, *de*preciation. And make no mistake about it, depreciation can happen. We know folks in New York who are under water on their condominiums. We know folks in California who are under water on their mini-mansions. And we know other folks in different parts of America who are under water on their suburban ranch-style houses in new suburban developments next door to even newer suburban developments. Of course, we also know people who have profited immensely on the ownership of a home and others who have lost tidy sums in stocks that *de*preciate much faster than homes.

If you haven't already purchased a home but are considering such a move, distinguish among single-family detached houses, condominiums, and cooperatives. The latter, by and large, are significantly worse investments than the former (although don't try to tell that to New Yorkers selling their co-ops to 30-something Wall Street investment bankers looking for a home for their million-dollar bonuses). The condo craze began to spread nationwide in the 1960s. The original idea was sound: providing concentrated housing in a highly desirable area. Beachfront property was so expensive, for instance, that it was out of reach for many homeowners as a site for a single-family home. But by developing a multi-story apartment building on a parcel of land that would otherwise be large enough only for one or two houses, developers were able to make beachfront living affordable for many more people while making the most lucrative use of expensive property. But as with many good ideas, the condominium concept was carried to an extreme. As other less innovative investors and developers jumped into the condo business, they first overbuilt even the most desirable areas. Then they began to apply the concept where it never belonged, in geographic areas that simply weren't desirable enough to generate the demand for such concentrated housing. Take a look at newspaper real estate sections from the late 1970s and again in the late 1980s. All the advertisements for distress sales and auctions of languishing condominium developments should give you a feel for the extent of the boom-and-bust cycle that afflicts many such undertakings. Certainly, single-family houses suffered some price declines as well during those times, but not to the extent that multi-family developments did. With population pressures for new housing abating, the difference in the investment potential between quality single-family housing and condominiums is apt to widen, not shrink.

Some investors, including both those who rent their homes and those who own them, indulge their appetite for owning real estate by purchasing vacation homes. For those who have decided to rent their primary home, this can be an effective way to add a real estate component to their portfolio. Houses that are intended for vacation or occasional use are often smaller and less expensive than year-round houses. But be careful if you intend to turn your vacation home into a money-making enterprise. The IRS has strict rules on the amount of personal use you can make of your second home if you rent it out; running afoul of those rules can be costly.

Another alert: Never, ever let a slick salesman convince you that buying a time-share is the same thing as investing in real estate. A time-share gives you the right to use a piece of property for a short amount of time or to trade your right to use one property for the right to use another. When you buy a time-share, you are buying a vacation, not a piece of property. As much as you may enjoy them, vacations have lousy investment potential.

Here's a final observation about real estate as an investment versus financial assets, such as stocks and bonds. Recall that the baby boomers are moving into an age when preparing for retirement begins to become more important. At the same time, many of those boomers who want to own a home already own one. Some will, of course, continue to upgrade into ever larger, more costly mansions. But we think that a large number of these investors already are electing to sit tight in homes they own while directing discretionary income toward stock and bond investing as a means of financing their retirements. That wave of money has created a noticeable surge in the demand side of the supply and demand equation for paper investments, which is one of the reasons for the mind-boggling rise in stock prices during the mid-1990s. While the pace of stock market gains can't continue at the 20%-plus levels of the past few years, we think the supply of money aimed at the financial markets will create more opportunities for appreciation there than in the housing market. Regional exceptions will occur, of course.

So where does all this leave you, the potential homeowner and stock investor? The best advice we can come up with is this: Buy a house because you want the space, the privacy, or the neighborhood that comes with it. If you do buy a house, pay careful attention to your real estate agent's warning about the three most important factors in real estate: location, location, location. If you buy a sound house in a desirable neighborhood, don't be afraid to leverage up a bit. Again, it's the cheapest money you'll ever borrow, so make the most of it and leave your cash reserves intact for deployment into other investments. And always leave a little for making those other investments. There is nothing like diversification in an investment portfolio. The point we really want you to take away is that the smart investor weighs alternatives carefully before plunging ahead.

OTHER FORMS OF REAL ESTATE INVESTMENT

REAL ESTATE INVESTMENT TRUSTS. Some things are beyond the scope of this book. We aren't going to tell you how to buy and manage a portfolio of apartment buildings or how to organize a syndicate to develop an office park. If you're that interested in real estate, you are far beyond our ability to help guide your decisions. But if, after buying your own home (or deciding not to), you still feel an urge to have a portion of your portfolio in real estate, there are two relatively simple ways to achieve that goal: real estate investment trusts and limited partnerships, although both have some problems. From our point of view, the better of those two alternatives is the REIT (rhymes with eat). Like a mutual fund, a REIT brings together a pool of capital to invest in mortgages, properties, or both. Income from the real estate or from the mortgages is divided among shareholders after the manager of the fund has paid the necessary expenses (including his fee). Most REITs have no defined life span; if a building that a REIT owns is sold or the mortgage on it is paid off, the REIT simply finds a similar property or mortgage into which it reinvests the proceeds. The shares of REITs are traded on the two major stock exchanges as well as on the NASDAQ market. REITs have enjoyed enormous gains in popularity—and in price—in recent years, and there are many to choose from. Certainly they provide a far more liquid approach to investing in real estate than owning a house or an office building. They also enjoy many of the other benefits that typically accrue to real estate, including preferable tax treatment and moderate protection against inflation. And, of course, they offer the investor something a house doesn't—the opportunity to diversify among several real estate properties in different geographical areas.

But (don't you get tired of always having to read about the downside of something that starts out sounding so good?) there are some more things, including disadvantages, that you need to know about REITs before phoning your broker. First, there are different kinds of REITs: mortgage, equity, and a blend of the two. Mortgage REITs are essentially lenders to real estate developers that don't directly own property, although the property serves as security for the loan. Equity REITs, on the other hand, buy property directly, often specializing in a certain type of commercial real estate, such as strip malls, office parks, and even nursing homes. Hybrid REITs blend both functions, owning property as well as lending to developers. These different kinds of REITs are intended to serve different investment functions. Mortgage REITs provide an income stream but have little opportunity for capital appreciation. Equity REITs are intended to appreciate over time; they also provide some income, but typically it is less than would be available from a mortgage REIT. One peculiarity of all REITs is that they are required by law to pay to investors as dividends 95% of their taxable income. Thus, you're going to wind up getting income—taxable to you—whether you want it or not.

A second disadvantage of REITs is that they are traded just like other stocks. The value of a share of a REIT reflects not only the value of the underlying properties or the income stream from the underlying mortgages, but it also reflects the perceptions of all the other investors who might own, or might want to own, REIT shares. Thus, while the value of the properties or the mortgages mightn't change at all, the value of the shares can rise and fall depending upon investor appetite for a particular REIT. In the long run and on average, the market for REIT shares, as the market for any other shares, should reflect something close to the true value of the assets it owns. But if you buy in the midst of a brief love affair between other investors and your REIT and have to sell after the fling is over, you could take a financial

Figure 9.2 A Wild Ride in Real Estate

Annual total returns (prices and dividends) of the National Association of
Real Estate Investment Trust's All-REIT index.

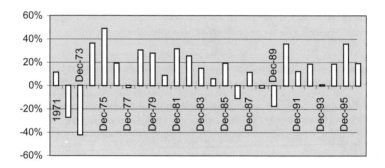

Despite erratic returns from year to year, the cumulative change in REITs
over the past 25 years has been sharply upward.

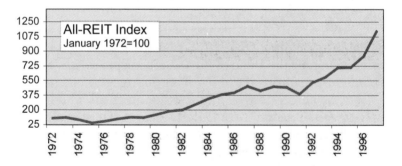

beating that wouldn't be reflected in the value of the under-lying asset. All we're saying is, just be careful and go in with your eyes open.

Which kind of REIT should you consider? Unless you specifically want taxable income, we'd prefer the equity REIT. After all, you are in real estate to own something tan-gible, aren't you? If you just want to lend money, you can probably do it with the same or better results and many fewer risks by buying bonds or money market funds. But not every equity REIT is going to be a worthwhile investment. For one thing, real estate investment fads come and go. Sometimes it's office parks, and other times hotels. If you buy a nursing home REIT when that kind of investing is the style and prices of such REIT shares are high, you could be deeply disappointed a few years later when the emphasis shifts to something else. Geographic diversity is a consideration, too. Some equity REITs specialize in a single state or even city. That's fine if that state or city is booming. But when the bust comes, it can be painful. Finally, most REITs are leveraged, with all that implies about risk and reward. You can find low-leverage or even no-leverage REITs, but you have to hunt for them.

Equity REITs, then, provide an easy but far from perfect means for the average investor to diversify his or her portfolio with a little real estate exposure. As you begin your screening of potential REIT investments, pay particular attention to the geographic diversity of each REIT's proper-ties. Also, do a quick check of your local newspaper's stock-price columns to ensure that a REIT you like is actively trad-ed. Some aren't, and it would be a shame to invest in some-thing you thought was liquid, only to find out when you want to get out that it isn't.

LIMITED PARTNERSHIPS. This is the other, less attractive way to invest in real estate (as well as other things, including oil and gas exploration). We can't say enough bad things about this approach to investing in *anything*. Like mutual funds and REITs, limited partnerships are a means by which several investors can pool their assets in an investment. In this case the investors are the *limited partners,* who are investing in a venture organized by *general partners.* Brokers who sell limited partnerships like to point out that the word *limited* refers to the liabilities of the investors; their liability is limited to the amount of money they invest. In other words, if something goes haywire, your maximum loss will be the money invested. The general partners, on the other hand, have unlimited liability, meaning that once the partnership's assets are exhausted, the general partners must bear any further losses. What the broker doesn't tell you is that there are lots of other limits on the limited partners, too, including control of the venture. You and your limited partners could, in theory, oust the general partners if you think they are botching the job. But in many cases it takes a two-thirds vote to do so, and limited partners are seldom organized enough to bring off such a move. What's more, the general partners have sufficient control of information about the project that you probably won't know they've botched it until it's too late to do anything about it but shed a tear.

Limited partnerships can look pretty tempting because the partnership arrangement usually provides for the limited partners to enjoy a sizable share of the profits that result from the venture. In the case of a real estate partnership, the development of an office building or shopping center could be involved. But if you read the prospectus that the partnership is required to give potential investors, you will notice lots of qualified language, such as "projected profits" and "anticipated profits." Those qualifiers are there for a good reason: Usually the profits are far smaller than the general partners originally "projected," but you won't find that out until you're a few years into the investment.

We arrive now at our biggest objection to limited partnerships: a nearly total lack of liquidity. It is easy enough to get into a partnership but will nigh impossible to get out. There is only a small secondary market for limited partnerships, so you could conceivably be stuck in a fruitless investment for 10 years or more; limited partnerships usually have finite life spans. If you can find someone willing to buy you out, it will often be at a ridiculously low price. Suffice it to say, there are better ways to invest in real estate, or nearly anything else you want to invest in, than a limited partnership.

PRECIOUS METALS.   Remember the stuff about supply and demand? Too much supply, not enough demand, and prices fall? Gold is a wonderful object lesson in supply and demand. The metal has been a traditional hedge against inflation, war, and pestilence through the centuries. As recently as the 1980s, when the United States was enduring some of the worst inflation in decades, the price of gold reached an astounding $800 an ounce as investors scrambled to find something that would retain its value. Well, the situation is considerably different today. Inflation is tame even in the face of strong economic growth and low unemployment. The Cold War is over, and there is no single strong enemy that threatens the United States. Finance is becoming increasingly global, and there is an abiding faith that governments and large financial institutions can measure and adjust the risks they take. In short, there is little apparent reason to own gold; hence, the demand for the metal is low.

Now, what about the supply side? Well, mining techniques that extract gold from the earth have become increasingly efficient, so it's easier than ever to get new gold. But far more important is the fact that some of the institutions that own more gold than anyone else have decided—and publicly announced—that they don't need nearly as much gold as they hold, and they want to dispose of it. Don't expect there to be a gold shortage anytime soon. So how does our supply and demand equation look these days? Huge supplies plus little demand equals bust! And sure enough, the equation

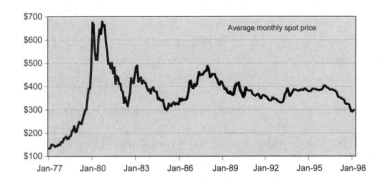

Figure 9.3 Gold: Big Party, Long Hangover

Prices in dollars per troy ounce.

works: In late 1997, gold slipped below $300 an ounce, and nobody knows where the bottom is.

Still, there are fanatics who just insist on owning gold. They have several choices. The simplest and most liquid form in which you can own gold is to buy shares in well-run gold-mining companies. The stock prices of such companies tend to fluctuate in tandem with the price of gold. If people do indeed flock to gold the next time there is some crisis, the price of gold will rise, and so will the price of your shares. The ease with which you can buy, hold, and sell gold shares becomes a prominent point in their favor, as you will see. But be careful about which stocks you buy. Extraction cost is everything in the gold industry. Mines with the highest extraction costs are the first to be closed as gold prices sink, and the last to be reopened. Only the most efficient can operate through thick and thin. Those are the stocks you want to own.

If you want to own gold as a hedge against inflation, stocks are fine. But if you are an apocalyptic, you'll argue that owning shares is pointless if the New York Stock Exchange collapses in the midst of a world financial crisis or is destroyed by a thermonuclear blast. You'll argue that you need the real stuff. That can be done fairly simply, too, by buying gold certificates issued by big banks and securities brokerage firms. You don't get to play with your gold or show it off, but you do own it. Of course, if the New York Stock Exchange fails or melts down to atomic cinders, the big banks and brokerage firms will probably go the same route. Ultimately, then, you may want to have gold stashed under the floorboards or in the car ready to head for the hills. In that case, you have few choices, none very good.

Gold is heavy, really heavy. We visited the gold vault deep under the Federal Reserve Bank of New York. The gold bars that are stashed there aren't very big, about the size of a brick. But it isn't any accident that the workers who move that gold around wear steel overshoes. Drop one of those things on a foot, and you're going to be in a cast for a while. You can buy minted coins made of pure gold, such as American Eagles, Canadian Maple Leafs, or South African Krugerrands. You will pay a modest premium for having someone convert gold ingots into pretty coins, but you will have real gold that is fairly liquid, assuming you don't bust the car's shock absorbers getting it home. You can even buy gold in ingot form if you're cheap enough to want to avoid the minting charge. The trouble is, once you take possession of your ingots, you must have them assayed before they can be sold again. And you still have the storage and transportation problem. What it boils down to is that either you really don't believe a crisis of earth-shattering proportions is going to destroy the financial system as we know it, in which case maybe you should consider real estate instead of gold as an inflation hedge; or else such a crisis is entirely possible, and it will be worth it to lug and store all that gold and get new shock absorbers (or a heavy-duty truck).

Silver has also been considered a hedge against inflation from time to time, and it benefits from having a wider range of industrial uses than gold. But if you thought hauling a pile of gold around was a burden, try silver. Because it costs far less per ounce than gold, you will acquire a hell of a lot more of it if you are planning to invest the same amount of money. You can, of course, buy silver mining stocks, but you are back in the same quandary you were in with gold: If you really need it, then you need the real thing. If you don't, find a better investment.

More recently a new player has come on the precious metals investment scene: platinum. Late in 1997 the U.S. mint began selling platinum coins, also called Eagles like their gold counterparts. While considered a precious metal, platinum is, like silver, used extensively in industry. Among its most important uses is as a catalyst in most automobile emissions systems. The sale of the mint's new platinum coins came on the heels of a remarkable rally in the underlying price of the metal that had driven the price to $479 an ounce at mid-year, the result of shortages of the metal coming out of Russia. The rally, which occurred as gold was still slumping, apparently convinced many investors that platinum prices were no longer tied to movements in gold prices. The reception that met the introduction of the platinum Eagles outdid even the Treasury's optimistic expectations. Unfortunately, shortly after the coins were introduced, the price of platinum joined gold's descent, at least in part on expectations that slower growth in Japan and much of the rest of Asia would reduce demand for platinum. As of this writing, the price of platinum was hovering just over $350 an ounce, and the first wave of investors who snapped up those new coins were sitting on tidy losses. The short lesson: It is tough to make money on precious metals.

DIAMONDS. Diamonds are a subject unto themselves. For years the supply of diamonds has been in the hands of a monopoly, and anything that is monopolized can be manipulated. That old monopoly looks like it may be breaking down, though. Some of the semi-nations created out of the old Soviet Union are big producers of diamonds, and they're putting them on the market without going through the monopoly. The implication is that more supply could be coming to market, and you know what increasing supplies do to prices.

Lest you think the stunning beauty of a flawless diamond makes it a worthwhile investment, consider that gem-quality diamonds have from time to time badly underperformed industrial diamonds. Our advice: Buy her a diamond because you love her, not as an investment.

SUGGESTED READING

Most bookstores will carry how-to books on investing in various aspects of real estate, ranging from simple rental properties to REITs. If you're serious about expanding your investment portfolio beyond owning your own home, pick up a volume that addresses the level of your interest.

Big-time real estate developers (which you probably aren't and never will be) are fascinating people with outsize egos and thick wallets. Reading about them can be fun even though you'll learn precious little to help you in your own real estate investing decisions. Donald Trump's self-adulatory works are the best known of these realty tales, but the far more perceptive and interesting work is about the Reichmann family: *The Reichmanns: Family, Faith, Fortune, and the Empire of Olympia and York* by Anthony Bianco (Times Books, 1997).

10 Collectibles Aren't Investable

"Let's face it, Charles, nothing *makes you 'reach for your wallet.'"*

This book, if you recall, is about making investment decisions. Here's an investment decision that is particularly easy: Say no to collectibles. Buy art, old coins, stamps, antique furniture, baseball cards, matchbook covers, autographs, or Barbie dolls solely because you want to own them. They look nice on your walls; they stimulate conversation; it makes you feel good to look at them, touch them, count them, or whatever.

Do not buy them to make money. Investing in collectibles takes the Greater Fool theory to its highest level. You are speculating (not investing) in something that is illiquid, incurs extremely high transaction costs, requires careful research, and is often highly vulnerable to fraud. There simply isn't any comparison between collectibles, no matter what they are, and legitimate investments such as stocks and bonds.

Yes, but—you sputter—some of these things really appreciate. Sure, we all can cite instances of impressive price appreciation in collectibles: Did you hear about the pre-1980 Barbie doll that sold for $4,000? The Roger Maris baseball card that brought $131,000? And, to top it all, the $53.3 million paid for Vincent van Gogh's painting *Irises*? These instances make news precisely because they are so unusual. What you don't hear or read about are the millions of dollars tied up in stamps, baseball cards, coins, and other such items that for all practical purposes are worthless today. You also seldom see much about the frauds that are out there: the Barbie dolls that have had their hairdos or body parts changed to conform to what "experts" say is the "right" Barbie for investment, or the flood of counterfeit baseball cards rolling off the presses.

The market for collectibles is highly fickle, often reaching its height at times of seeming prosperity when inflation is providing some people with more money than they know what to do with. That cash finds its way into "hard" assets rather than financial assets, driving prices up to phenomenal heights before the inevitable collapse occurs. But the price gains are often for very rare or very perfect specimens, whether they are dolls, coins, or art. Frequently, such specimens are already priced high enough that the average investor has no business spending that much without intimate knowledge of the nuances of the trade. In short, investing in collectibles is highly risky and requires at least as much time and effort, with much less assurance of long-term success, as putting money to work in other, more predictably lucrative assets.

That's not going to stop dealers and other advocates of various collectibles from trying to persuade you otherwise. The worst of the dealers will argue that stocks and bonds perform sporadically, that you have to either be able to predict takeovers or mergers or trade on inside information to make money in those markets. They will tell you that paper investments are difficult to understand and that, in the end, all you have is a piece of paper. Don't ask why they are so willing to take your pieces of paper, either checks or currency, for their wares. Often, they will invoke the blessing of some of the well-known apocalyptic sages who assert that a sackful of old coins will stand you in good stead when we run into the inevitable hyper-inflation that will destroy the world as we know it. If you run into one of these guys, turn and flee. The best test of any dealer in collectibles is to ask him about the investment potential of an item. If he tells you he doesn't know and that in any case you shouldn't buy something simply as an investment, you are in the right place.

Obviously, we can't deal with every collectible on its own merits. We are constantly astounded when we learn that people collect some of the things they do. But because Old Master paintings get more media attention than any other class of collectible, let's take a trip through the world of art collecting to see how it works as a potential investment market. The details of other collectibles will be different, but we think you will encounter most of the same problems on some scale regardless of what you are collecting.

ART FOR MONEY'S SAKE

The good news is that, yes, you can make money collecting art, and it isn't confined only to the Old Masters. In 1992, Andy Warhol's pop art *210 Coke Bottles* fetched an amazing $2.09 million at auction in New York. Four years earlier the same painting had sold for $1.43 million. Not counting commissions—which can be very substantial in the art world—that's a tidy profit of 46% in four years.

The bad news is that it takes money to make money in the art market. Unfortunately for most of us, the art that is most likely to appreciate in value—the Old Masters, the Impressionists, and the Postimpressionists—has already appreciated so much that it's out of our league. You can be pretty certain that the people with enough money to buy that caliber of art didn't make their money by investing in art from the beginning; they made their fortunes some other way and are only now indulging a taste for art.

For the rest of us, the prospects aren't so good. Art experts counsel that the collector with less than $1 million—that's right, $1 million—to spend will have to be content with contemporary art. The trouble is, experts can't agree on how likely it is that most contemporary art will appreciate. On the optimistic side, you have experts who figure that perhaps 2% of contemporary art has some shot at rising in value in coming years. But that estimate is pooh-poohed by others who cite a Stanford University study of art auctions at Sotheby's and Christie's between 1973 and 1978 which concluded that less than .01%—yes, one hundredth of one percent—of contemporary art has any resale value at all. Moreover, the experts add, the situation has gotten *worse* in the intervening two decades. So there you have it: Your chances of losing

Figure 10.1 Fine Art Does Appreciate

Art Market Research in London prepares an index of art prices. The figures below show the average annualized price gain of certain types of art collectibles over a 10-year period. The index does not take into account transaction costs, which would greatly reduce the annual returns.

	Annualized Gain Over 10 Years Ended Dec. 31, 1997
Old Masters paintings	2.7%
19th-century European paintings	-0.5%
French impressionists	7.8%
Modern European painting	-3.2%
Contemporary masters	11.5%
European porcelain	6.9%
Chinese ceramics	1.5%
English silver	5.1%
Continental silver	3.2%
French 18th-century furniture	8.2%
English 18th-century furniture	6.6%

money by investing in contemporary art range from 98% to more than 99.99%. Now, how much do you want to invest?

TRANSACTION COSTS IN ART MAKE BROKERAGE FEES LOOK CHEAP

We'll start our art investment program with a visit to a gallery to look at some contemporary paintings. The biggest variety of art and some of the best can be found in the gallery neighborhoods of Manhattan. But you don't have to live in or travel frequently to New York to shop for contemporary art. Most large cities have at least a few galleries handling works of regional artists. In any event, as an art investor you will be deeply interested in the prices of art. The pieces hanging on the wall will have price tags that reflect very little of the actual worth of the painting itself. Instead, the price mostly consists of what it will take for the artist to pay the rent on his studio and the gallery owner to pay the rent on the gallery. That's obvious from the commission structure between the gallery and the artist. If the painting sells, the gallery gets about 50% of the total price, or less if the artist is "hot."

What do you get when you buy the picture? The piece of art, to be sure, but probably not the frame, although the gallery will frame it for an extra charge. And you don't get the copyright to the picture. That belongs to the artist, who will collect any royalties if the picture enjoys the rare degree of popularity that results in its commercial use. You can obtain the copyright from the artist, but, again, that costs extra. You should get a warranty of title and authenticity, and a certificate stating the name of the artist, the title of the work, when it was done, and how much you paid for it.

Prices in the art market aren't fixed any more than prices in the auto or real estate markets are fixed. But the art market is different from the auto dealer's lot or the multiple-listing service that markets houses. Art galleries usually have agreements that give them exclusive representation of an artist, so there isn't any effective competition. The gallery, the artist, and the customers who bought earlier works by an artist all have a vested interest in seeing that prices rise. Still, the price tag on the gallery wall is the best that the gallery thinks it can get for the piece; you probably can and should get a 10% markdown from that price. Hard bargaining might net you another few percentage points or maybe a free frame, but that's about all you can expect.

Some novice art collectors attempt to skirt the gallery system by going directly to the artist's studio to negotiate the purchase of a new work. If the artist isn't represented by a gallery, this approach could lead to obtaining a painting at a much lower price. But with that lower price comes a reduced likelihood that the art piece will appreciate because the artist obviously isn't getting the kind of exposure she would if she were represented by a gallery. If the artist is represented by a gallery, she usually has a legal obligation to pay it a commission on the sale of her work whether or not the gallery handles the sale.

Another popular way to purchase art is through auction houses. The trouble with auctions is that they're a smug world of secret codes and unwritten rules where professionals have all the advantages. Moreover, they take place at a set date and time, so you must be available, either in person or by phone, to bid on pieces. Your choices are limited to the art being auctioned, of course, and you must do your home-work before the auctioneer begins his spiel. The appeal of an auction is that commission rates are lower than the 50% charged by galleries. Typically, an auction house charges a 20% commission (10% paid by the seller and 10% paid by the buyer).

While most auction houses strive to project a snooty aura, for most of them business is down from the 1980s boom, and they're desperate for customers. Walk right in. They're happy to set up new buyers with an auction expert—something of an academically trained salesman—to answer questions. Don't be reluctant to take advantage of auction-buying perks, such as socializing with other collectors or indulging in the crab that is served on big silver trays at some auction events. Here are some tips for the auction scene:

- Auction houses categorize their offerings, and you can tell from the words they use how the ranking works; "masterpieces" obviously are better than "important" pieces, which in turn are loftier than "fine" pieces. As in buying homes, it's always best to buy the cheapest item in the best neighborhood, rather than the other way around.

- Read the catalog description carefully. "Attributed to Rembrandt" doesn't quite mean Rembrandt. "School of Rembrandt" indicates the painter was a pupil of the master. But paintings from the hand of an artist identi-fied as being from the "circle of Rembrandt" or a "follower of Rembrandt" might as well be anonymous.

- Tiny symbols in the auction catalog next to the title of a piece, such as triangles or check marks, tip off buy-ers to check the fine print. They flag that the auction house is actually the owner of the property or has lent money against it, which makes the auction house expert's advice suspect.

■ Never get egged into a bidding war with an invisible opponent. It's perfectly legal for an auction house to invent bids, up to a point. To create momentum, the auctioneer is allowed to call bids that don't exist up to the seller's secret minimum price, called the "reserve" price. Assume a painting is listed in the catalog at $4,000 to $6,000. Buyers don't know it, but the seller has agreed to take anything above $3,000. The auctioneer will begin, "Do I have $2,500 for this? Yes. Then, $2,750, I have $2,750. Do I have $3,000? Yes"—even though there's no bid. It's called "bidding from the chandelier," and it's legal as long as all the fake bids are below the reserve price. The reserve is generally 65% to 80% of the low estimate.

■ Auction catalog photos routinely err on the side of flattering the merchandise. In the auction world, there's a saying: "The camera adds 10%." With paintings, a picture won't tell you if it's cracked, relined, or overcleaned. Condition is an extremely important determinant of value.

A less popular but effective way through the art labyrinth is to hire freelance consultants who will, for a commission, help you find art that you want to own. A good consultant can cut down immensely on the time and effort required to make a purchase and will handle many of the details that are unfamiliar to the novice buyer. Most freelance consultants are paid on a commission basis, ranging from 10% to 35%. The lower the commission, the more likely you will be billed for additional expenses. But beware the consultant who represents certain artists and steers you toward them. Also, many consultants can obtain sizable discounts from galleries. Your commission payment to the consultant should reflect the consultant's cost for the work, not the gallery's list price.

NOW THAT YOU HAVE IT, WHAT ARE YOU GOING TO DO WITH IT?

We will assume that you have found a painting you like, have measured it carefully to be sure that it will fit your wall, and have purchased it. Getting it home is your responsibility, although the gallery will help arrange suitable shipping. Your job is to protect your artwork by storing it or hanging it carefully and insuring it. Not all paintings or artworks hold up well over the years. Some very expensive contemporary art has suffered from such infirmities as flaking or fading paint. But overall, your biggest concern should be insurance of your valuable investment. Unfortunately, insuring a work of art will probably be a colossal headache because objective values are virtually impossible to determine. Suffice it to say, it will be expensive, and that expense will mount depending on the kinds of losses you want included in the coverage. You can control the expense to some extent by taking on larger deductibles, which in effect is self-insuring a portion of the artwork against loss.

GETTING RID OF ART

For whatever reason, you have decided to sell your prized painting. How to go about it? Well, you can visit the gallery where you bought it. There's a minute chance that if the artist has done well, the gallery will repurchase it from you, although probably at a fraction of your purchase price.

There's a good chance that the gallery won't offer you anything. After that, you can resort to the auction houses or consultants who might handle a sale. But in those cases there will be commissions to pay, ranging up to 40%. In short, if you do manage to sell your art, it will probably be at a loss. And, unfortunately, while the government will gladly tax any gains you make by selling art, it won't recognize a loss unless you can convince the IRS that you are a professional art investor. Don't try it. As a practical matter, however, passing muster with the IRS won't be a problem for most investors because the sad fact is there simply *isn't* a secondary market for most contemporary art.

That leaves you with the only remaining alternative: giving it away. You can pass it along to your heirs through your will, in which case it is in the heirs' best interest to have the art appraised at the lowest possible value. To give you an idea of the frequently mistaken notions of the value of art, the IRS's Art Advisory Panel reviewed 673 artworks that collectors had bequeathed their heirs from 1985 through 1987. Remember now that the appraisals should have shown the lowest possible values to minimize estate taxes. The IRS panel questioned the appraisals of about half the total works reviewed and concluded that a quarter of those were *overvalued* by an average of nearly $29,000.

Some collectors try to give their art to museums or charitable organizations so they can take a tax deduction for the contributions. If the piece is really excellent, a museum curator might want it; but if it is that good, you probably could sell it at auction for more than the tax deduction will yield. In the case of art donated to a charitable organization, you will want the work to be appraised as high as possible. Rest assured that a deduction for donated art will raise an eyebrow or two at the IRS and may well trigger an audit that otherwise would not occur.

Well, that about covers art from the investment point of view: high transaction costs, high maintenance and insurance costs, an illiquid or nonexistent secondary market, and unfavorable tax treatment. It's enough to make commodities sound like a good deal.

SUGGESTED READING

Each collectible, be it coins, baseball cards, or fine art, generates its own library of books that can be useful for the novice collector. But buyer beware: The authors of most of these tomes are aficionados who have a badly biased view of the investment potential of their particular hobby. Coin collectors reading some of the popular books on that hobby, for instance, will be regaled with tales of fantastic profits made by coin collectors. But they won't hear anything about the thousands of numismatists who, while clearly enjoying the hobby, have sunk thousands of dollars into collections that nobody else wants. And you certainly won't get a true picture of the time and effort that must be invested to assemble even a modestly worthwhile collection of anything. Our advice for the novice collector is to start small. Visit your local library, whose reference collections may well have current periodicals as well as basic books about collecting. Use those resources to find out about local clubs of collectors and spend some time at their meetings. Talking to other collectors is a valuable, low-cost way of finding the best, most reliable sources of information.

11

Tax Strategies for Investors

STEIN

"Please go on with the explanation of your expenses and try to ignore my facial expressions."

Reprinted with permission of Eli Stein.

We'll be the first people to tell you (as if you didn't already know) that taxes are among life's worst financial headaches. The laws are confusing, the IRS is fearsome, and, in the end, taxes are costly. As an investor you're going to become aware very soon of just how confusing and costly taxes can be. But take heart! It isn't all bad news. In 1997, Congress and the Clinton administration passed the most significant tax legislation in more than a decade. The good news is that the Taxpayer Relief Act of 1997 is *very* investor friendly.

But before we explore how life has gotten a little less taxing for investors, let us look at some rules to guide you in thinking about taxes. We've noticed over the years that many investors have a slightly loony view of taxes. They have an irrational hatred of paying taxes. Perhaps it's a gut reaction or they just haven't thought very carefully about what they're doing, but in their extreme efforts to avoid paying taxes, they make bad investment decisions. We know of many otherwise smart people who have been hammered by "tax-sheltered" investments, especially limited partnerships, that have become neither tax sheltered nor good investments. The result: They ended up earning and keeping less than if they had simply pursued an investment program on its own merits and forgot about taxes. Hence, the following:

First Rule: Never, ever make an investment decision based principally on tax considerations. Find other, more profitable goals. Try to beat the overall market. Challenge yourself to produce a higher return than some well-known mutual fund manager. But don't put a lot of effort into trying to beat the IRS. It's getting harder to do, and, frankly, it isn't worth the effort.

Second Rule: Keep good records. The IRS loves records, and its agents know how to use them. You should, too. Of course, as a smart investor you already know the wisdom of maintaining good records. Keeping careful track of your actual expenses in running your portfolio, including purchases of books (be sure to record what you paid for this one), publications, and software, is the only way you are going to know your real return. The IRS allows investors to write off expenses "for the production or collection of income" and "for the management, conservation, or maintenance" of income-producing property.

Meticulous record keeping is especially important when selling portions of a single-stock holding or mutual fund. The rules that apply to the sale of an individual security are different from those that apply to the sale of mutual fund shares. Many investors wrongly assume that the costs of acquiring a sizable position in a single stock over time can be averaged when a portion of those shares are sold. Wrong! The IRS wants to know specifically what the shares you sold cost you. If you don't know, the tax guys will assume you sold the first shares you acquired, which often will have the largest gain and generate the most tax. Mutual fund shares can be accounted for in that same fashion, *or* they can be averaged to determine a single cost-per-share (providing, of course, that you have religiously recorded the purchase amounts and dates).

As we'll see shortly, the record keeping burdens of home ownership have been eased considerably under the new tax law, which allows a homeowner in most circumstances to sell a house at a profit of up to $500,000 without paying any taxes. Since you needn't save all those receipts for home improvements to boost the total cost of your house, and thus minimize your taxable gains, many homeowners are going to quit keeping those kinds of records. But before you toss that folder of receipts into the trash, keep in mind that nobody can predict what will happen to real estate prices and inflation over the next decade or two. Should you, for whatever reason, wind up living in the same house for that period of time, you might (should we say happily?) find that your house generates *more* than $500,000 profit (or $250,000 if you're single).

Third Rule: Never assume you know what the tax laws are. Tax lawyers admitted to us, after passage of the 1997 legislation, that it will be months or even years before they know exactly how the new rules will be applied. The process works like this: Congress makes a law, the IRS draws up rules to enforce it, and the courts interpret whether the laws and rules are appropriate. Your attempts to interpret current tax law could get you into a lot more trouble and expense than it takes to consult a qualified tax expert. If the tax consequences of a potential investment strategy aren't entirely clear to you, consult that expert before you implement the strategy.

CAPITAL GAINS TAXES ARE BETTER THAN INCOME TAXES

Not all taxes are created equal. Indeed, one of the principal effects of the 1997 tax law changes is to make them even more unequal. What was already favorable treatment for capital gains over ordinary income became considerably more favorable when the top capital gains tax rate dropped from 28% to 20%. There was no corresponding reduction in ordinary income tax rates, which remain at 38% in the highest income brackets. When all is said and done, which would you rather pay, 20% or 38%? Of course, not all of us are so fortunate to make enough money to fall into that top ordinary income rate, but the point remains the same: All other things being equal, you're better off making money through capital gains—price appreciation—than you are through income such as dividends and rent payments. This fact of life argues strongly in favor of stocks—specifically growth stocks that don't pay dividends—over bonds, except for municipal issues, especially among investors in high tax brackets.

Stocks have another advantage at tax time, too. You can choose when to take your capital gains. Interest payments from bonds come regularly whether you want them or not, and you are liable for taxes on that income when you receive it. Capital gains, on the other hand, occur only when you sell the item that has appreciated in value. You may watch ecstatically as one of your stocks climbs from $5 a share to $50, but until you actually sell it, there's no tax on that gain. What is more, you can to some extent coordinate the sale of appreciated property, such as stocks, to coincide with the sale of depreciated items. The effect is to minimize or even neutralize the tax bite on the winning stock at the

Figure 11.1 Uncle Sam Can Get Very, Very Greedy

Stated Top Marginal Federal Income Tax Rates

A taxpayer's marginal rate today may actually be significantly higher than the stated rate in this table. That's because of "hidden" rate increases buried in the tax law, such as the phaseout of personal exemptions and limitations on itemized deductions.

1925-28	25%	1954-63	91
1929	24	1964	77
1930-31	25	1965-67	70
1932-35	63	1968	75.25
1936-39	79	1969	77
1940	81.1	1970	71.75
1941	81	1971-80	70
1942-43	88	1981	69.125
1944-45	94	1982-19	50
1946-47	86.45	1987	38.5
1948-49	82.13	1988-90	28
1950-51	91	1991-92	31
1952-53	92	1993----	39.6

Source: House Ways and Means Committee

same time you purge your portfolio of the dog(s) that crept in when you weren't paying attention.

NO TAXES ARE BETTER THAN CAPITAL GAINS TAXES

Even the more favorable treatment of stocks doesn't compare with the windfall that came to homeowners in the 1997 tax legislation. Suddenly many investors are finding that their single largest asset can be sold at a huge profit without *any tax liability!* A couple owning a home they bought 12 years ago for $150,000 that is now worth $485,000 can keep the entire profit of $335,000 (less, of course, realty fees and commissions). That's on top of the other huge incentive the government gives you to buy a home: the tax deductibility of mortgage interest and real estate taxes. And considering that the typical home buyer acquires that asset with only 20% down, appreciating property is one of life's best investments. But remember that we just said *appreciating* property. We all know people who bought real estate at the peak of the last big real estate boom; for them, none of this brings any joy. Their property values still are far below their purchase price, and, unfortunately, they won't get a tax credit if they sell at a loss.

With the good comes the bad, and that's true of tax treatments of real estate, too. While the legislation confers immense benefits on most homeowners with profits, it severely penalizes the homeowners who have *immense* profits. Prior to 1997, a homeowner selling at a large profit could shelter that gain from taxes by rolling it over into a more expensive home. Not anymore. The rollover provision died in 1997, and any profits in excess of $500,000 on a home sale are now taxable. The capital gains rate applies if, as one would assume, the house had been held more than 12 months.

So what does all this mean to you? If you don't own a house, should you buy one? If you do own one, should you sell it?

It all depends. As we explained earlier in the book, a house is not the best way to achieve real estate diversity in an investment portfolio since it is a play on a single, very confined market: the neighborhood in which the house sits. But houses are, by and large, fairly safe (not necessarily lucrative) investments if held over some period of time. And they do enjoy the advantages of leverage, tax deductibility, and, now, tax-free profits. We'd prefer that you make your own decision about house buying based on such factors as how much space you need, where you want to live, and whether you're willing to put up with the headaches of home maintenance. Those things are a lot easier to assess than the profit potential and tax consequences of owning a home.

Now, about selling. Real estate has recovered considerably in many parts of the United States recently. You may be hearing from the neighbors about the fantastic prices for which nearby homes recently sold. If you're tempted to cash out, just remember two points. First, you have to live somewhere. How much of your profits will you really keep if you have to buy another house? Will rent end up costing you more than your tax-deductible mortgage payment? Second, once you've gotten the money out, you have to do something with it. Do you know of a better place to put that money than where it is now, especially with real estate prices in your neck of the woods rising? Certainly the tax law will immensely benefit empty-nesters who no longer want the headaches of owning a big house. But for everyone else, the answers need careful thought.

Deferred Taxes Are (Often) Better Than Taxes Paid Now

You were, of course, always taking full advantage of whatever retirement plans your company offered or that you were eligible for as a self-employed individual. If you weren't, you aren't as smart as we thought you were. And even if you were, the 1997 tax legislation provides more choices to at least delay paying taxes on income set aside as part of a retirement plan. Make no mistake about it, neither the old schemes nor the new ones are adequate vehicles to fund the kinds of retirements we all hope to enjoy. You'll have to supplement them with other investment programs. But given the tax advantages of the programs that are out there, you should be using them as fully as possible.

The programs go under a variety of names and numbers. There's the 401k, the Keogh, the Roth IRA, and the regular IRA. They're all designed to be tax advantaged (that's different from tax free) in that earnings from investments in these plans, whether capital gains or ordinary income, compound tax free until you begin to withdraw money, usually for retirement purposes. At that point the money is taxed as regular income. Presumably, though nobody is guaranteeing it, you will be in a lower tax bracket then. Meanwhile, the advantage of compounding those earnings each year instead of peeling away 20% or 38% in taxes every April can be awesome.

Some investments are particularly suited to inclusion in a tax-advantaged portfolio if you have the option of selecting what goes into it. (Not everyone has that luxury; some corporate plans have extremely limited choices.) On balance, income-producing assets are better for a tax-advantaged plan than assets that will gain in price. (That's because you can't get any tax advantage for the capital gains since those gains will be taxed as ordinary income when the money is withdrawn.) But in many cases an investor will want or need the income to meet living expenses, in which case bonds and similar investments must be kept outside the tax-advantaged portfolio. Zero-coupon bonds issued by corporations or by the Treasury are best suited to a retirement plan because an investor thus avoids paying taxes on accreted, or implied, interest. But zero-coupon municipal bonds—indeed, all municipal bonds—have no place in a tax-advantaged portfolio; they already are, for the most part, tax exempt.

Some of you will be lucky enough to be employed by a company that contributes the maximum amount possible to a qualified retirement plan, thus leaving you to use the savings from your salary to establish an investment portfolio outside the confines of a retirement program. Others of you will have to contribute some of your own money to qualify for matching company contributions. And some, of course, will have only the contributions that you make out of your salary. But whatever the case, make the maximum possible use of any such plan even if it means that you must delay setting up your own non-tax-advantaged investment portfolio. Only an estimated 60% of all employees eligible take advantage of such plans, yet this is probably the single most important basic investment decision anyone can make. Not only does it help fund your retirement, which more than likely is your biggest investment goal, but it does it with the minimum possible tax bite.

MUTUAL FUNDS AND TAXES

Just as you have hardly any control over the investment decisions made by the managers of mutual funds you own, you also have little to say about the tax consequences of their investment strategies and tactics. A mutual fund is required to pay out to shareholders virtually all the dividends and gains it realizes in a given year. Thus, each year you will receive a statement from your fund showing the amount of capital gains distributions and dividends. Dividends are taxed as ordinary income, and capital gains, provided they come from assets held more than 12 months, are treated under the capital gains tax. This distinction applies to tax-exempt municipal bond funds as well. The income from those funds may be exempt from federal, state, and local taxes, but the capital gains that result when the manager sells a bond at a profit are not exempt. That's why you should avoid municipal bond funds if reducing taxes is high on your list of priorities for some reason. Buying and holding the bonds directly lets you determine if and when to take capital gains taxes on what is otherwise a tax-free investment.

You can control some "taxable events"—you gotta love the silliness of this particular bit of jargon—that arise with mutual funds. For instance, you must remember that each time you transfer from one fund to another, you trigger some tax consequences: a gain or loss on the shares you owned in the fund you sold and a new cost basis on the shares of the fund you bought. (The exception, of course, is when the funds are held in a retirement account where current profits and losses don't matter; they'll be taxed later at ordinary income rates when you begin withdrawals.) The record keeping and calculations aren't so difficult if you invest a lump sum to buy all your mutual fund shares at one time. But if you dollar cost average, you will accumulate shares at different prices for as long as you do this. The situation becomes even more complex if you take advantage of the dividend reinvestment plans that many funds offer. Ignoring or forgetting about those reinvested dividends can be painfully expensive. Consider the example of someone who buys shares in a mutual fund for $20,000 and, over the years, reinvests a total of $10,000 more in dividends. The fund shares are then sold for $35,000. Many investors figure that they owe taxes on the $15,000 difference between the original purchase price and the final sale price. Wrong! The reinvested dividends added to the initial $20,000 investment give the fund owner a $30,000 cost basis, and she owes taxes only on the $5,000 gain above that. Lest you think the IRS has fallen down on the job, remember that each year's worth of reinvested dividends were taxed along the way.

For most investors the best approach to mutual fund record keeping is to treat it the same way as buying individual stocks: Note the purchase, sales price, and date each time a transaction occurs. You can't stop the payment of dividends and capital distributions from the fund, but you can control the amount of taxable gains and losses each year by choosing specific shares to sell. Otherwise, the IRS takes control and assumes, as it does with individual stock sales, that the first shares you bought (and often the ones that have appreciated the most) are the first ones you sell. But mutual fund investors do get one break that investors buying and selling individual stocks don't get: They can, if they choose, use the "average cost" or "average basis" method of determining taxable gains or losses. The method requires that you calculate the average per-share price of all your shares in the fund. Be warned, however: Once you have used this method, you must continue to use it for the same fund in the future.

Don't avoid mutual funds just because of this seemingly complex tax treatment. Just do as we said at the beginning of this chapter: Keep good records.

TAX CONSIDERATIONS IN SELECTING INVESTMENTS

In making selections for your non-tax-advantaged portfolio, always be sure to weigh the effect of taxes on total return. The easiest example to illustrate this point is with bonds. We won't include junk bonds in this analysis simply because few investors should be holding such dangerous instruments outside of a fund. Instead, we'll put before you a menu of other bonds: Treasuries, municipals, and corporates. We'll consider first the tax treatment of each; then we'll weigh that along with the risks and yields.

The income from Treasuries is taxable at the federal level but not at the state and local level. If you buy municipals issued in your own state, income from them is apt to be exempt from all taxes. Income from munis issued in other states won't be taxed at the federal level but will face state and local taxes. And the income from corporate bonds will be taxed by just about anybody who can tax it. Clearly munis issued in your own state have the upper hand in the battle to reduce taxes.

But remember the first rule we gave you at the outset of this chapter: Don't make an investment decision based mainly on tax criteria. If you are a conservative investor, which investment makes the most sense? If you know something about the municipal bond market and the rapidity with which ratings can change for the worse, you might feel more comfortable with the Treasuries—especially if you live in a state like Florida that has no state and local income taxes, which evens the odds a little. If, on the other hand, you live in a place like New York with its punishingly high income taxes, you will almost certainly be swayed toward muni bonds issued in New York, even though they do stand at considerably more risk than Treasury bonds. In any case, do a quick calculation to compare transaction costs, especially if you use Treasury Direct to buy newly issued bonds at no charge. But don't always assume a muni bond issued in your home state is a better bet than one issued elsewhere. If you live in Florida, all muni bonds are created equal (at least similarly rated ones are) since there is no local and state income tax to avoid. Even if you live in states with moderately high state and local taxes, you may still find that a muni bond issued by another state yields enough additional to make purchasing it worthwhile instead of investing in your own backyard. You may find that when you compare highly rated corporate bonds with either Treasuries or munis, the yield on the corporates won't be high enough to justify the extra risk even before you take taxes into account. Even higher-yielding corporate bonds (though not junk) will have a hard time competing with the after-tax yields of similarly risky munis.

Some people make this whole process much more complex by weighing the relative merits of Treasuries or municipal bonds against stocks. We think that's an exercise in frustration and suggests that you don't yet have a good grip on your investment program. By and large, bonds are about income while stocks are about capital appreciation. Since they aren't or shouldn't be used interchangeably, there isn't much point in pursuing questions about which is the better investment. If you are serious about using bonds as a capital appreciation tool, you need to be thinking about zero-coupon issues. They rise and fall the most in price as interest rates rise and fall. If you want capital gains from bonds, that implies you think you know something about where interest rates are headed. Good luck. Taxes, whether capital gains or ordinary income, are the least of your worries.

KEEPING IT ALL IN THE FAMILY

To judge by the way the IRS acts, there are lots of investors out there making quiet arrangements to dupe the government one way or another. That explains the lengths to which the tax authorities have gone to eliminate what they believe are unfair or deceptive related-party sales. If one of your favorite stocks has inexplicably fallen 50%, for instance, you may want to take the loss for tax purposes but still hang on to the stock somehow. It would be tempting, wouldn't it, to sell it to your wife or husband. That way you get the loss, but the stock stays in the family. No go, says the IRS. Even if you made the sale in good faith (a likely story), you won't be allowed to deduct the loss. Curiously enough, though, that little strategy can work if you sell the depreciated stock to an *in-law*. The IRS must believe all those mother-in-law jokes and figures you'd never take such a chance with your favorite stock.

Kids don't get any break from the IRS, either. Children under the age of 14 who have income in excess of a certain amount (and that amount, which is adjusted annually for inflation, is awfully small) will be taxed at the parents' top rate. Children 14 or older, however, will be taxed only on their own income. There is a way around the so-called kiddy tax; it involves giving the child investments that don't throw off any, or at least much, income, such as small-growth stocks. In this way the child can have a substantial asset that doesn't suffer from the parents' high taxes. Also, government savings bonds, on which interest accretes but isn't paid until maturity, can be effective vehicles for avoiding the under-14 tax as long as maturity (the bond, not the kid) comes at age 14 or later.

There is one foolproof way of avoiding capital gains taxes on assets that have appreciated substantially, but it isn't pleasant to contemplate: Leave those assets to your heirs. If they inherit the assets, the cost basis becomes the value of the asset at the time they inherit it, completely eliminating from capital gains taxes the amount of appreciation that occurred while you owned it. Say you bought a block of stock for $20,000, and on your death it was worth $80,000, a $60,000 gain. When your heirs inherit that stock, their cost basis becomes $80,000, and if, for instance, they sell it for $90,000 two years later, they owe taxes (at the capital gains rate) only on $10,000, not the $70,000 that it has gained since you first bought it. (Estate taxes, however, are figured on the value of the asset at the time of the donor's death, not the original cost of the purchase; you may face a substantial estate tax bill as a result.)

If you want to be around to pass out the goodies, you can avoid capital gains taxes by giving away appreciated assets. The same sort of cost-basis adjustment occurs. However, gift taxes are due on any single gift of more than $10,000 in any one year. And, of course, you lose any income or dividends the investment might have generated, so be sure you don't need the money. There are some trust arrangements that convey ownership of assets to your heirs but allow you to make use of them (such as living in your house) while you are still alive. This sort of thing falls more into estate planning than investment decisions, so we won't go into detail. But just knowing that such arrangements are possible should give you confidence to keep up a vigorous investment program for as long as you can.

DOING THE WASH

If we have seemed a little biased toward stocks earlier in this chapter, it's probably because we are—but not for tax reasons. Indeed, we think it's only fair that we give bonds their due, too. With bonds you can accomplish something you can't do with stocks—a wash sale. The IRS doesn't like wash sales. It figures you are trying to get away with something, and, truth be told, you are. A wash sale occurs when you sell something that has fallen in value, usually a stock, to establish a loss for tax purposes. But you, we, and the IRS know that you really think the stock is going to do well in the long run. So after dumping it to take the tax loss, you buy it back. Not only has the IRS subsidized your loss, but you now own the same stock at a lower price. The IRS says you can't do that. If you sell a stock at a loss, you must wait a minimum of 31 days before buying it back if you want that loss to count on your tax return. You also can't buy more of the same stock less than 31 days before you sell your current holdings for a loss. You could, of course, buy another stock in the same industry, but individual stocks don't tend to perform exactly alike, so that might be risky. Besides, IRS wash sales rules forbid the purchase of a "substantially similar" investment.

But bonds offer you an opportunity to escape the 31-day rule. That's because bonds of similar quality and duration do tend to behave in a similar manner. So you can change the vehicle without changing the effect. Say, for example, you bought a 10-year A-rated corporate bond two years ago and interest rates have gone against you. The price of the bond has fallen. You sell it and take your loss for tax purposes. Then you turn right around 15 minutes later and buy an 8-year corporate bond with an A rating issued by another company for almost the same price at which you sold your first one. You now own a substantially similar asset, and you have a loss to offset some gains.

There are ways to avoid having a penalized wash sale in stocks, although they entail a bit of risk. One way is to buy the same amount of stock you already own (known, appropriately enough, as "doubling up"), wait at least 31 days, and then sell the original stock. During that time the price may fall further, of course, resulting in a doubling of your loss. And if you sell and then wait more than 31 days, the price of the stock might soar far above what you sold it for. That's probably what the IRS hopes will happen to punish you for trying to evade paying your fair share.

Call options can help. Suppose you bought a stock at 20 and it fell to 15. You want the tax loss, but you don't want to give up the stock because you're still convinced that one day that baby is going to fly. Solution: In late November (at least 31 days before the end of the year) buy a March call option on your stock with a strike price of 17.5. Before the year ends, sell your stock to establish the tax loss. No less than 31 days later you can exercise the call option (if the price of the stock is above 17.5) or let it lapse and buy shares in the open market (if the price is below 17.5). The strategy allows you to double up at only about 10% of the cost of buying more shares. It also allows you to take your tax loss without losing your grip on that nifty stock, and, if you like, to earn interest on your sale proceeds for nearly three months until the option is exercised or expires.

Index

A

Adjustable rate bonds, 165-66
Age and investing
    middle-aged investors, 69-71
    retirement age investors, 71-72
    young/new investors, 67-69
American Association of Individual
        Investors, 53
American Depositary Receipts
        (ADRs), 245-46
American Stock Exchange, number of
        listings, 83
American Telephone & Telegraph
        (AT&T), 104
Analysis of market. *See* Stock market
        valuation
Annual report, 132
    important items of, 134
Annuities
    taxation, 215-16
    variable annuities, 215-16
Arbitragers, role of, 262-63
Art as investment, 317-25
    auction purchases, 320-22
    consultants, use of, 322
    gallery system, 319-20
    losses and contemporary art, 318-
        19, 324
    price gains, 317, 318
    selling art, 323-25
Asset allocation
    aim of, 55
    with bonds, 61
    dynamic rebalancing, 58
    and future assets, 57
    information sources on, 78-79
    mutual fund portfolio, 214-15
    non-stock examples, 56-57
    with real estate, 61
    reshaping problem portfolio, 77-78
    risk factors, 63-66
    and risk tolerance, 58
    with stocks, 61

strategic asset allocation, 58
tactical asset allocation, 58-59, 75-76
value of, 56, 75
Asset allocation portfolios
    extremes of, examples, 62
    middle-aged investors, 69-71, 73-74
    rebalancing portfolio, 72-74
    retirement age investors, 71-72, 74
    simple example of, 59
    young/new investors, 67-69, 72-73
Auctions, art, 320-22

B

Baby boomers, 296-97, 303
Balanced funds, 217
Balanced target funds, 218
Banc One, 122
Banks
    bank brokers, 39
    money managers at, 227-28
Bank stocks, 122
Barron's
    closing prices, 91
    as information source, 52, 115, 119
    mutual fund information, 198, 199,
        210, 217
    for P-E ratios, 89, 129
    Roundtable, 132
    software reviews, 131
    for trend information, 132
    200-day moving average, 86
Bear market
    and Federal Reserve, 86
    and mutual funds, 197
Biotech funds, 220
Biotech stocks, 119
Blue chip stocks, 100-105
    decline potential of, 102-4
    GM example, 103
    IBM example, 101-3
    risk factors, 64
    selection of, 108, 110

after inflation returns, 18, 20, 22
projecting future needs, 23
real rate, monitoring of, 50-52
S&P index since 1920s, 75
small stocks since 1920s, 76
after tax returns, 18
and transaction costs, 36-42
Revenue bond, 172
Risk
  agency bonds, 64
  blue chip stocks, 65
  bonds, 148, 152-55
  business risk, 98
  vs. chance, 29
  collectibles, 65-66
  commodities, 66
  corporate bonds, 64
  currency risk, 241-43
  economic risk, 97
  financial risk, 99
  foreign investments, 62, 64, 68,
    239-43
  individual attitudes toward, 30-33
  information risk, 99
  interest rate risk, 98
  liquidity risk, 99-100
  and margin accounts, 139
  market risk, 98
  municipal bonds, 64
  options, 66
  real estate, 65
  and short sales, 140-41
  small company stocks, 65
  time factors related to, 20-22, 28,
    29, 47
  Treasury bonds, 63-64
  zero-coupon bonds, 64
Risk capital, meaning of, 273
Risk reduction
  and dividend reinvestment plans,
    142
  limit orders, 141
  stop loss order, 141-42
Risk tolerance
  and asset allocation, 58
  and market dips, 84
  self-assessment, 32-33
  tests, 30-32
Russell 2000, mutual fund benchmark,
  210

S

Safety
  bonds as, 145
  government agency bonds, 162-64
  over long term, 21
  savings bonds, 160-62
  Treasury bonds, 153, 156, 181, 182
Sales calls, avoiding buying over phone,
  8-9
Savings bonds, 160-62
  Series EE, 160-61
  Series HH, 161-62
  tax advantage, 161
  yields, 160-61
Schwab & Co., Charles, 39-40, 228
Science/technology funds, 221
Screen, 129-32
  analysis of investment potential, 131
  information from company, 132-33
  mutual fund analysis, 208-11
  with P-E ratios, 129-31
Sears Roebuck, 104
Secondary markets, bonds, 146, 161
Sector funds, 221
  cautions about, 216
  international, 250
Securities and Exchange Commission,
  99, 134
  registration of investment advisors
    with, 226-27
  on trading options, 265-66
  on wrap accounts, 232
Selling stock, 136-38
  and losses, 136
  P-E ratio for, 137
  portions of shares, 138
  technical analysis for, 137
  valuation techniques for, 137
Sentiment indicators
  as contrary indicator, 90
  limitations of, 90-91
  stock market valuation, 90-91
Series EE savings bonds, 160-61
Series HH savings bonds, 161-62
Shadow portfolio, of mutual funds, 212
Short covering, 140
Short-intermediate municipal bond
  funds, 222
Short municipal bond funds, 222
Short sales, futures, 260

U

Unit investment trusts (UITs), 206, 234-35
  with bonds, 234-35
  operation of, 234-35
  with stocks, 235
U.S. multinational companies, 244-45
Utilities, dividends of, 126
Utility funds, 221

V

Vacation homes, tax rules, 302
Value averaging
  process of, 46
  results of, 46
Value stocks, 121-23
  benefits of, 121, 123
  operation of, 121-22
  P-E ratio, 123
  selection of, 123, 133
  compared to small-growth stock, 121
Vanguard 500 Index Portfolio, 205-6
Vanguard Group, 228
Vanguard's Wilshire 5000 Equity Index, 203-4
Variable annuities, 215-16
  fees, 216
  negative aspects of, 215-16
  tax-deferred treatment, 215
Vinik, Jeffrey, 199-200, 211

W

Wall Street Journal, The, 94
Wal-Mart, 108, 109
Wash sale, 341-43
  avoiding penalties, 342-43
  prohibitions, 342
Wasting asset, 267

Wealthy
  money management firms, use of, 42
  risk tolerance of, 32
Webs, 207
Westinghouse, 104
Wilshire 5000 Equity Index
  index fund based on, 206
  mutual fund benchmark, 210
"Window dressing," 136
Women, risk tolerance of, 32
World income funds, 222
Wrap accounts, 231-34
  choosing programs, 233
  fees, 231-32, 234
  reasonable restrictions rule, 232
  sponsoring firms, 231
Writing an option, 261

Y

Yield curve, 150-52
Yields
  and bond price, 147
  corporate bonds, 173-74
  high and risk, 148
  and maturity of bond, 149
  savings bonds, 160-61
  Treasury bonds, 156, 157, 160
Young investors, asset allocation for, 67-69, 72-73

Z

Zero-coupon bonds, 174-77, 176-77, 186
  benefits of, 174-76, 338
  forms of, 175
  interest-rate risk, 176
  for retirement plan, 334
  risk factors, 64, 182
  taxation, 176
Zero-sum markets, 259